The Fear of Sinking

The Fear of Sinking

The American Success Formula
in the Gilded Age

Paulette D. Kilmer

The University of Tennessee Press
Knoxville

Material quoted from R. Gordon Kelly, ed., *Children's Periodicals of the United States*, reprinted with permission of Greenwood Publishing Group, Inc., Westport, Conn.

The paper in this book meets the minimum requirements of the American National Standard for Permanence of Paper for Printed Library Materials.
∞
The binding materials have been chosen for strength and durability.

✸ Printed on recycled paper.

Library of Congress Cataloging-in-Publication Data

Kilmer, Paulette D., 1949–
   The fear of sinking : the American success formula in the Gilded
Age / Paulette D. Kilmer. — 1st ed.
      p. cm.
   Includes bibliographical references and index.
   ISBN 0-87049-939-4 (cloth: alk. paper)
   1. Success in popular culture—United States—History—19th
century. 2. United States—Social life and customs—1865–1918.
I. Title.
BJ1611.2.K55 1996
302'.14'097309034—dc20   95-41826
                                              CIP

In loving memory of my grandfather,
Henry J. Kilmer,
who taught me how to tell stories; and my brother,
Vaughn J. ("Bunky") Kilmer,
who shared my zeal for learning and books

Contents

Acknowledgments

This book grew out of years of research and thinking. Many people have helped me. At the University of Illinois in Urbana-Champaign, Dr. James W. Carey, formerly dean of the College of Communications; Dr. Clifford Christians, director of the Institute of Communication Research; Dr. Wallace Farnham, an emeritus professor in the History Department; and Dr. Howard S. Maclay shaped my thoughts.

Dr. Dwight Teeter, Jr., dean of the College of Communications at the University of Tennessee, Knoxville, has been my mentor since my undergraduate days at the University of Wisconsin—Madison. His lively sense of humor, his dedication to learning, his willingness to help others, and his practical suggestions have inspired me. His comments increased the clarity of this manuscript.

At the University of Tennessee Press, Meredith Morris-Babb, acquisitions editor, and Kimberly C. Scarbrough, acquisitions assistant, gave me invaluable editorial advice and much encouragement.

This book probably never would have been written without Dr. Ed Lambeth's kindness. He arranged for me to work for the School of Journalism at the University of Missouri in Columbia. The library there contained many original documents essential for this study. Librarians at the University of Illinois, the University of Missouri, and the State Historical Society of Wisconsin helped me locate rare potboilers and other documents. Michael Strahan, the reference computer services librarian at Northern Michigan University, cheerfully searched for new information and missing details. My students also have been supportive. I am particularly grateful to Mark Johnson, Tammy Johnson, Paul Puotinen, Bonnie Star, and Joseph Urban.

The seeds of this book were sown during my undergraduate and master's degree studies at the University of Wisconsin—Madison; and

Dr. John McNelly, emeritus professor at the University of Wisconsin, always offers useful advice.

Many friends have encouraged me to write this book. Margo Wilson, a true friend in all ways, has helped me develop ideas. Over the years, Dr. Donald Dennis and Jane Dennis have given me help, advice, and fellowship. Members of the Community United Church of Christ in Champaign, Illinois, especially the Reverend Jack Goode, his wife Diana Goode, the Reverend Karen Bush, and her husband Scott Bush, nurtured me spiritually.

Of course, my family, too, has been involved in this creative odyssey. My brother Nick and his wife Kayla offered moral support and took me to the movies when I felt overwhelmed. My father's wit and direct criticism challenge my complacency. My mother's optimistic observations and amusing repartee kept me in good spirits.

Passing through the Eye of the Needle

In democratic countries, however opulent a man is supposed to be, he is almost always discontented with his fortune because he finds that he is less rich than his father was, and he fears that his son will be less rich than himself. Most rich men in democracies are therefore constantly haunted by the desire of obtaining wealth, and they naturally turn their attention to trade and manufactures, which appear to offer the readiest and most efficient means of success. In this respect they share the instincts of the poor without feeling the same necessities; say, rather, they feel the most imperious of all necessities, that of not sinking in the world.

—Alexis de Tocqueville, 1840

The plastic, chrome, and styrofoam conveniences of the late twentieth century do not mask the discontent with their material lives that Americans express in addictions. Some drink. Some "do" crack. Some eat compulsively. Some work out maniacally. Some "shop till they drop," as if finding the right purchase at the mall will tell them who they really are. Hoping to connect with something larger than themselves, most seek insights into the mysteries of the universe from popular culture and religion. Somehow identity becomes synonymous with an occupation, and income provides a yardstick for achievement. The American obsession with success began at Plymouth Rock and continues to this day. This over arching desire to be the best shapes all arenas of the past and present life of our nation.

Popular culture and religion both probe the assumptions underlying twentieth-century definitions of success. These definitions emerged gradually, in the stories told to the public by reporters, singers, actors, fiction writers, and ministers. Within the webs of their narratives, writers experimented with reality to amplify those psychological truths essential to the survival of the Republic. Joseph Campbell's works—particularly *Myths To Live By*—assert that every society needs a body of archetypes (repeated cultural patterns) embedded in myths (sacred stories believed to be true). "Myths and fairy tales are one of the most characteristic ways in which archetypes manifest themselves, and the mythological motifs . . . are paradigm archetypal images."[1] This book explores the role popular culture, by repeating crucial motifs that teach the people lessons of the heart, has played in maintaining values.

No amount of technology or academic knowledge can divest the human mind of its need for narrative closure. Through archetypes, myths enable people "to interpret the contemporary world as experienced in terms of relevance to our inner life."[2] For example, social historian Paul Boyer traces Bible stories about the end of the world in popular culture from antiquity to the present. Moreover, he and others have interpreted every significant moment in American history in light of this prophecy creed. The body of narratives applying the millennial prototype to world conditions continues to influence domestic politics and foreign affairs. Americans construct their values using biblical models. While the prophecy paradigm specifies a blueprint for the last hours of life on earth, the success archetype tells citizens how to fulfill their earthly needs without jeopardizing their souls.

As Carol S. Pearson notes, "People seem to have lost their souls. They may have material possessions—the right house, the right car, the right job, the right clothes; they may even have a stable family life and be religious. But inside themselves, they feel empty. Even when they go through the right motions, it is movement without meaning."[3]

The plots of many folktales constitute testing grounds for working out the relationship between physical existence and mystical aspirations. Moreover, this tension between flesh and soul inspired writers of both potboilers—stories written to pay the bills—and newspaper articles in the late nineteenth and early twentieth centuries to incorporate the Cinderella archetype in their works. In the classic rags-to-riches model that permeated society and inspired these authors, a steadfast adolescent protagonist saves a wealthy benefactor, whose kindness in turn enables the worthy hero or heroine to rise into the middle class. This theme we call the success prototype, paradigm, or archetype. Although sometimes (as in Horatio Alger's inspirational adventure stories) a success motif dominates a plot, generally archetypes blend into the narrative seamlessly. Each generation of writers interpreted the paradigm differently, clarifying or elaborating upon past cultural values in light of present contingencies.

Between about 1870 and 1910, the success prototype in such works paid special attention to biblical injunctions against amassing treasures. Characters (like real people) worried about losing their souls and their reputations through greed. Even those who did not attend church still embraced Judeo-Christian mores. Through social osmosis, religious values had permeated popular culture. Even Cornelius Vanderbilt, the richest man in the nation in 1877, "though not much of a church man[,] was never skeptical."[4] Backsliders believed that the diligent earned respect as well as a berth in paradise through hard work and good deeds while the lazy, pampered rich went to hell. However, as rampant geographical expansion and a deluge of inventions shook the country, individuals were faced, on a scale unknown to prior generations, with temptations to pursue private gain, despite the cost to others. By the twentieth century, the motif "passing through the eye of the needle" came to serve as a metonym for the moral embedded in the "rags-to-riches" model.

The biblical parable was explicit. When a wealthy man asked what he should do to serve God, Christ told him to give away all his material possessions. As he left, Christ concluded: "Truly, I say to you, it will be hard for a rich man to enter the kingdom of heaven. Again, I tell you, it is easier for a camel to go through the eye of a needle than for a rich man to enter the kingdom of God" (Matthew 19:23–24).

The passage retains its power, despite the fact many people no longer read the Bible. James W. Carey refers to religious metaphors as vanishing mediators, which fall away once secular changes have been absorbed into a culture.[5] Metaphors as evocative as "passing through the eye of the needle" become permanent parts of the collective unconscious (the shared feelings and symbols deep below the personal or individual unconscious). For Carl Jung, myths illuminate psychological reality and place the physical world in perspective as merely the most obvious plane of existence. In *The Great Code: The Bible and Literature,* Northrop Frye points out that, although archetypes and electrons remain invisible, they nevertheless constitute entities just as real as any physical objects.

Jung's elevation of imagination and intuition to vital survival skills contradicted the nineteenth-century emphasis upon technology and expediency. Folklore and science both explain natural phenomena. Storytellers rely upon their creativity to leap over gaps that baffle scientists. Myths, Jung concludes, emerge from the *unus mundus* (one world) or all-encompassing mind, as he calls the collective unconscious that contains both *logos* (science) and *mythos* (mysticism).[6]

The success paradigm, like Jungian archetypes, provided categories for organizing experience. Repeatedly, the dialectic between science and mysticism surfaced in popular narratives of the late nineteenth century and early twentieth century. The mutations of the Cinderella paradigm reflect Jung's observation that, although archetypes transcend racial or ethnic differences, they are geographically and culturally shaped.[7] In other words, regardless of heredity, members of the same community draw upon the same prototypes to understand reality. For example, Americans appreciate the spiritual warning encoded in the biblical image of "passing through the eye of the needle."

Scholars have argued about the origins of this metaphor. Some would translate the Greek word for *camel* as the similar term for *rope*. Although this explanation retains the warning that those who are rich on earth probably will not enter heaven, the image of a tailor toiling to thread a rope through a needle is hardly as graphic as that of a sweaty, dusty nomad pushing a stubborn camel through a tiny hole. Indeed, many agree with the opinion expressed in *The Interpreter's Bible* that most literal interpretations mute the passage's dramatic impact.[8]

Today some theologians suggest Christ repeated an inside joke by describing a gate in the wall of Jerusalem, not a sewing needle. The small portal, called "the eye of the needle," prevented armies and undesirables from sneaking into the city after dusk. Many in Christ's audience had laughed at travelers who had arrived too late to enter the main gate. The penalty for being tardy was having to unpack the dromedary. Some ministers intensify the drama by making the gate so small the camels had to go through it on their knees. Although the owner lost face, it was not impossible to shove the uncooperative beast though the small aperture. "But anyone who has witnessed a camel arising or settling down and has heard its raucous cries of complaint at changing its position will appreciate the superb irony in the notion that a camel could ever make it through the eye of a needle."[9] This substitution of a sewing needle for a gate may reflect the impact of popular culture upon the literal meaning of the motif.

Many Americans consider the Bible the source of sacred narratives. People live in a mythological universe created subconsciously through generations of cultural interaction.[10] The reinterpretation of archetypes requires psychic energy, and, throughout time, humans have made the development of the spirit a characteristic pattern of behavior.[11] Joseph Campbell analyzes the Bible as a source of laws, symbols, and metaphors relevant in defining the meaning of life. The arts and social institutions, including schools and newspapers, regenerate themes vital to the preservation of the community's Judeo-Christian values. Admonitions concerning the dangers inherent in acquiring wealth date at least from the time when Israel's rivals (Egypt, Babylon, Assyria, and Phoenicia) prospered at Israel's expense: "They [possessed] the power and domination that the Israelites themselves desperately longed to possess and would certainly have regarded as a signal mark of divine favor if they had possessed it. The only recourse [was] to show this heathen success in a context of demonic parody, as a short-lived triumph that has all the marks of the real thing except permanence."[12]

Centuries later, Americans still denounce "heathen success." In fact, according to Frye and Campbell, a common plot dialectic pits wealth against loyalty. In the Gilded Age, songs, serials, and sermons often reprinted by newspapers demonstrated that material wealth could not replace love, and the love of God was paradigmatic. Magazine fiction and dime novels traced the unsavory histories of those foolish enough to forsake family and friends to attain riches. Ironically, those who fretted most about the corrupting power of gold had the least chance of earning enough cash to afford either luxuries or temptations. The distinction between actuality and possibility remained shadowy, because viewing the humdrum present as a prelude to an exhilarating future helped people to persevere. Although many said wealth led to sin, most dreamed of making a million dollars. Such contradictions helped individuals to cope with despair by assuring them their present poverty was noble; moreover, daydreams strengthened their resolve and nurtured their hopes.

Popular culture provided a stage for experimenting with the success prototype. This book analyzes the success paradigm in popular plots, success tracts, and news accounts. Instead of focusing on one genre, as other scholars have done, here we examine the plot strategies of forty-one authors who employed the rags-to-riches model in ten genres of fiction, in success tracts, and in news items that pleased the masses between the Civil War and World War I. By concentrating on the public image of such writers in the mass media, this volume also seeks to discover how the authors themselves wished to be remembered. Most either wrote biographies and essays about their craft or consented to be interviewed about their flamboyant lives as well as about their serial novels.

The popular tales filled a cultural need and coexisted with literature. Instead of comparing the tales with the timeless works of great authors, this book focuses on the ephemeral pieces, analyzing them within the social context of the Gilded Age. Our question, then, is not what constituted good or bad writing, but rather what purposes formula stories served for readers. While Cawelti makes insightful points about particular genres, often by emphasizing the most aesthetically pleasing works, this study examines the success model as it appears in the most pedestrian, as well as in the loftiest, exemplars of many genres.

What role did popular tales play as carriers of archetypes, once advances in technology during the Gilded Age had led to a merger of oral and print narratives? Oral culture, of course, remained separate from the world of print. In fact, in the late nineteenth century, three forms of narrative thrived: spoken stories, written tales, and a hybrid of oral and print modes (the bardic tales).

Just as the bards of bygone eras sang ballads, popular authors (including newswriters) entertained and educated readers with the traditional lore essential to emotional grounding in society. Formula or bardic tales deliberately repeat ethically relevant motifs. This book critically assesses the emergence of bardic tales as a counterpoint to the evolution of objectivity and the establishment of journalism as a profession.

Chapter 1 contrasts news accounts and bardic plots as prescriptions for life. Chapter 2 presents the methodology and cultural implications of the research. Chapter 3 considers the forces that compelled publishers to embrace the success archetype. Chapter 4 focuses on how writers of the works under discussion here codified the Cinderella model to create different genres. Chapter 5 analyzes how that model was incorporated into stories designed to teach children how to become adults. Chapter 6 explains the fact that fiction and biography often coincided, as people unconsciously organized experiences around the success prototype stored in the subconscious narrative pool that binds a community together. Chapter 7 examines how newspaper reporters and popular bards invoked the success paradigm in disaster accounts. The last chapter compares how journalists and other popular authors measured the wealthy against the success archetype. Rich and poor, young and old alike unconsciously gleaned popular culture to find the affirmation of their beliefs.

Chapter 1

News and Fiction

Prescriptions for Living

S uch opening phrases as "Once upon a time" or, in a newspaper, "The following story comes well authenticated from Trenton, Tennessee," alerted nineteenth-century readers to expect an outrageous sequence of events, followed by a moral. Editors of the time often launched bizarre reports with declarations of their veracity. For example, in October 1883, the *Alexandria (Louisiana) Town Talk* assured readers that trustworthy folks in Tennessee had witnessed the following train of events:

> A young man, long past maturity, had no beard at all. Then one day he noticed a lump on his neck a few inches beneath his chin. The unsightly wen resembled a large walnut. He asked the doctor to remove it. As the doctor made the incision, a matted, spongy substance popped out. The wad was a "closely matted and coiled mass of hair." It seems that the beard, which should have been spread over the young man's face, had concentrated in this one spot and grown beneath the skin. The hair was removed, and the opening soon healed, and the strange development became unnoticeable.[1]

Henry Nash Smith explains in *The Virgin Land* that such narrative codes point to a plane of reality where concepts and emotions fuse to form symbolic images.[2] Parables fascinate readers by posing plausible explanations that make the improbable incident sound factual. Their plots appeal to the reservoir of archetypes upon which each member of a community draws in interpreting messages. The cited news item generated conversations as well as guffaws; Sunday scientists and poets may have debated whether that freakish lump could have formed. Men with no beards or light beards may have felt comforted.

Such tales articulate affective truths rather than physical realities, however. The imagery resonates within the heart. Like a fairy tale, such a story works through symbolism. Indeed, the strange phenomenon reinforces the moral of Alger's rags-to-riches tales: be satisfied with middle-class affluence. The figures in the story represent values. For instance, the mature lad might be the nation and the lack of a beard the blindness of the population concerning wealth. The matted lump could be monopoly, covetousness, or the unhealthy acquisition of physical treasures. The physician may represent the bard, editor, minister, or other seer who lances the canker by cutting through the facade of unwise preoccupation with social climbing. The scar's final healing, of course, is the inner peace that awaits the community once no one hoards power or money and everyone avoids vice (and, in consequence, everyone ascends to the middle class).

This news account resembles a fairy tale in a number of striking ways. The central character has no name. The location could be Anywhere, U.S.A. The protagonist struggles and then proves himself worthy by having the wen removed. The doctor plays the role of the benefactor. The implicit moral—"the opening soon healed, and the strange development became unnoticeable"—promises redemption to those who lance the boils festering on their souls.

Sometimes, of course, false hopes and phony piety blind people. Mark Twain and Charles Dudley Warner coined the phrase "The Gilded Age" to describe the hypocrisy of their day, which was rooted in unrealistic expectations. Their novel, *The Gilded Age* (1872), satirizes the scramble for political renown, industrial power, and economic advancement through speculation. To Twain and Warner, the Gilded Age sparkled with a patina of noble values that glittered in speeches but crumbled when citizens took action. Many historians have agreed with the novelists. Certainly the historical record contains examples of greed. The Robber Barons, for example, gained prestige and aristocratic status through unscrupulous ploys more despicable than the chicanery of petty thieves.

The disparity between the Robber Barons and ordinary citizens has stimulated economic analyses of the forces of production in a capitalist society. For example, in *Mechanic Accents*, Michael Denning viewed the dime novels produced between 1840 and 1893 as helping to maintain class lines by blinding workers to their social immobility and by encouraging their unrealistic hopes of rising through diligence.[3] His "Unknown Public"—the million anonymous immigrant laborers and farmers, mostly Irish and German—bought the ten-cent thrillers. During the Gilded Age, Christine Bold concluded in a related study, the publishing industry discovered the money-making potential of formulas and forced writers to utilize predetermined plot lines, stunting their artistic development.[4]

For the first time in history, cheap paper and fast presses made it possible to write down what in earlier times would have been spoken or sung. By creating a mass market for stories, the publishing industry's innovations led to an increase in the number of a new variety of strolling minstrels. When stories became commodities to be bought and sold in a market, writers found new economic and occupational niches. The demand for entertaining reading enabled hundreds of authors to work independently as producers of cliff-hangers (serials composed of episodes that end suspensefully), paperbacks, feature articles, and news briefs.

The proliferation of magazines and books concerned both those who equated reading with spiritual well-being and those who denounced popular bards as mouthpieces of the devil. Popular culture became enmeshed in this argument over the social role of reading as the arena in which the desire to acquire wealth might be reconciled with the need to feel pure in spirit. Some ministers preached to the populace through cheap fiction. Like citizens, many preachers assumed making too much money incited ruthless behavior and obscured the futility of seeking fulfillment in owning things.

Editors hired cultural bards because plots containing the success archetype satisfied a demand in the marketplace. Nevertheless, although the writers lived on their earnings, they did not consider their work merely a means of paying bills. Interviews with them indicate many took pride in their ability to please readers who sought escape from drudgery and disappointment in eagerly awaited installments detailing a modern Cinderella's quest for happiness in a wicked world.

While both readers and writers shared in the struggle to survive financially, factors other than economic ones fueled public interest in the rags-to-riches paradigm. For instance, changing technology, which multiplied the mechanical dangers the public faced daily, made the success prototype a refuge from modernity. This was especially true because the process of invention enticed individuals to acquire material possessions. Innovation was viewed ambivalently, as both creator and destroyer. Each wave of technological advancement exposed citizens to new threats, as well as to new pleasures and sources of wonder. Often, euphoria over time saved, money earned, or physical barriers surmounted repressed recognition of the anxiety introduced into the community by the new technology. The timeless Cinderella paradigm recalled a safe day when elves rather than machines made shoes and when frogs taught rude princesses lessons in decorum. The popular plots reassured those who felt overwhelmed by the stresses of everyday life. In fantasy, they briefly attained the success that often eluded them in the real world.

Frequently, progress intensified the misery of the poor, even while raising their standard of living. The urban Cinderella tales inspired optimism amid ugliness. Sunny plots about lucky folks who vanquished villainy, overcame their troubles with grit, and thereby earned the respect of kind strangers, provided a sanctuary for desperate people trapped in poverty. Like mystic chants, plots repeated a cherished archetype that promised better times ahead—times when justice would prevail against perfidy and the deserving would live happily ever after, secure in the knowledge the wicked had danced to death in flaming shoes or—in Victorian parlance—been annihilated by Demon Rum or Tempter Tobacco.

Before journalists were expected to be objective, reporters as well as fiction artisans exposed the sins of Demon Rum and invoked the magical power of words to redress social injustices. The Corliss Engine did not dethrone Cinderella. The ability to transform raw materials into such wonders as refrigerated railroad cars, bicycles, and ice-cream bricks did not relieve humans of their need for narrative closure. Indeed, the world remains a blank stage until the players codify their experiences in scenarios. Language provides the means of understanding life. For the throngs of anonymous readers, writers recycled ancient archetypes and myths that had sustained people for centuries. The story, and not the facts, prevails; because, without a narrative frame, societies collapse.

Past, present, and future coalesce in the web of archetypes implanted in cultural myths that bind society. A primary set of plot lines, distilled from centuries of exposure to the Cinderella tale, evolved around the notion that, without honor, money was worthless. Alger's adventures retold that tale from a male perspective and illustrated the effects of changing technology on individuals as well as on progress. Indeed, authors employed technology to update the ancient art of balladry. They sang the ballads people longed to hear. But, instead of lutes, they stroked typewriters. Instead of congregating in marketplaces to listen to a strolling bard, people read modern versions in new formats (news, serials, mysteries, adventures, romances, and horse operas) that recast proven values and symbols in modern guises recognizable to even the most obtuse spectator.

The new technology enabled writers to skip back and forth between the very separate worlds of traditional oratory and contemporary print. The hybrid was not always beautiful, but, in the age of the useful and the practical, it gave believers a bit of whimsy, a corner of fantasy, a dose of imagination. This was allowed only because it improved the reader's character or brought her or him one step closer to passing through the eye of the needle—that is, to laying up trea-sures both in heaven and on earth.[5]

The formula for balancing the desire for material goods with the need for spiritual well-being evolved as a part of the success arche-type. The bardic tales combined elements from novels and fairy tales into a new form, a hybrid that conveyed archetypes to reinforce val-ues. Writers adapted bardic tales to genres that appealed to the mul-titudes: dime thrillers, mysteries, domestic fantasies, romances, and idea novels. In *The American Myth of Success: From Horatio Alger to Norman Vincent Peale,* Richard Weiss observes, "Their writings re-flect the craving for stability in a society in the throes of transforma-tion."[6] Regardless of the format, these updated fairy tales denounced money as the root of all evil and illustrated how excessive wealth drove youths into billiard parlors, theaters, and race tracks.

The success paradigm helped people to negotiate reality by pro-viding interpretations of what it meant to be rich. Popular bards cau-tioned that no one was truly rich without the love and esteem of fam-ily, peers, and colleagues. Gold could not replace fidelity.

Soon, however, the presence of thousands of wealthy families chal-lenged the folk wisdom concerning amassing material goods. Steel mogul Andrew Carnegie and the Reverend Russell Conwell sug-gested prosperous individuals might attain salvation by serving as ex-emplars of success. Such individuals, by sagely investing the fortunes entrusted to them by God, could help the poor lift themselves up by their bootstraps. The meaning of the Cinderella paradigm fluctuated to accommodate progress. People sought to maintain their spiritual health amid massive upheavals in their understanding of the world. The rags-to-riches formula guaranteed constancy; but, to see that the success archetype continued to function as a viable link between past and present, the popular bards employed modern images in explicat-ing it.

John G. Cawelti, author of *Adventure, Mystery, and Romance: For-mula Stories as Art and Popular Culture,* and other scholars have demonstrated the cultural significance of formula writing. James D. Hart, in *The Popular Book: A History of America's Literary Taste,* and Frank Luther Mott, in *Golden Multitudes: The Story of Best Sellers in the United States,* trace the history of writing for the multitudes.[7]

Feminist scholars have made significant contributions to our under-standing of such writing. By adjusting standards to reflect crucial histori-cal contingencies, Jane Tompkins, in *Sensational Designs: The Cultural Work of American Fiction, 1790–1860,* enlarges the traditional liter-ary canon to include romance writers. Her imaginative work proves it can be profitable to evaluate narratives using criteria other than those associated with literary masterpieces. Mary Kelley has studied the private diaries and papers of a dozen popular women writers to probe the social role of romances. Her analysis in *Private Woman, Public Stage: Literary Domesticity in Nineteenth-Century America* reveals the human side of these often-neglected creators of best sellers about women's struggles to provide happy homes for their children.[8]

Although some critics consider potboilers to be inferior works of literature, the analysis reported here demonstrates the bardic tales belong in the category of popular culture rather than in that of timeless classics. The essential differences between bardic tales and novels arise from the authors' and the readers' purposes. Popular bards breathe new life into the shared wisdom of the community, wisdom contained in the traditional formulas that impel individuals to aspire to serve forces larger than themselves and, concomitantly, to affirm their membership in society. Novelists, on the other hand, give readers a highly personalized, unique view of the human condition that provides intellectual stimulation and aesthetic pleasure.

Readers of all ages have found, and still find, intellectual satisfaction in novels and emotional grounding in formula tales. In the twentieth century, these bardic tales have inspired radio, television, and motion picture dramas. In the nineteenth century, children encountered the success archetype in several arenas. Their parents read to them from the Bible and from magazines that repeated popular plots. Their teachers taught them to recite from *McGuffey's Readers*, which reiterated the same values codified in the success archetype: thrift, perseverance, loyalty, integrity, honor. Aphorisms warned that money, unless invested honorably, corrodes one's soul. Rhymed exercises extolled diligent workers who surmounted obstacles and ultimately earned the respect of their neighbors, as well as modest remuneration. At church, ministers preached about the folly of squandering heavenly treasures to acquire objects. Some pupils won Sunday-school books given as prizes at picnics and socials. Others checked out volumes with character-building plots from the church library.

In fact, the Cinderella paradigm appealed so strongly to the popular bards that many of them recast their own life stories to fit the same imaginative formula they had written and rewritten so many times for publishers. Perhaps the power of this cultural icon—the image of a hard-working protagonist who deserves to succeed—seduced the writers so completely they could not see their own experiences except in ways that fit the cherished paradigm. They emphasized personal incidents that conformed to the same hallowed pattern their readers had found amusing and fulfilling for decades.

During the Gilded Age, newspapers, biographies, and cliff-hangers repeatedly echoed that same pattern, which promised good would prevail over evil. Editors deified community leaders, turning them into personifications of the success archetype. Obituaries and retirement stories praised diligent citizens who attained middle-class respectability but were too honest to make a fortune through speculating or profiting from the misery of others.

Reporters cast disaster accounts in the language of the pluck-and-luck myth. Fires served as almighty levelers. The rich and the poor suffered together. Money vanished. Only faith endured. Moreover, those endowed with integrity stood the test of the loss, while those pampered by a lifestyle of ease or sloth sank into oblivion. Devastation strengthened the true-hearted, who transformed their sorrow into opportunity. Individuals as well as towns arose from the ashes stronger than ever, according to editorials. Bardic tales similarly depicted fires and other tragedies as painful but invigorating chances to discover the inner strength that would revitalize a protagonist's life.

In addition to framing disaster accounts in terms of the archetypes that reinforced social mores, reporters reminded readers of the tension between materialism and spirituality. Stories about the sad consequences of spoiling sons and daughters underscored the pernicious effect of money on families. Both newspapers and publishing houses deplored the foolishness and decadence of the rich. Treasures of the heart, editors warned readers to remember, endured long after gold had lost its luster. Both bardic tales and news items pointed out that honor, public esteem, and fidelity could not be bought. The bards gradually reinterpreted paradigms to preserve traditional values.

Chapter 2

The Magic Formulas
of the People's Press

B etween the Civil War and World War I, the clamor for romances, cliff-hangers and other popular genres made publishing a big business dependent upon consumers who tried to justify reading for pleasure as somehow uplifting. Many people preferred success tales over literary masterpieces. Talented novelists suffered from the lack of public support for their work. Even *Moby-Dick* (1851), Herman Melville's masterpiece, failed commercially: "The last three decades of Melville's life were silent. He lived inconspicuously in New York City and spent twenty years working as a district inspector of customs there."[1]

Critics feared the impact of the quick sales of the formula tales upon literary giants such as Melville. The editor of *Blackwood's Edinburgh Magazine* accused popular authors of reducing fiction to a product so dependent upon crowd approval that in 1899 novelists, like hat makers, rode the crest of fashion.[2] Nathaniel Hawthorne had drawn similar conclusions in 1855, when he complained in a letter to his publisher that the demand for "innumerable editions" of Maria Susanna Cummins's romance, *The Lamplighter* (1854), proved "America [was] given over to a d——d mob of scribbling women." The fact that he read the "scribbling women's" work underscores their popularity. The dominance of "trash," Hawthorne declared, had blunted readers' taste, making it impossible for him to succeed. Yet he praised "Fanny Fern," the author of the sentimental love story, *Ruth Hall* (1855), for "[writing] as if the Devil were in her; and that is the only condition under which a woman writes anything worth reading."[3] Both Hawthorne and the editor of *Blackwood's* compared these morality tales to classics.

The commercial fiction resembled extended fairy tales more than novels, however. Unlike novelists, who shared their personal insights into human nature, those who wrote books to please the multitudes built plots around archetypes. Thus, collectively, they created a distinctive body of narrative—the people's press.

The people's press combined the format of the novel with the conventions of the fairy tale, the parable, and the legend to delineate the meaning of material and spiritual success. In fact, some best sellers barely qualified as novels, because they were constructed as tales expanded to fill publishing agendas, rather than as literary works. The spinners of the magical formula stories entertained the masses, taught melodramatic lessons, relied on stock characters, and repeated the repertoire of predictable but nevertheless exciting situations that reassured readers rather than challenged their moral sensibilities. The popular bards used the press as a channel for the stories they wrote reflecting the fears and aspirations of their specific moment in the cavalcade of time. New technology enabled nineteenth-century yarn spinners to capture in print those ancient plots that in prior generations would have been passed on orally. Thus a new narrative format emerged, blending oral conventions and written structures to create permanent artifacts that reinforced cultural mores.

Many authors, including the Reverend Charles M. Sheldon, who wrote *In His Steps* (1897), served morality rather than art.[4] The pastor asked his congregation, "What would Jesus do?" His characters answered the question by earning, at the same time, a living and praise from the community. In its era, Sheldon's success parable outsold everything except the Bible and collections of Shakespeare. The editor of *Blackwood's* called the book "lumps of sugar," noting that "they [copies of the book] cover the face of America like a swarm of locusts."[5]

The popularity of books like *In His Steps* (1897) reflected the public fascination with that illusive cultural mandate, success. Of course, for religious people, success meant surviving financially while following the laws recorded in Genesis I. Even those who did not attend church respected the biblical moral code. However, the blend of religious and secular language invoked to describe success confused educated citizens, as well as those who had been instructed only by hard knocks.

What Is Success?

The *Random House Dictionary of the English Language* defines *success* in three ways. First, it is "the favorable or prosperous termination of attempts or endeavors." Second, the word implies "the attainment of wealth, position, honors and the like." Third, the term signifies "a successful performance." The circular nature of the third definition reflects the fog surrounding this word. Everybody wants to succeed, to "turn out successfully"—that is, to "attain desired results . . . to thrive, prosper, grow or the like . . . to attain success in some popularly recognized form, as wealth or standing."[6] Success is a public as well as a personal goal.

Even today, democracy and the open-market economy prevail because popular bards translate (via formula tales conveying the rags-to-riches archetype) the notion of *success* as implying capitalism and altruism. Capitalism prescribes the mechanism and the rules for earning a living. Altruism, unselfish concern for the welfare of others, offers those who are prosperous opportunities to justify themselves by sharing their wealth with those who deserve compassion.

In the late nineteenth century, most people considered poverty to be the consequence of sloth. Hence, altruism and philanthropy usually symbolically sanctioned the status quo, simply by defining the circumstances that merited—or did not merit—intervention. Mere suffering or privation did not justify intercession. In fact, many believed, to qualify for financial assistance, a beneficiary had to earn respect and thus indicate loyalty, courage, and purity of spirit. But why do some prosper while others languish? The answer to this question was embodied in the Protestant work ethic, which Max Weber concluded transformed jobs into religious duties: "The most mundane tasks become devotional."[7] Hard work and chance, not economic swings, determined one's fate.

Popular culture often provides an arena within which people struggle to reconcile reality with revered myths. A myth is a story people believe into actuality. Myths convey the pivotal values of the community and emphasize action over character. Their importance lies in their power to motivate people.

The primary capitalist myth recasts "Cinderella" in other rags-to-riches stories. This is a sacred tale; the public often equates it with fundamental values like patriotism and family love.[8] Time and place remain fuzzy. During the Gilded Age, Horatio Alger and scores of other popular authors retold the cherished myth that sanctioned capitalism and upheld the nation's dominant value system. For instance, E. D. E. N. Southworth's romance, *Ishmael; Or, In the Depths* (1863), and its sequel, *Self-Raised; Or, From the Depths* (1864), follow one boy's victory—Alger (Cinderella) style—over poverty. The last sentence in the preface of the former book declares: "[Ishmael is] a guiding star to the youth of every land, to show them that there is no depth of human misery from which they may not, by virtue, energy and perseverance, rise to earthly honors as well as eternal glory."[9]

The rags-to-riches tales written by Alger, Southworth, and their colleagues conveyed a paradigm, instantly recognizable in a brief set of symbols. Like fairy tales, these stories made time and place indistinct, often interchangeable. While fairy tales impart universal truths, Ian Watt explains in *The Rise of the Novel* (1957), novels focus on specific individuals living in a particular place at a specific time. Alger's occasional minute details of the street life in Chicago or New York merely set the story firmly in the nineteenth century, giving it the guise of reality.

Alger wrote more than a hundred books about hard-working protagonists who overcome formidable odds to attain middle-class status. The plots start with a sequence of trials, which correspond to Cinderella's stoic effort to do her housework thoroughly and cheerfully, despite the cruelty of her stepmother and stepsisters. The Alger hero wins the respect of a benefactor through an act of bravery made possible only by improbable coincidence. Cinderella, too, proves herself worthy by sorting out poppy seeds from a pail full of beans of various sizes or by some equally strenuous task.

Once the fortuitous coincidence occurs, Cinderella, or Alger's Cinderfella, passes through a sequence of trials. Cinderella at midnight must relinquish her glory as the belle of the ball to return to being a drudge. Cinderfella also must avoid temptation and prove himself worthy. After a waiting period in which Cinderella keeps working at home and Cinderfella toils in the office or on the street, a magic moment of revelation arrives. Cinderella's tiny foot fits the slipper, proving her birthright, which the jealous stepmother has hidden from her. Cinderfella's true identity is revealed when the benefactor recovers his dead father's stolen will. Both Cinderella and Cinderfella triumph through hard work and gumption. Without coincidence and luck, neither would prosper.

The Cinderella story appealed to literary masters as well as to the forgotten writers who devoted themselves to entertaining readers eager for adventures and romances. Cinderella assured everyone that, amid the rush of change caused by technological innovation, the important things—the root values—remain the same. In *The Self-Made Man in America: The Myth of Rags to Riches* (1954), Irvin G. Wyllie analyzes the literary lions of the late nineteenth century who wrote about success and business.[10] Both popular bards and literary dons exposed the tension between business acumen and morality. Literature rose above the moment. The popular tales celebrated the present so indulgently that most lost their relevance within a generation.

Language, of course, changes over time. In addition to trying to understand the appeal of incidents that seem unbelievable today, modern scholars sometimes must translate dialects nearly impossible to decipher. For example, in describing the adventures of "Deadwood Dick," Henry Nash Smith expresses doubt that the character Old Avalanche really embodies "a genuine northern mountain man," as the roster of characters in the beginning of the cliff-hanger promised. This true-hearted but goofy sidekick often turned handsprings instead of walking and jabbered in a dialect "Wheeler intended to be outrageously funny, but is now unreadable even under the urging of scientific inquiry." Old Avalanche's black goat, Florence Nightingale, accompanied him everywhere. "This character appears repeatedly in the 'Deadwood Dick' series and does not improve on longer acquaintance," Smith concludes.[11]

Both novelists and popular bards defended morality against corrosion by rampant financial success. William Dean Howells drew a compelling portrait of a successful tycoon in *The Rise of Silas Lapham* (1886). Howells shaped American attitudes toward literature while serving as an editor at the *Atlantic Monthly* and later at *Harper's Monthly*. In his book, *Criticism and Fiction,* as well as in his *Harper's* magazine column, "Easy Chair," he propounded the "dicta of this age (1870–1910): that art must serve morality, that it should teach rather than amuse, and that truthfulness to American life would inevitably picture the smiling aspects of experience."[12]

The popular bards agreed with Howells that writers should show the uplifting side of life while simultaneously reassuring readers that goodness paid off. Even Henry James, who denied that morality was relevant in realism, focused on themes that appeared as exciting plot thickeners in the thrillers—psychology, phantoms, artists neglected, and childhood defiled. James "never attempted to portray the 'downtown' strongholds of business, the subject that he felt loomed largest in the buzzing, heedless democracy of late-nineteenth-century America. He predicted that reputations would be made by those who could capture the turbulent worlds of commerce and industry for fiction."[13] However, unlike the popular writers, James never wrote for story papers. He moved to Europe because he considered the United States an artistic desert.

Several decades later, Lewis Mumford debunked the notion that the arts had stagnated during the Gilded Age.[14] Instead of looking at the significance of the artists within the cultural context of the late nineteenth century, Mumford evaluated them in light of their relevance to the 1930s.

Mumford, Howells, and Mark Twain considered James's preference for the Old World short-sighted. The popular bards, too, struggled to reconcile their respect for the Old World as the bastion of manners and culture with their need to glorify the New World as the land of unlimited potential. Many resolved the conflict in favor of the United States, depicting villainous foreigners and decadent Continental mores. Both novelists and bards felt compelled to investigate social evils. For example, Herman Melville's short story, "Bartleby the Scrivener," traces the sad history of a "forlorn Wall Street clerk whose successive refusal to work, to move, to eat—lead inexorably to his death in the New York City prison, the Tombs."[15]

Like Melville, romance writers (such as Gene Stratton Porter) and religious bards (including E. P. Roe) worried about the consequences of social barriers. Of course, Melville differed from the popular writers in many ways. While most people today associate him with *Moby-Dick* (1851) and his South Sea island tales, in fact he wrote about poverty and bad luck as well as about adventure. Such masters as Melville, James, and Howells perceived the scramble for success in terms of real or at least credible situations. The popular writers, in contrast, selected realistic details to add variety to their repetitions of the enduring myth that, for lucky-plucky ones, respectability lies just around the corner.

How Does Society Mandate Success?

Just as most critics study the authors of classics, many historians concentrate on economics or politics rather than psychology. The bardic tales emphasized feelings and idealism rather than reality. "The success myth has always joined the promise of material rewards to a supernaturalistic cosmology and remains rooted in the belief that, in a universe of reason and law, man is free to decide his own fate."[16] The sentimentality and didacticism in the plots of these Gilded Age stories reflected the domination of morality in public discourse during that era. For example, those debating monetary questions invoked the rhetoric of morality—civilization, laissez faire, and natural laws.[17] Opponents of silver referred to it as a demonic influence. Christianity permeated the symbols used by many politicians, if not their daily practices. Some people were obsessed with the relationship between morality and success, and nearly everyone, regardless of income level or place of residence, was interested in that topic. Success stories, as well as advice on how to get ahead, circulated through many channels, including sermons frequently printed in newspapers and pamphlets.

Ministers, industrialists, and entertainers all believed in the success paradigm. Some published their "secrets" of success. The Reverend Russell Conwell praised the power of hard work, tempered with righteous luck. Having earned an estimated $2 million lecturing on *Acres of Diamonds* (1887), he used most of that money to found and maintain Temple University in Philadelphia so needy but worthy students could rise into the middle class. Many readers of *Acres of Diamonds* expected also to listen to Conwell proclaim the probability of finding riches in the back yard. This success tract appeared first in pamphlet form and later as a book. Andrew Carnegie, who made his fortune in the steel industry, wrote *The Gospel of Wealth* (1900) to tell the rich how to motivate the poor to prosper through self-improvement. Even the circus entrepreneur, P. T. Barnum, wrote inspirational tracts. In fact, dozens of self-help manuals codified the same formula that inspired Alger.

Critical reaction to this flood of idealism often emphasizes the economic and social disparities between the rags-to-riches dream and the brutal realities of everyday life in the period under consideration. In fact, literary historian Vernon L. Parrington calls the Gilded Age "the Great American Barbecue," a time in which the pretentious and the pompous reduced art to vulgarity.[18]

George Santayana mistakenly dismissed the period as a time of "wishful thinking." In his essay, "The Genteel Tradition," Santayana declares that American intellectuals have bifurcated minds that separate thought from experience. He personifies the "genteel tradition" as a bespectacled grandmother whose age and peculiar notions about propriety limited her vision. This passive, useless, decorative esthete pales beside the vibrant businessman. "This division may be found symbolized in American architecture: a neat reproduction of the colonial mansion—with some modern comforts introduced surreptitiously—stands beside the sky-scraper. The American Will inhabits the sky-scraper; the American intellect inhabits the colonial mansion. The one is the sphere of the American man; the other, at least predominantly, of the American woman. The one is all aggressive enterprise; the other is all genteel tradition."[19]

According to Santayana, poetics battle with pragmatism in the split American mind. He attributes this unfortunate schizophrenia to Calvinism, which has entombed the intellect in the past. Moreover, highbrows confuse traditional pap with the arts; while lowbrows, like dogs begging at a banquet table, lap up tidbits dropped by the nabobs. Such lowbrows do not participate in drafting the community's cultural agenda, any more than the mutts help plan the banquet menu. Indeed, in Santayana's view, the complacent intellectual class had been so debilitated by the excesses of Calvinism that their morals had suffered irreparably.

While in the past scholars tended to emphasize the intellectual class at the expense of the lowbrows, today's cultural historians recognize that the common people shaped, as well as benefited from, culture. In *Work, Culture and Society,* Herbert G. Gutman points out that the cultural heritage of individual laborers affected job performance and subtly changed the nature of the workplace.[20] Immigrants and Americans born in this country resisted the transition from a premodern to an industrial lifestyle and took refuge in traditional modes of expression: ballads, tales, and other folk arts.

Lawrence W. Levine refers to a "shared public culture" less rigidly divided into spheres based on sophistication than today's artistic domains.[21] In fact, prior to the turn of the century, he notes in *Highbrow/Lowbrow,* crowds made actors repeat pet lines, booed, and occasionally rioted when actions or accommodations displeased them. Thus they participated in, as well as watched, performances. Before 1900, Italian opera, Shakespeare, and European masterpieces interested all classes. The nation's cultural diversity, reflected in regional variations and ethnic enclaves, did not, until after the Gilded Age, split the population into a hierarchy based on education or class. According to David Paul Nord, although workers retained traditional mores and customs, many found solace in reading.[22]

These workers found insights into the meaning of existence, as well as entertainment, in the plots that reinforced their values. Walter R. Fisher believes people feel compelled not only to read but also to tell stories. He refers to *homo narrans,* the storytelling animal, to underscore the linguistic imperative of narrative closure.[23] A century ago, critics debated the impact of stories upon the multitude. Some called novels and magazine serials "opiates of the public." Nevertheless, at this time doubt gnawed at millionaires, scientists, farmers, factory hands, and everybody else confronted with the massive changes transforming the United States into an industrial society during the Gilded Age.[24] Uncertainty about the nature of faith, the role of the church in the community, and the meaning of personal success cannot be dismissed as the product of a clash between old and new values. Instead, the anxiety about what it meant to be an American working-class person reflected a metamorphosis of traditional mores—indeed, the creation of the modern mindset. Emphasizing the wealthy and obviously influential sectors of society obscures the crucial part the average individual played in all arenas of life. One idea—the millennium—galvanized all classes, and even the most pedestrian products of the popular press reflected the renewed interested in religious questions.

In fact, the proliferation of periodicals and cheap books for mass audiences reflected "the overall ubiquity of reading as a working-class activity."[25] Newspapers and magazines designed to appeal to the multitude proliferated. During the 1880s, as cities grew, evening editions catering to laborers increased by 112 percent. The U.S. Census Office in 1895 reported that readers could select from ten times as many periodicals and newspapers as their counterparts had had to choose from in the 1850s. Such boons as cheap paper, lucrative advertising, and the Postal Act of 1879 encouraged the creation of magazines for national distribution. The expanded audience bought paperbacks, cheap books, and other mass-produced works containing formulaic plots. The range of literary interests encompassed bardic tales, inspirational tracts, how-to pamphlets, and masterpieces, including the works of Defoe, Shakespeare, and the Bible.[26]

Most critics have judged the formula plots as novels and found them wanting; however, the popular plots merit consideration as a body of narratives separate from the classics. The very elements that make the serials appeal to the anonymous multitude disqualify them from consideration as novels. The popular plots appropriate structures from past oral traditions, from fairy tales. Readers predict what will happen and, in so doing, enjoy anticipating the triumph of virtue and the downfall of vice. The stock characters, the lexicon of actions and clichés, instill a sense of control over the random forces of evil.

Although the formula plots echoed the same success archetype, they were not identical. Many writers developed the formula creatively to make each story different. Some drew upon history. Others relied upon humor and local color. Many used multiple plots to keep the story fresh. To assume formula literature is by definition junk is to overlook the cultural role played by such fleeting tales in reinforcing values and providing a stage for experimentation with social change.

The stories analyzed in the course of research for this book are listed in the appendix. Each was examined individually, within a historical and cultural matrix. This chapter describes eleven major categories of works known as "potboilers." Popular-culture expert John G. Cawelti points out that popular literature differs from the serious genres of tragedy, comedy, and romance in that the classics "tend toward some kind of encounter with our sense of the limitations of reality, while formulas embody moral fantasies of a world more exciting, more fulfilling, or more benevolent than the one we inhabit."[27]

All the books studied present idealized visions of life. For example, instead of seeing the fatal blight of urban poverty, as Stephen Crane did in *Maggie: A Girl of the Streets* (1893), Alger, Roe, and Wiggin envision cities where hard work pays off and determination makes it possible to rise above destitution.[28] Roe, a Presbyterian, often found inspiration in newspaper clippings for his pious, sentimental, domestic romances, including *Opening a Chestnut Burr* (1874) and *He Fell in*

Love with His Wife (1886). "Religious fiction became an appropriate solace in this time of crisis because it helped writers forget about difficult Biblical or otherworldly dilemmas. To secularize sin and salvation was to make them more manageable, to retrieve them from the doubtful realm of metaphysics and to anchor them in perceivable reality."[29]

The forty-four works analyzed in this study (see appendix) were selected from titles suggested by James D. Hart in *The Popular Book: A History of America's Literary Taste,* by Frank Mott in *Golden Multitudes: The Story of Best Sellers in the United States,* by Edmund Pearson in *Dime Novels; Or, Following an Old Trail in Popular Literature,* and by Quentin Reynolds in *The Fiction Factory; Or, From Pulp Row to Quality Street.*[30]

An extensive analysis was made of the plot of each work. The focus on narrative skeletons made it possible to obtain some objectivity in a highly subjective enterprise. Scholars argue over the meaning of symbols in literature but agree upon the sequence of events. No matter who does the plot summary, the incidents remain the same. Spot checks of more than a hundred popular works indicated that each selection was representative. Published interviews with the authors, as well as articles written about them, provided insights into their aspirations and motives. These writers repeated the success archetype in a myriad of long stories in all the genres.

Across genres, certain patterns of belief were evident. The most pervasive theme was the question for ordinary people of their personal worth and responsibility in the efficient, anonymous, mechanized realm created by the professional and the scientist. Indeed, "the surrender of inner freedom, the discipline of deviant impulses into rapturous conformity and the consequent achievement of both worldly success and divine grace merge into a single mythical process, a cosmic success story."[31]

Doubts about the new technological world inspired religious motifs even in secular works like dime novels, horse operas, and mysteries. The popularity of "Old Sleuth," a detective character created by Harlan Page Halsey, coincided with the rise of urban America. "Old Sleuth" and his companions employed the scientific method to solve crimes. These detective stories demonstrated how science might be harnessed to promote law and order. In fact, Twain noted in *The Galaxy* (1871) that most folks read their sermons rather than heard them; thus they learned the Gospel of Christ "through the despised novel and Christmas story, NOT from the drowsy pulpit!"[32]

Throughout the Gilded Age, religious novels commanded attention because readers encountered the consequences of piety and hypocrisy daily. "Like any popular books, no matter what their subject matter . . . , these religious works appeal to the prevailing needs, desires and interests that the widest reading public also holds during its non-reading hours."[33] Before 1850, the plots focused on the inner turmoil of the protagonist. By the Gilded Age, authors had discovered the golden formula that linked wealth with spiritual growth and often works "contained love affairs pivotal in the conversions of the central characters."[34] The religious books in this investigation—Roe's *Barriers Burned Away* (1872), Wallace's *Ben-Hur: A Tale of the Christ* (1880), and Deland's *John Ward, Preacher* (1888)—all depict a cosmos in which the mysteries of heaven evaded human comprehension but nevertheless provide respite from the world's cruelty.[35] Of course, contradictions and coincidences abound, as the protagonists struggle to overcome temptations.

Lucky coincidences assist protagonists in the idea portraits, too. The stock characters play the sketchiest possible roles in these stories. In his commentary on "ideas in the Eighties," Mott includes all books (even *Ben-Hur*) containing "theses and a jumble of notions."[36] I excluded from his broad category stories that do not emphasize ideas over personalities to specify a plot type with a particular kind of story line.

Mott notes the dissatisfaction with social conditions that churned in intellectual circles during the 1880s. Reform movements inspired Sheldon to write *In His Steps* (1897) and Bellamy to imagine an industrial utopia in his Social Gospel novel, *Looking Backward* (1888).[37] Wiggin reminded readers of the true meaning behind yuletide frivolity in *The Birds' Christmas Carol* (1887).[38] Phelps surveyed heaven three times in *Gates Ajar* (1868), *Beyond the Gates* (1883), and *The Gates Between* (1887).[39] Twain and Warner wrote a two-volume parody, *The Gilded Age* (1873), to expose the absurdity of the primary capitalist rags-to-riches myth.[40]

In addition to mysteries and dime novels, domestic fantasies appealed to readers. The action in these family stories typically hinges on either the fortuitous or the disastrous appearance of a stranger. Cawelti called domestic novels that were reflective of social or historical contexts "social melodramas." These works "combine the emotional satisfactions of melodrama with the interest inherent in a detailed, intimate and realistic analysis of major social or historical phenomena."[41] George Cable's *John March, Southerner* (1894), since it depicts a particular place frozen in time, fits Cawelti's criteria for social melodrama. However, the book also belongs among the legion of domestic formula plots because each stock character behaves with the certainty promised by the success archetype.[42] Moreover, Cawelti's scheme reduces the domestic formula to a feeble cousin of realism. The repetitions of stock events did not aim to convey an accurate image of a real situation. The echoes vibrate with the resonance of the original, but most vary slightly from it.

A few stories satirized cherished cultural myths. In *Phemie Frost's Experiences* (1874), Stephens caricatures easterners' preoccupation with aristocracy, depicting the heroine's misconceptions through such devices as foiled assignations with a Russian prince. Stephens's parody resembles the typical women's romance and domestic novel in its emphasis on the importance of the home. However, unlike authors of domestic novels, which also glorified marriage, Stephens and the other romance writers focused on lovers rather than on several generations of characters. Her humorous variation on the success paradigm gave readers something to think about. The story unfurls on two levels. The physical details provide a link between the real world and the realm of the tale, so that the plot embodies a magic carpet to places far away from the drudgery and the disappointments of daily life. The characters seem to exist in a parallel universe just as tangible as the reader's milieu. Nineteenth-century readers probably imagined themselves in the world of the heroines. Janice Radway suggests that romance readers actively rather than passively consume books.[43]

Nevertheless, readers sometimes put down romances or cliff-hangers long enough to devour how-to pamphlets proclaiming the gospel of success. Hart and Mott contrast these tracts with the era's fiction. Both popular plots and motivational tracts reinforced the same values. P. T. Barnum's *The Art of Money-Getting*, a pamphlet originally published in 1858, later was reprinted as part of his autobiography, *Struggles and Triumphs* (1884). Carnegie's *The Gospel of Wealth* (1889) and Conwell's *Acres of Diamonds* (1887) articulate popular Gilded Age definitions of success.[44]

Despite the popularity of the inspirational writers, the name synonymous with the success archetype belonged to Alger, the author of adventure stories for boys. He has become so completely associated with the rags-to-riches paradigm that today some people think he was a fictional character!

Tracing the Cinderella archetype across genres a century ago provides insights into the narrative roots of American culture.[45] The formula plots offered a safe space to experiment with change. Today television, Harlequin romances, and the tabloids serve the same function as serial plots and cheap books did a century ago. The success prototype encouraged readers to prove their self-worth by performing acts that perpetuated majestic forces larger than any individual.

The repeated plots told people who they were while reminding them of their communal affiliations. James W. Carey points out that individuals rely upon culture to supply the palette for painting portraits of their experiences.[46] That private picture must form part of the mural of the larger society's identity and history. To relate one's individual story to the narratives of others requires absorbing a shared set of symbols, which ground all personal legends in the communal chronicle. "It is to enlarge the human conversation while deepening self-understanding."[47]

Why Study Success?

Studying formula tales reveals cultural facets of the Gilded Age impossible to fathom solely by examining economics or institutions. And analyzing the conditions that made the success archetype powerful a hundred years ago clarifies the meaning of prosperity today. The repeated plots and stock characters offered readers in a different era predictability in a world full of nasty surprises. Today predictable television characters give fans a sense of control over their complex environments, by creating a set of fantasy relationships in which everyone behaves according to the script rather than according to the rules of economic competition, which require that one lose so that the other may win. The link between the past and present sometimes bent but seldom broke because plots were flexible. Writers molded situations to the public's expectations. In fact, the story lines repeated in the modern mass media tie present forms to their predecessors. Television provides a forum for discovering cultural identity. Humans assess their worth and determine their niches in society largely by considering what others before them have been and done.

David Thorburn says television fits into the flow of narration that started with speech and will end only with extinction.[48] He traces the symbolic transformations of a warrior's sword as the tribe's fortunes fluctuate. Ironically, after the last battle has been lost, the sword survives in a museum as the artifact of a defunct people. According to Thorburn, paradigms evolve similarly, changing with the community and sometimes outliving it through acculturation. The content, rituals, and symbols of modern television, for example, began with early storytellers, including Shakespearean theater, Punch and Judy, and the rain dance. The roots of television are sunk deep in history. Of course, radio plays and motion pictures also developed on the tree of narration planted by the individual who first attempted to tell what happened on a hunt or to explain why the sun sets. Joseph Campbell's studies of myths as channels for bonding support Thorburn's idea.[49]

Identical stock characters and archetypes saturate television, nineteenth-century potboilers, and fairy tales. Television, as an arena for storytelling, connects the late twentieth century to all past times. Fiske and Hartley call this narrative undertow the bardic function, and Newcomb and Alley compare television to the chorus in a Greek tragedy that expresses the community's feelings.[50]

All societies, Campbell and Thorburn agree, develop a storytelling network to connect them with their past and offer wisdom for negotiating the present and planning for the future. Thorburn calls this continuous stream of stories a "consensus narrative" shared by all members of society. It is the pipeline to the nation's collective unconscious. This locus of common thought, the consensus narrative, tends to be conservative. It replays society's lore in symbols the public seeks to bridge the turbulent present and the nostalgic past where repeated stock characters, familiar plots, and established story conventions preclude despair.

The repetition of ideas via symbols in plots satisfies psychological and social needs that defy scientific explanation. Formula stories operate at a subconscious level. Their triteness comforts readers. Their clichés embody signposts of the inner self and, like a road map to cultural identity, reveal the meaning of life. Sometimes writers immerse paradigms in humor, because laughter releases tension and enhances one's sense of well-being. Just like the last century's potboilers, situation comedies frequently invite people to laugh at circumstances that scare or disgust them. As long as humans care about their lives and their ties to others, they will ground their existence in their community's narrative consensus.

Reversing Thorburn's phrase reveals an important dimension of the metaphor. While a *consensus narrative* preserves the social body by maintaining a set of traditional values, a *narrative consensus* gels when the members of a group clarify the purposes of their lives by creating stories that cast the success prototype in contemporary terms. The threadbare plots connect the present with the past and so provide narrative closure. No single repetition cures broken spirits, but constant exposure to the success archetype helps people develop an emotional immunity to despair. Despite the upsets and betrayals they endure, protagonists persevere. The success paradigm guarantees spiritual rewards for goodness and promises cosmic justice despite the machinations of the powerful. Banal plots persist because they help individuals cope with the shattering of their illusions. Thus formula tales, as channels of popular culture, should be judged according to their efficacy in preserving and codifying values.

Chapter 3

"Book Soap"

Clean Thoughts for Clean Folks

When the bottom fell out of the cheap paperback industry during the recession of the late 1880s, entrepreneurs bought thousands of books wholesale to give away with their products. In fact, the combination of soap and books proved so profitable that a new trademark, "Book Soap," appeared. Soap manufacturers, John Tebbel estimates in *A History of Book Publishing in the United States*, offered their customers two million volumes. The ubiquity of books inspired the invention of a vending machine "with a crank that produced, for a nickel, a novel that could not be made to sell at higher prices."[1] Patent medicine distributors gave free sets of books to those who invested fifty cents in their curatives. Shoppers who spent fifteen cents received a complimentary novel. "Book Soap" authors included Edgar Alan Poe, Nathaniel Hawthorne, Emily Dickinson, and popular American authors as well as Charles Dickens, Sir Walter Scott, and other Europeans.

The unlikely combination of books and soap is only one of many contradictory features of life in the years between 1870 and 1910. Social contradictions abounded. For example, although the invention of efficient machines and the upsurge of labor unions created leisure time and thus precipitated an appreciation for recreation, people nevertheless associated hard work with clean living. By claiming to engage only respectable authors, publishers milked the quest for purity dominant in many social and civic circles.

Although the "Book Soap" trademark implied an affinity between fiction and wholesome thinking, some educators feared that books in fact corrupted readers. For instance, in 1870, *Hours at Home* observed that only "lazy, not very clean" boys who indulged their physical senses read novels.[2] On the other hand, generations of church leaders had appreciated the power of the printed word as a means of spreading the gospel. Some writers, Richard Weiss suggests in *The American Myth of Success*, tried to inculcate an appreciation for conscience and restraint in readers, to prevent the nation's blessings from becoming curses.[3] Indeed, many regarded Bible reading as an integral part of their religious responsibilities but worried about encountering Satan in popular literature.[4]

To Anthony Comstock, director of the New York Society for the Suppression of Vice, "popularized nastiness" was spreading an "epidemic of lewdness through the channels of light literature" among the country's 22,000,000 youths. In 1873, after little deliberation and no hearings, Congress enacted the Comstock Act to prohibit obscene mail. As a special agent of the Post Office Department, Comstock rid the mails of anything he deemed unsavory. In 1875, Comstock's society was empowered to arrest those who violated New York's anti-obscenity law.

Comstock wrote *Traps for the Young* (1883) because he feared that nickel novels, "so-called monthly libraries of cheap literature," as well as newspapers, "all . . . [exerted] a silent influence in the wrong direction." The "devil seeds" sown by such publications yielded a harvest of crime and shame. Comstock warned, "unless the restraining forces of religion and morality keep ahead of all other considerations, the ship of state will soon be dashed to pieces upon the boulders and quicksands of immorality." The minions of decency freely mixed metaphors in their tirades against story papers and dime novels. This "vampire literature," Comstock concluded, distracted the weak and encouraged backsliders to devote the Sabbath to E. D. E. N. Southworth or "Ned Buntline" instead of to God.[5]

In 1885, the editor of the *Zion's Herald* of Boston told the Lake George Conference of Librarians that books exerted a greater influence upon readers than human companionship because they "[touch] our whole being, intellect, heart and executive purpose. . . . They lay hold of our highest and most sacred sentiments and color our views of the life beyond."[6] This critic believed books could either purify or corrupt the mind. In *The Fiction Factory*, William Wallace Cook, who also wrote under the names John Milton Edwards and Stella Edwards, attributed his twenty-two successful years as a writer to his ability to establish a Borateem connection to fiction for his readers. "The life of today sets a pattern for the fiction of today. The masses demand rapid-fire action and good red brawn in their reading matter. Their awakened moral sense makes possible the muck-raker; and when they weary of the day's evil and the day's toil, it is their habit to divert themselves with pleasant and exciting reading. And it must be CLEAN."[7]

This chapter analyzes how literary, technological, and spiritual metaphors updated the success archetype and, in doing so, helped to keep religion a potent force. The artisans of popular culture recast biblical imagery, including the proverb claiming cleanliness was next to godliness, into guidelines for effective living. During the Gilded Age, the strange combination of soap and books reflected uncertainty about the role of publishing. Was it a means of making money or a pulpit for uplifting readers? Indeed, the famous Reverend Henry Ward Beecher endorsed Pears soap.[8] Publishing firms of all sizes sought manuscripts that would instruct rather than merely amuse people. The serials and cheap fiction reassured powerless folks that, ultimately, goodness would prevail, despite the transformation of the republic from an agrarian commonwealth into an urban society where citizens shared institutions with strangers as well as with acquaintances.

Towns ceased to be social islands when technology tied them inextricably to each other and to cities.[9] In *The Railway Journey: The Industrialization of Time and Space in the Nineteenth Century*, Wolfgang Schivelbusch points out that railroads connected the isolated hamlets in a continuous network. As shipping enabled folks to buy produce from distant areas, goods lost their distinctively regional traits.[10] The regularity of the train schedule shattered the sense of neighborhood and privacy that once had prevailed in the countryside. Time as well as distance shrank when the telegraph, functioning in tandem with railroads, emerged as a vital instrument for sending signals down the track.[11]

In improving communication capabilities, the railroads, the U.S. Postal Act of 1879, and the telegraph created a consumer public whose members, no matter where they lived, were united by reading the same things, by perusing the same advertisements, and by purchasing the same merchandise.[12] Moreover, by collapsing time and space to a series of dots and dashes dependent upon the content of the communiqué rather than the distance it traveled over the wires, the telegraph freed messages from the constraints of transportation. Of course, the speed made news a commodity. Current events spanned global, national, and local arenas. People read about myriads of political rallies, sensational murders, oddities, and scandals.

For two years, nearly everyone in the United States read about Samuel Tilton's charge that the Reverend Henry Ward Beecher had seduced his wife. "For thousands of Americans, [Beecher] was no less than a modern oracle."[13] His ability to incorporate middle-class values into his Social Darwinist messages made him popular. Beecher's defenders converted the scandal into a verbal gladiators' battle between the church and skeptics. Beecher's attorneys denounced Tilton as a modern Judas. Many people considered attacks upon the widely published and highly respected man of God to be assaults on Christianity. Instead of trying the minister, the court put religion on trial. Although editors explained that covering Beecher's alleged improprieties empowered the populace to cleanse the public arena, skeptics viewed the dailies as rumor mongers.

The Beecher scandal flashed across the country. The radical feminist Victoria Claflin Woodhull, the era's flamboyant, self-proclaimed "bad girl," condemned Beecher for hiding behind his clerical robes instead of defending free love. In fact, dispatchers sometimes manufactured news where none existed. For example, the telegraph operator in Austin, Nevada, inadvertently passed along an April Fool's Day hoax as a real event. The *Austin (Nev.) Reese River Reveille* reported on 2 April 1875 that Beecher had "jumped overboard and was crushed to death by the wheels of a ferry boat" on his way home from his trial. On the next day, an item on an inside page of the *Reveille* exposed the deception but praised the telegraph operator for "his zeal to give [people] the news" and urged readers to "commend the *Reveille* for its desire to give them the latest intelligence."[14]

The modern demand for accuracy and objectivity simply did not exist a hundred years ago. Newspaper articles established the context for events and commented on their significance to the community. Often writers used language and rhetorical devices, which twentieth-century readers expect to find solely on the editorial page.

For example, the editor of the *Reveille*, in the erroneous notice of Beecher's death, listed the minister's contributions to philosophy and literature. He admitted, despite "all his faults [Beecher] is a great man, and by his words if not by his acts, has been a moral teacher of extraordinary power." Nevertheless, in the back pages of the edition, the editor declared: "An Austin lady, when she read the report of Beecher's suicide last evening, said she felt kind'er sorry for Beecher; but the papers would now have room to publish those nice recipes about how to make rutabaga waffles and potato-pound cakes." In a paragraph sandwiched between a brief account of the adventures of a desperado, Chevaz, who committed three robberies in one day, and a notice about the impact of the recently minted twenty-cent gold piece, the editor quipped: "Beecher said in his testimony yesterday that his manner in Tilton's house was pretty much the same as in his own home. That's just what Tilton charged—only too much so!"[15]

Thanks to the telegraph, even communities in the Far West and the South knew of the preacher's alleged forbidden love for one of his flock. Journalists and popular bards, as well as down-home pastors, speculated on the sins of the celebrated orator of Brooklyn's Plymouth Church, the most powerful seat of Congregationalism in the United States. The ambiguous resolution of the case in a hung jury satisfied nobody.[16] Even after the trial had ended, the indignant continued to lambaste Beecher. For example, in 1883, the editor of the *Alexandria (La.) Daily Town Talk* joked, "Henry Ward Beecher says 'Four-Fifths of the inhabitants of Heaven are women.' It is the Beecher idea of Heaven."[17]

Despite being ridiculed, Beecher—brother of the courageous reformer, Catherine Beecher, and the famous writer, Harriet Beecher Stowe—remained the earthly embodiment of his congregation's cherished values. When Henry died in 1887, civic and religious leaders contributed testimonials to a memorial volume featuring a picture of "Plymouth's Dying Pastor—A Faithful Wife's Untiring Vigil."[18] The faithful had dismissed the adultery charges because they considered Beecher to be God's emissary. Besides commanding space in news columns, the Beecher-Tilton scandal inspired countless authors of potboilers to mete out justice to hypocrites whose faults led to their downfall. Since public bards scrutinized the papers for ideas with which to embellish the success archetype, the suggestion of Beecher's guilt, rather than the actuality of his situation, fired their imaginations. None referred to him directly. Instead, they created a stock villain, the depraved minister whose greed and duplicity doom him and others. By reducing criticism of Beecher to attacks on the authority of the Bible, Beecher's attorneys deflected accusations that the parson had traded spiritual rewards for physical ones.[19]

Ironically, by transforming him into a living icon of righteousness falsely accused by the wicked press, the scandal strengthened Beecher's hold over his flock. His admirers considered him the "outstanding pulpit orator of his day," while his rivals discredited him, claiming his immense popularity arose from "his sentimental and high-flown rhetoric in sermons on political, social and religious subjects."[20] Beecher lectured passionately in England against slavery and published many collections of his sermons. Reporters covered his crusades. Moreover, the print media provided a stage for Beecher and a legion of public heroes, including his father Lyman Beecher, a Presbyterian minister, who had given blistering temperance and anti-Catholic speeches. All news stories, regardless of their factual content, of course, rely upon readers' collaboration for meaning.

Both newspapers and magazines told the tale of the minister and Mrs. Tilton. How writers interpreted events depended upon their loyalty to Beecher and their need to preserve his image as God's emissary. If Brother Henry couldn't pass through the eye of the needle, who could? The ambivalence of the jury reflected doubts fueled by progress during the Gilded Age. In the blaze of electric lights, the thunder of the Bessemer steel furnaces, and a myriad of mechanical assaults on the natural world, old values provided a refuge amid change.

At least figuratively, religious metaphors returned to individuals control over their volatile world. As a living icon of the church during his trial for adultery, Beecher served as a mediator between progress and tradition. Even his transgression reflected the tension between old ways, represented by the sanctity of marriage, and new ideas such as free love. He led his congregation down a middle road between Darwinism and Calvinism. Beecher's optimistic sermons reassured them that their faith could not be shaken by secular accomplishments. He spoke to both the orthodox and the liberal in his sermons, quoting the Bible but also describing incidents of street life in New York and Brooklyn. Criticizing such a beloved preacher amounted to blasphemy.[21]

Throngs of tourists filled the pews of the Plymouth Congregational Church. They had read Beecher's sermons in newspapers and magazines. His relaxed pulpit style contrasted with the traditionally staid demeanor of most clergy. He shocked conservatives by telling jokes and thus encouraging his flock to laugh in God's house. Paul Carter, author of *The Spiritual Crisis of the Gilded Age*, observed Beecher's "popular preaching was open to the same criticism that in a later day has been leveled at television: if it had something for everybody it had not much for anybody."[22]

"Damned Pleasing?"

Just as theologians accused Beecher of insulting religion with his pulpit antics, critics called publishers peddlers of illicit goods. Beecher's sermons, like the popular plots, simultaneously entertained and instructed the public. Although some may never have heard of "Book Soap," which gave customers an engaging story as well as a cleaning agent, most read in pursuit of practical as well as frivolous goals. The vigilant equated listening to Beecher with reading trashy thrillers. However, their disapproval did not prevent the multitude from admiring Beecher or from buying cheap publications with religious overtones. Eventually the nation's social, civic, and intellectual leaders praised Beecher.

Beecher's trial also clarified technology's role in solving mechanical problems but not ethical ones. By 1875, the complexities of life had made it difficult to arrive at simple determinations of right and wrong. The question of whether Beecher had sinned proved to be not nearly as significant as the consequences of publicly acknowledging flaws in an eminent preacher whose diligence had made his church well known across the nation. Beecher embodied the ambitious protagonist in story papers and cheap novels who reaped both material and spiritual rewards. These rough-hewn plots reminded readers that tradition applauded constancy. The old values provided a refuge from mechanical assaults on the natural world.[23]

Change and society functioned symbiotically. Many believed that without inventors, progress could not occur and that without progress, society would stagnate. Therefore, as new time-saving tools replaced older ones, people appreciated the rise in their standard of living but regretted the loss of control over their world that accompanied increasing mechanical sophistication. They felt compelled to harness technology to make the powerful machines serve God rather than Satan. Gadgets had to be as commercial and useful as "Book Soap" to guarantee that inventions would promote virtue instead of creating temptations.

Metaphors convey stories in a distilled form and invest practical objects with purpose, thereby reducing the impersonal forces of production to manageable entities. Of course, these figures of speech draw upon the stockpile of past associations. Familiar metaphors, John F. Kasson notes in *Civilizing the Machine,* often attribute inventions to divine providence.[24] For example, during the Revolutionary era, patriots saw in machines a means of securing their destiny; they believed that, unlike the Old World, the new Republic had broken free of the cosmic laws governing the engine of the universe. In America, all things seemed possible, because God had blessed the Yankees with ingenuity as well as with abundant land.

From colonial times to the present, figurative language has blended pastoral images with industrial technology. For example, in the Gilded Age, "iron horses" raced through the imagination. Workers toiled in "beehives of industry." "King Coal" eventually deposed "King Cotton." The Social Gospel advocate who wrote *In His Steps* (1897) referred to himself as one of "God's phonographs . . . with a personality of his own."[25] Indeed, while the Reverend Sheldon worried about "building up the edifice of man," the "Hokey-Pokey Man," Samuel F. Dunham, constructed a new dessert—or rather applied the principles of efficiency to an old treat. He "laid by a snug fortune" selling ice-cream "bricks" or "hokey-pokeys" for a penny.[26]

Although bricks of ice cream may seem trivial, they were the example par excellence of convenient and sanitary packaging. The profusion of inventions during the years between the close of the Civil War and the beginning of World War I offered citizens gadgets that each inventor claimed were useful. Some (refrigerated railroad cars, ether, and skyscrapers) proved very valuable indeed. Others, however, were ludicrous. For instance, the talking doll evolved around 1890, according to children's advocate Kate Douglas Wiggin. Initially, through the miracle of electricity, this four-foot-high babe babbled, "Mama! Papa!" Toy makers soon felt compelled to improve upon their lifelike creation, so they gave the doll an angelic voice and an altruistic message "fitted to the needs of the present decade." Now, the child who played house learned a lesson. To the question, "Do you want a piece of candy?" the doll responded, "Give brother *big* piece; give me little piece!"[27]

The doll's response ignored human nature but reflected the cultural mandate to make play pragmatic (and women self-sacrificing). Wiggin resented false sentiment and "devoutly hoped [that the mechanism would] horrify by-standers by demanding, 'Give me *big* piece! Give brother little piece!'" At least, then the doll would sound like a real child. The author of *Rebecca of Sunnybrook Farm* sympathized with tots: "Think of having a gilded dummy like that given to you to amuse yourself with. Think of having to play, to play forsooth, with a model of propriety, a high-minded monstrosity like that!"[28] She believed in allowing youngsters to explore the world by going outside and getting dirty. Wiggin feared that contrivances like the electronic talking doll would stifle children's imaginations.

While expensive toys may have stifled children's budding sense of wonder, playthings for grownups occasionally proved deadly for all ages. Attempts to make amusements "useful" led to new hazards, especially in travel. Every innovation in transportation has taken its toll. The improvement of roads both enhanced mobility and introduced the possibility of being run over. Horse-and-carriage accidents claimed victims prior to the carnage inflicted by railroads. Bicycles also incited fatal carelessness. Of course, with increasing complexity, the dangers snowballed. During the Gilded Age, public conveyances evolved from the horse and buggy to the tram to the automobile. By-standers as well as drivers got hurt.

Consider the fate of wagon driver Julius Citron, who, on 7 October 1907, waited for the streetcar before dawn, until an automobile of the "long, low racing" variety struck him, hurled him through the air, and vanished into the darkness. When Patrolman Lawless stepped in front of the auto (which was going thirty miles an hour) and waved his arms for it to stop, the chauffeur "merely laughed" and "steered straight for" the officer, who jumped out of the way just in time. No one saw the vehicle's number.[29]

Besides decrying automobile accidents, intellectuals worried about the hidden threats some stationary marvels posed. For instance, most hailed the Brooklyn Bridge as a symbol of national unity and a tri-

umph of engineering. Yet, to Henry James, the graceful blend of gran-
ite arches and steel cable signified a spider ready to suck the very life
out of the common people who were supposed to benefit from it. In
Darkness and Daylight: Lights and Shadows of New York Life (1891),
Helen Campbell asserted that this engineering feat turned those unlucky enough to live in the tenements beneath the bridge into noc-
turnal zombies who took outings on holidays to see the sun. The
Brooklyn Bridge, Alan Trachtenberg concluded, ascended metaphori-
cally as well as physically in 1883. Artists and intellectuals responded
ambiguously to the technological feat made necessary by the expansion of industry. Was the bridge "a helping hand" extending across
the water? Or was it a blood sucker?[30]

Although it did not roar and could not move, the Brooklyn Bridge
symbolized possibility and inspired dreams. Painters and poets paid it
tribute. While workers who risked their lives to construct the link between Brooklyn and Manhattan remained mostly unnoticed, crowds
flocked to Philadelphia to see another wonder, the mighty Corliss
steam engine at the Centennial Exposition in 1876. The Corliss ruled
like a Cyclops over the "mechanical forms crouched low along the
nave resting on huge iron paws, their hoppers yawning for victuals."[31]
Writers ransacked mythology to pay homage to the Corliss engine and
its metal kin.

In fact, Kasson says, Americans reconciled their love for nature
with their reverence for machines by depersonalizing Mother Nature,
making her into the Grand Cosmic Engine. At the same time, the
country ironically began personifying inventions. John C. Kimball told
readers of the Unitarian *Christian Examiner* in 1869 that inventors,
not artists, embodied moral superiority because their works yielded
concrete results. To this Prophet of the Practical and the Useful, God
reigned in heaven as the almighty inventor and Jesus Christ served as
his chief mechanic.[32]

Frequently, such metaphors reinforced the success archetype.
Even God worked, and Christ toiled in the practical tasks reserved
for mechanics. All the popular print arenas indulged in evocative figurative language. News and fiction alike reiterated the traditionally sacred theme: the righteous triumph, and the wicked fall. Nevertheless, to some critics, including Comstock, it seemed the popular bards
were "conspirators against the nation's highest hopes for the future":
"There is at present a strong competition among writers and publishers of cheap books and papers to see which one can excel the others
in unclean stories."[33] He worried about the evil influence of reading,

beginning with the Sunday paper and progressing through dime novels and story papers to reprints and subscription books: "Novel-readers are like opium smokers: the more they have of it, the more they want of it, and the publishers, delighted at this state of affairs, go on corrupting public taste and understanding and making fortunes out of this corruption."[34]

Although *The Hour* magazine claimed "millions of young girls and thousands of young men are *novelized* into absolute idiocy," what individuals read during the last three decades of the nineteenth century remains shrouded in mystery, partly because readers often chose materials considered trivial at best and vile at worst.[35] Despite the criticism of the popular bards, a mania for reading spread across the United States in the 1870s, according to John Tebbel, author of *A History of Book Publishing in the United States.*[36] With mandatory public education and the construction of libraries, literacy increased. This increase, together with the discovery of inexpensive ways to manufacture paperbacks, precipitated the reading boom.

Fiction dominated publishers' lists of new books between 1880 and 1909. Of course, reprints accounted for some of the trade. But until 1910, when the category of "literature and collected works" (classics, essays, etc.) edged out the category of "fiction" by a small margin, fiction dominated according to Tebbel. Readers frequented bookstores as well as newsstands in train depots, pharmacies, hotel lobbies, and department stores. Some ordered thrillers, romances, and other potboilers from the fiction factories by mail while others purchased subscriptions for cheap books from door-to-door sales agents. All these outlets published some works that, being designed to appeal to the masses, were destined to vanish.

Most books celebrated the success archetype (the formula for being simultaneously solvent and altruistic). No one knew which titles would merit literary longevity. Best sellers, better sellers, and popular tracts that fascinated the multitude filled a cultural need. However, momentary relevance did not guarantee permanence. Indeed, in *Adventure, Mystery and Romance: Formula Stories as Art and Popular Culture,* John Cawelti noted that social melodramas, such as E. P. Roe's *Barriers Burned Away* (1872), which was inspired by the Chicago Fire, focus so tightly on current circumstances that, after a generation or two, readers cannot relate to the plots.[37]

The Booksellers: A War on Trash?
Publishers of classics, as well as firms specializing in popular genres, profited from the mania for "book soap." In fact, most publishing

houses claimed their reading lists protected the innocent from the filth hidden between the lurid covers of the dime and cheap novels. By repeating the success paradigm and scrupulously echoing the moral code of the era, potboilers competed for respectability with masterpieces that pondered universal truths. The rest of this chapter examines the publishing industry as a whole. Cheap publishing firms, with reasonably priced editions, made available to even the poorest readers literature that was destined to greatness. Moreover, people could easily read both the contemporary fairy tales and the classics.

By the mid-1870s, the avalanche of newspapers, magazines, and cheap books precipitated a backlash against reading fiction, especially cliff-hangers. Leading publishing houses took advantage of the attacks by claiming to protect neighborhood dealers from the garbage produced by unscrupulous entrepreneurs whose shoddy wares flooded back alleys. Nevertheless, even the most highly regarded firms marketed best sellers containing the success archetype. Nearly a third of those books, Frank Luther Mott observed in *Golden Multitudes,* "fall pretty definitely outside the literary pale."[38] The term *best seller* was coined in 1910 to indicate extensive sales. It never reflected quality. Moreover, no readily defined public assured commercial success. Every year the list of best sellers included sugary romances, intellectual treatises, and literary masterpieces.

For instance, in 1894, five very different stories achieved best-seller status. With *Trilby,* George du Maurier proved that the public had an appetite for frank sexual material.[39] With schoolboy charm, by posing questions to business tycoons in clever cartoons, William H. Harvey promoted the gold standard in *Coin's Financial School.*[40] With *The Prisoner of Zenda*, a king-for-a-day fantasy, Anthony Hope escaped from reality.[41] With *Beside the Bonnie, Bonnie Brier Bush,* the Reverend John Watson, under the pseudonym Ian Maclaren, saluted his highland home in Scotland.[42] But the one entry destined to remain popular a hundred years later was Margaret Marshall Saunders' canine rags-to-riches story, *Beautiful Joe,* which has sold well over a million copies since 1894.[43]

Edward Weeks limits his best-seller list for the years 1875–1934 to titles selling half a million copies. Because he felt that Weeks's standard was too rigorous for the years prior to 1875 and too loose for those after 1934, Mott "set the figure required to make a book a best seller at one percent of the population of the continental United States."[44] In *Golden Multitudes,* Mott includes 234 works appearing between 1662 and 1945. His "Better-Sellers List" contains selections that created a stir in their time. Some of them, including Mark

Twain's *Tom Sawyer* (1876) and Somerset Maugham's *Of Human Bondage* (1915), became classics.[45]

This study focuses on books with plots built around the success prototype that, for the most part, did not prevail as literature. Today some, including *Mrs. Wiggs of the Cabbage Patch* (1901) and *The Hoosier School Master* (1871), are appreciated as Americana.[46] A few continue to command attention, proving that Alger's success formula remains relevant. *The Little Princess* (which first appeared in *St. Nicholas* magazine in 1888), *Freckles* (1904), and *Ben-Hur* (1880) still can be found in library collections.[47] Despite libraries' lack of interest in most clean tales popular a century ago, as recently as 1994 customers could still order the *Frank Merriwell* series from bookstores in either cloth or paperback.[48]

Booksellers hoped that every work ordered would catch the public's attention. They purchased volumes from major houses and regional presses. Although after the Civil War firms also flourished in Boston, Philadelphia, and Chicago, New York remained the publishing center. Authors gained prestige, and publishers made profits in proportion to their abilities to please the multitude who unconsciously sought the affirmation of reading as a route to improvement. No one could predict which works would become best sellers.

Not even the previous publication of a highly popular novel guaranteed a new title a place in the spotlight. Given the popularity of *Ben-Hur* (1880), Lew Wallace's biblical Horatio Alger tale, Harpers expected his new book, *The Prince of India* (1893), to do well indeed.[49] Through parables that embody its plot, *Ben-Hur* had blended action with spiritual insights and practical life lessons so effectively that half a million copies had been sold between 1880 and 1890. After an initial flurry of interest, no doubt due to the celebrity of the Civil War general, readers ignored the new work.

Many other houses also sought authors like Wallace who spoke to the common people. Macmillan launched the modern western genre with Owen Wister's *The Virginian: A Horseman of the Plains* (1902).[50] Lothrop made money on reporter Irving Bacheller's backwoods humor in *Eben Holden* (1900).[51] Doubleday, Page published Gene Stratton Porter's "Cinderfella" tale of the Michigan forest, *Freckles* (1904).[52] Scribners released *Little Lord Fauntleroy* (1886), by Frances Hodgson Burnett, much to the horror of boys who were forced to wear velvet suits trimmed with lace collars and cuffs after their mothers saw the illustrations of the American urchin whose goodness redeemed his English aristocratic grandfather.[53]

Loring charmed readers of all ages with John Habberton's *Helen's*

Babies: With Some Account of Their Ways, Innocent, Crafty, Angelic, Impish, Witching and Repulsive. Also a Painful Record of Their Actions During Ten Days of Their Existence, by Their Latest Victim (1876). Habberton wrote the first ten thousand words to keep his wife abreast of domestic events transpiring while she was ill. When the family story went out of print in 1932, merchants marketed it in dime stores. Mott concluded, "Dated though it is, *Helen's Babies* is still full of charm and chuckles."[54]

Besides humorous domestic novels, people liked social melodramas about reform movements with plot incidents that applied old values to recent crises and generated viable alternatives. Appleton introduced the public to Hall Caine's world of clerical intrigue in *The Deemster* (1888).[55] Ralph Connor, in *Black Rock* (1898), described a minister's crusade to save miners in the Canadian Northwest from the Demon Rum.[56] Mme. Sarah Grand [Frances Elizabeth (Clarke) McFall] mentioned syphilis in her idea novel that promoted women's rights, *The Heavenly Twins* (1893), in which a starry-eyed maiden regretted marrying a penitent rake.[57] *Anne of Green Gables* (1908), created by Lucy M. Montgomery, knew better.[58] In fact, she rose, in rags-to-riches fashion, from being an indigent orphan to become a member of the middle class.

The Cheaper the Better?

Eventually, the old-line publishing houses sold paperback versions of their hardcover selections to prevent competitors from undercutting them. These firms mostly pirated French and English novels until the 1880s, when they added American works. However, the International Copyright Law of 1891 ended the heyday of cheap publishing. Raymond Howard Shove, author of *Cheap Books Produced in the United States,* explains that the cheap publishers should not be confused with the dime novel houses.[59] Titles varying in literary sophistication and priced lower than their counterparts in the general market were called "cheap books."[60] Dime novels, in contrast, sold for a set price, repeated popular plot formulas, emphasized action over literary merit, and had orange covers or lively illustrations on their jackets. They preceded cheap books, which were bound in cloth, had paper covers, or came without a jacket. Moreover, while dime novels merely promised thrills, the cheap libraries claimed to offer classics.

The switch from rag to pulpwood paper made it possible to print cheap books. Although many publishers thought that the cheap houses would destroy the book trade, Charles Dudley Warner, Twain's collaborator on *The Gilded Age* (1873), believed such ventures as Cassell's "National Library" democratized reading by enabling poor people to buy books. Warner told *Harper's* magazine in 1886: "For the price of a box of strawberries or a banana, you can buy the immortal works of the greatest genius of all time in fiction, poetry or science."[61] Others besides Warner appreciated the fact that the "cheap" press offered access to classics in science, theology, and scholarship, as well as literature. In fact, *Publishers Weekly* surmised that "people want books just as they want dry goods and groceries."[62]

By the late 1880s, American novels surpassed their foreign counterparts in popularity. The traditional houses had established paperback libraries of their own. Scribners featured native works in its "Yellow Covers." Houghton Mifflin created the "Riverside Line" while Ticknor established the "Ticknor Paper Series." Some were satisfied with the free volumes offered by the Book Soap Company, but others sought quality in their books and paid fifty cents for the Ticknor and Scribner's volumes. Although publishing profits rose, authors frequently earned less than two hundred dollars per book.[63] The low compensation many writers received reflected the cultural preference for the practical and the useful over the artistic. Indeed, the popular bards made more money than most of the literary geniuses because they answered a demand.

The capitalist economy, based on supply and demand, encouraged materialism, which quickly stimulated greed. Giving away books to induce customers to buy soap illustrated one way of increasing sales by appealing to the desire to get something for nothing. Alexis de Tocqueville in 1830 noted the American delight in bargains. He concluded that, in the United States, bargain hunting was as indigenous as corn or eagles: "They do for cheapness what the French did for conquest. . . . Cheapness is the sovereign law of commerce."[64] Peterson bragged that it was the "Cheapest book house in the world." The firm's catalog, located at the back of E. D. E. N. Southworth's *Victor's Triumph* (1875), promised "A SWEEPING REDUCTION!" in the price of clothbound books that had sold for $1.50 to $1.75. Customers were offered "MRS. SOUTHWORTH'S WORKS IN CHEAP FORM" for fifty cents.[65]

The Potentate of Cheapness, Theophilus Beasley (T. B.) Peterson, opened a book and news shop in 1845 in Philadelphia. Within a decade, he had established himself as a publisher, and in 1858 he made his brothers, George and Thomas, his partners. Although George died in 1861, the firm remained T. B. Peterson and Brothers. Madeleine B. Stern, in her *Publishers for Mass Entertainment in Nineteenth-Century America,* concluded that the leaders of the book world respected T. B. Peterson's honesty and ability. As his company made its fortune largely off the success fables of "those damned scribbling women," it seems quite appropriate that T. B. himself was characterized as "one of the self-made men" in the American publishing industry.[66]

The Petersons succeeded so greatly that, by 1874, their company was the largest cheap publishing concern in the country with plates for over a thousand titles. "Cheap" did not necessarily mean mindless. The Petersons reprinted classics by foreign authors such as Alexander Dumas, Charles Dickens, and Gustave Flaubert. In 1873, the *New York Tribune Extra* series of scholarly studies, including *Tyndall on Light*, Beecher's *Compulsory Education,* and Young's *Solar Physics,* sold briskly. The *Tribune Extras* resembled modern newspaper supplements and were not books. Nevertheless, they "[pointed] the way for cheap 'libraries,' which shortly sprang up in profusion."[67] Domestic romances shared catalog space with classics and how-to books. In fact, these publishers heeded the timeless warning not to place all one's eggs in a single basket. Stern calls T. B. Peterson an innovator, pointing out that he pioneered the creation of promotional materials featuring portraits and biographies of his writing stars.[68]

Although often associated with the potboilers of the era, Petersons also offered prospective book buyers a potpourri of titles, including inspirational tracts, humorous sketches, English and French novels, and how-to manuals such as the "LIST OF THE BEST COOK BOOKS PUBLISHED": *The Family Save-All,* by a Practical Housewife; *The Queen of the Kitchen, or The Southern Cook Book*; *Francatelli's Modern Cook Book* "with the most approved methods of French, English, German and Italian Cookery with Sixty-two Illustrations"; and nine other homemaking tracts, each priced at $1.50.[69]

To promote their work, the popular bards depended upon catalogs placed at the end of cheap books. The list of self-improvement tracts suggests that, a century ago, individuals felt compelled to justify reading as a character-building activity. Time-management studies indicated that workers performed their jobs more effectively if they participated in leisure-time activities outside the workplace. Therefore, vacations, parks, and school recesses reflected the cultural mandate to value things according to their utilitarian consequences. Even if no one ordered from the catalog at the back of the romance, its presence gave readers permission to enjoy the book because it proposed opportunities for self-improvement.

During the Gilded Age, physicians began to stress that exercise was a necessary part of staying healthy enough to improve physically and mentally. Sports-related books invited readers to master active amusements that formerly had been the province of the rich alone. For example, many aspired to distinguish themselves in the elite hobby of hunting for fun and fitness rather than for food. One dime handbook reduced the aristocratic pastime of hunting to something that the average bricklayer could afford to pursue. Perhaps, those who wished to dream about hunting rather than actually doing it ordered *Frank Forester's Sporting Scenes . . . And Characters,* "By Henry William Herbert [in] A New, Revised and Enlarged Edition, with a Life of the Author, a New Introductory Chapter, Frank Forester's Portrait and Autograph, with a full length picture of him in shooting costume and seventeen other illustrations, from original designs by Darley and Frank Forester [in] Two Vols." for four dollars.[70] The advertisement revolves around the dashing expert, who may become either a role model for the novice or a romantic figure for the daydreamer.

Humor sold briskly, too. For $1.50, wags could purchase three of "Q. K. Philander Doestick's Funny Books": *Doestick's Letters, Plu-Ri-Bus-Tah, The Elephant Club,* or *Witches of New York.* "Harry Cockton's Eight Laughable Novels," priced at seventy-five cents in paper, included *The Fatal Marriage, Sylvester Sound,* and *Valentine Vox—Ventriloquist.* Those who trusted the discretion of the editors could mail eighteen dollars to Petersons to purchase the twelve-volume "Illustrated" set of "American Humorous Books."[71] These books seem useless until one realizes that many provided material for oratory contests as well as entertainment for family reading time. Often the titles touched upon marriage, work, and improbable encounters.

Such manuals opened the escape hatch of whimsy. For example, regional humor took readers away from their neighborhoods to destinations reached only via the portals of the imagination. Seventeen "Humorous Illustrated Books" advertised in the catalog at the back of Southworth's *Victor's Triumph* included *Major Jones' Courtship and Travels* (by William Tappan Thompson) "in one Vol., [with] 29 illustrations" ($1.75); the side-splitters, *Piney Wood's Tavern or Sam Slick in Texas* (by Philip Paxton), *Simon Suggs' Adventures and Travels* (by Johnson Jones Hooper) "with 17 illustrations," and *High Life in New York* "by Jonathan Slick [Ann Stephens] with Illustrations" at $1.50 each; and *Major Jones' Georgia Scenes,* "[with] 12 Illustrations," at $1.00 for cloth or $0.75 for paper. No doubt, bargain-hunters chose the paperback version of *Raney Cottem's Courtship,* "with 8 Illustrations," at $0.50.[72]

While humor books usually wove platitudes and proverbs into their warp of silliness, some selections in the catalog offered readers serious information. Individuals of all ages recited passages in speaking contests. They clipped material from newspapers and collected cheap volumes of humor and poetry. Poetry lovers saved money—a truly American thing to do—on *Beautiful Snow! [The] New & Enlarged Edition* "with other poems never before published, by J. W. Watson, with Original Illustrations by Edward L. Henry. This New and Enlarged edition . . . contains, besides all the Poems that were in the original editions of *Beautiful Snow* and in *The Outcast and Other Poems,* many New and Original Poems . . . which have never before been published and are fully equal to the Poem of 'Beautiful Snow.'" The advertisement mentioned "Beautiful Snow" eight times in one paragraph.[73] Those who ordered the book bought the right to tell their friends that they owned the original version most children recited in school. Later, the poem was mostly forgotten!

The *Victor's Triumph* catalog lists numerous prose selections promising advice and social education or exposure to masterpieces. Of course, "New and Good Books by the Best Authors" puffed readers' egos through testaments describing the accomplishments of their favorite authors.

Some prospered by writing about reforms. W. T. Witmer repeated a truism that popular bards also believed: tobacco or alcohol ruins lives. In his fable, *Wild Oats Sown Abroad*, he appealed to the parochial distrust of Europe as the source of carnal corruption. Self-improvement tracts included *The Ladies' Guide to True Politeness and Perfect Manners,* by Miss Leslie. "Every lady should have it. [In] cloth [with a] full gilt back[,] $1.50." The details about the binding emphasized the book's material worth and implied whoever bought it got a bargain.

Those seeking an education could read *Coal, Coal Oil and Other Minerals in the Earth,* by Eli Browen. One book, *Popery Exposed: An Exposition of Popery as It Was and Is,* mirrored religious prejudices of the Gilded Age.[74] Besides giving readers evidence to use in conversation, these books satisfied psychological needs, massaging the reader's ego with supremacist nonsense.

Religious pamphlets echoed the archetypal success motif that material objects endanger spiritual well-being. For example, the four volumes of "Green's Works on Gambling" denounced that vice, described the speculator's lifestyle, and suggested reforms. Many villains drank, smoked, cursed, and gambled. Reformers also wrote didactically. For example, T. S. Arthur's *Six Nights with the Washingtonians,* "Illustrated"; and *The Latimer Family; Or, The Bottle and the Pledge,* denounced "the Siamese twins," drinking and gambling. *T. S. Arthur's Great Temperance Stories* or all four series of "Dow's Patent Sermons" showed readers the grim future that awaited drunkards.[75]

The cheap religious books generated an interest in self-education. Many who could not afford to go to night school could order primers from Petersons and other inexpensive publishers. Those planning to lecture about faith or reforms, including temperance, no doubt benefited from the two-dollar "Model Speakers and Readers," among them *Comstock's Elocution and Model Speaker,* "Intended for the use of Schools, Colleges and for Private Study, for the Promotion of Health, Cure of Stammering and Defective Articulation. By Andrew Comstock and Philip Lawrence. With 236 Illustrations."[76] Perhaps displaying such books strategically attested to a family's prestige and so impressed visitors.

"How-To" Handbooks

Dime novel houses produced nonfictional wares similar to Petersons' self-improvement and religious books. In fact, Beadle and Adams started their business with "songsters," biographical sketches, and rule-books for games. The expectation that reading would teach individuals essential social and commercial skills inspired this how-to literature, including reprinted sermons and essays on morality. In 1872, the Beadle subsidiary branch of Adams, Victor and Company brought out the Reverend T. De Witt Talmage's *The Abominations of Modern Society.* The cover reminded buyers that he also had written *Crumbs Swept Up.* The *Publisher's and Stationers' Weekly Trade Circular* promised, "The book deals with morals and conditions in New York City written in Talmage's lurid style."[77]

A two-page advertisement for Talmage's pamphlet appeared later that same year in the "Home-Born Book of Home-Truths," *Get Thee Behind Me, Satan!* by Mrs. Wirt Sikes, whose *nom de plume* was her maiden name, Olive Logan. The author of *Photographs of Paris Life* and *Women and Theaters* commented on vanity, flirting, wardrobe, free love, servant girls, marriage, and children. A leading trade journal predicted that Logan's "woman-book . . . shall breathe the spirit of true love and the sweet sanctities, which grow out of Christian marriage."[78]

Realizing women were interested in marriage and housekeeping, Beadle and Adams issued the *Dime Recipe Book: A Directory for the Parlor, Nursery, Sick Room, Toilet, Kitchen, Larder, etc.,* and the *Dime Cook-Book, or, Housewife's Pocket Companion Embodying What Is Most Economic, Most Practical, Most Excellent.* The editor of the firm's *Home* magazine, Mrs. Metta Victor, had written both manuals in 1859, one year before Beadle and Adams released their first novel. Six years later, she wrote *The Housewife's Manual: or, How to Keep House and Order a*

Home; How to Dye, Cleanse and Renovate; How to Cut, Fit and Make Garments; How to Cultivate Plants and Flowers; How to Care for Birds and Household Pets, etc.[79]

Housewives also cared for the sick. They scanned dailies, magazines, and cheap publications for health-care information. Of course, healing ailments and administering basic first aid were essential practical arts in long-settled as well as frontier communities. Charles E. Rosenberg, in *The Care of Strangers: The Rise of America's Hospital System,* points out that prior to the Civil War, most patients relied upon relatives or neighbors to take care of them.[80] The concept of the hospital as a positive institution rather than as a variety of the detested almshouse emerged between 1870 and 1910, partly as a way in which philanthropists and Social Gospel reformers fulfilled their mission of stewardship to help the poor help themselves. Since many people before the twentieth century either distrusted hospitals or could not take advantage of clinics, the dime publishing houses hired writers to impart rudimentary medical knowledge. "Drs. Warren, Donna, Parker, et al." collaborated on the *Dime Family Physician and Manual for the Sick Room; With Family Diseases and their Treatment, Hints on Nursing and Rearing, Children's Complaints, Physiological Facts, Rules of Health, Recipes for Preparing Well-Known Curatives, Etc.,* published by Beadle and Adams.

In addition to the tracts for women, Beadle and Adams published a "Young People's Series" featuring pamphlets about etiquette, letter writing, dreams, ballroom dancing, poetry, beauty secrets, and fortune telling. The list contained both respectable and shocking items and thus served the hidden agenda of appealing to youths' curiosity and sense of fun, while still promoting self-improvement. Like the thrillers, many how-to pamphlets emphasized respect for propriety and the inner life. For example, the *Dime Book of Etiquette* provided readers with "A Practical Guide to Good Breeding and Complete Directory to the Observances of Society." Some writers raised eyebrows by offering outrageous instructions. The *Dime Fortune Teller,* for example, offered "Peeps into Futurity" and tips on "Fortune Telling by Cards . . . [reading] a Person's Character by Means of Cabalistic Calculations, Palmistry or Telling Fortunes by the Lines of the Hand . . . [or] . . . by the Grounds in a Tea or Coffee Cup" and, most useful of all, "How to Tell Your Fortune by the White of an Egg."[81]

Another series focused on "Games and Pastimes:" football, cricket, swimming, skating, chess, riding, driving, and croquet. Games taught children to persevere, constructively to harness their energy, and to value their mental and physical skills over material things. The mandate to education and hence to improve the character of children induced dime-novel houses to produce such biographical series as these: "Biographical Library," "American Sixpenny Biographies," "Men of the Time," and "Lives of Great Americans." These narratives blended excitement with behavior becoming in role models who pursued honor and spiritual integrity, not wealth. Besides Abraham Lincoln, General Ulysses S. Grant, and Joseph Garibaldi, "the Liberator of Italy," authors described *Tecumseh, the Shawnee Chief; Pontiac, the Conspirator, Chief of the Ottawas;* and Revolutionary War heroes like "Mad Anthony" Wayne and Ethan Allen. Edward S. Ellis contributed the *Life and Times of Daniel Boone, the Illustrious Pioneer, Indian Fighter, Scout and Hunter* to Beadle's "American Sixpenny Biographies."[82]

The company also marketed collections of humor, speeches, and songs. In *Main Street on the Middle Border,* Lewis Atherton noted that, although small-town residents bought cheap prints rather than oil paintings, they could not replace the local musician or orator with a machine. In the rural areas, musical talent or speaking ability earned individuals prestige—so long as they did not shirk their responsibilities. Teachers required students to memorize verses for socials, which began with box suppers and ended with spelling bees and entertainment performed by the children and their parents. Often homemade prizes were awarded. "Music and oratory thrived on even the newest of town frontiers."[83] Churches sponsored choirs and debating societies. Despite strict Protestant prohibitions against dancing, communities broke the monotony of winter with "balls," borrowing the city word to describe their hoedown.

These amusements created a demand for books of songs and oratory about the hazards inherent in coveting earthly rather than heavenly treasures. This dire message about success was delivered in lighthearted pieces like *Bob Harrison's Comic Songs, Jokes and Ethiopian Dialogues, Beadle's Dime Book of Fun,* and the *Paddy Whack Joke Book;* or in anthologies for amateur orators called "Speakers" and "Dialogues."[84] People ordered songbooks, including *The Old Arm Chair* (1860), *Stand by the Flag* (1859), *Bobbin' Around* (1860), *Kiss Me While I'm Dreaming* (1866), *Heathen Chinee Songster* (1871), *Girls, Don't Fool with Cupid Songster* (1871) and *Crusader's Temperance Songster* (1874).[85]

The titles of the dime manuals do not always indicate their place in the "book soap" pantheon of the Gilded Age. However, the content of these self-help tracts clearly reveals their respect for clean living. Like the rest of the book industry, the dime houses offered readers information, narratives, and advice in conformity with the expectation that reading was to be educational. The desire to create wholesome amusements reflective of the community's moral standards generated the market for songbooks. Moreover, since the lyrics reinforced the values of patriotism, respect for parents, and the rewards of hard work, singing augmented social education by echoing the success paradigm. Children learned their ethical obligations at school as well as at church. The crusade for purity often shaped their play. Songbooks bridged the gap between didactic and recreational activities. In addition to hymns, people sang folksongs, ballads, nonsense tunes, and, eventually, popular ditties. All these musical channels preserved values by giving people avenues for expressing their hopes and desires as well as their fears. Lyricists often borrowed details from news accounts to blend archetypes and current events in their tunes.[86]

The Fiction Factory

Songbooks encouraged people to socialize, but bardic tales gave them solitary pleasure. Although ministers and educators frowned upon fiction and condemned the formula plots as not only useless but also destructive, Peterson defended popular stories that resembled fairy tales more closely than novels:

> In supplying your wants and taste in the reading line, it is of the first importance that you should give special attention to what is popularly designated entertaining reading matter. No library is either attractive or complete without a collection of novels and romances. The experience of many years has demonstrated that light reading is essential to even the most studious men and women, furnishing the mind with healthful recreation; while to the young, and to those that have not cultivated a taste for solid works of science, it forms one of the best possible training schools, gradually establishing in a pleasant manner that habit of concentration of thought absolutely necessary to read understandingly the more ponderous works, which treat of political economy, the sciences and of the arts.[87]

Naturally, Petersons acquired the correct "light" volumes for every library by converting story-paper adventures into cheap books. The serials of many popular authors were republished as novels after appearing in periodicals. Writers depended upon exposure in magazines and newspapers to attain popularity. While some of Petersons' novelists had entertained readers in the 1840s and 1850s, countless new authors appeared during the Gilded Age. Probably, many who ordered these books had already read the serials in the *Ledger* or some other story paper. The repetition of the success plots, as with any popular-culture artifact, fulfilled individuals' ritual need for recognition of the mores that bound them to the rest of society. By affirming traditional mores, Mary Jane Holmes sold over two million volumes of her domestic novels during the Gilded Age. In 1905, the *Bookman's* obituary of Holmes asserted:

> While the highly cultivated public is one of varied tastes, the far greater public, which critics do not recognize, holds fast to certain primitive ideals both ethical and literary, which are unchanged amid the clash of Romantics and Realists, of Naturalists and Symbolists. These last may rage together and imagine a vain thing, but the boy or the girl who is trained in a district school and who lives the simple life holds fast always to certain fixed ideas, which from generation to generation remain immutable.[88]

The community forms the context for the development of narrative formulas. Many authors develop plot recipes that are known to please readers. Faith Baldwin and the Harlequin writers attest to the endurance of escapist, romantic tales. Bards contribute to the popular press for numerous reasons. Many nineteenth-century women preferred embroidering plot skeletons to stitching dishtowels. Robert Bonner, the publisher of one of the foremost story papers, the *New York Ledger,* sent his writers general instructions. Nevertheless, the author's personality and idiosyncrasies made every romance, adventure, or mystery unique.

Of course, some writers garnished the narrative bones more skillfully than others. For example, Southworth and Holmes repeated motifs without lapsing into the production of a stream of interchangeable stories. They strove to recreate the myth so seamlessly that readers rediscovered the moral each time they read a version of it. Readers chose a book because they knew how the story would end, but they expected surprises en route to the satisfying conclusion. The narratives grew from the archetypal frame to become historical, domestic, or romantic tales in which the stock characters took on new identities. Southworth and Holmes so deeply saturated their stories with mundane details that readers no longer relate to their tales; nevertheless, their particular personalities set their novels apart from those of their contemporaries. In contrast, Laura Jean Libbey wrote the same story in the same wooden way for decades.

In *All the Happy Endings*, Papashvily concluded that, regardless of their fondness of whimsy or their contrived plots full of amazing coincidences, Southworth, Holmes, Hentz, and many of their colleagues wrote sincerely. Moreover, they approached their work seriously and respected their readers. Libbey, however, spent as much time promoting herself as a personality as she did writing. Papashvily observed that Libbey's characters were interchangeable, something that was not true of many other romance novelists.[89]

William Wallace Cook, who used many pseudonyms, earned over $100,000 in his "Fiction Factory." He referred to his products as factory-made, not to admit their inferiority but rather to emphasize that, like all laborers, he efficiently worked long hours every day. In his home, he built an office equipped with a typewriter, files, and clippings from newspapers and periodicals. *Publishers Weekly* praised Cook's last book, *Plotto*, as a "brain saving devise" of 1,800 "time-tested formulae" from 4,000 years of storytelling. Authors used these plot skeletons "with the same ease that standardized parts are fit in machine shops."[90] Although Cook knew at the outset a half-dozen of the major incidents in the plot, he tried to make each story better than the last one. His publishers reviewed and criticized his manuscripts to help him understand the public's sensibilities. Critics have considered serial writing sterile, but Cook took pride in his work:

> A bright bit of dialogue would evoke a chuckle, a touch of pathos would bring a tear, an unexpected incident shooting suddenly out of the tangled threads would fill him with rapture, and for the logical but unexpected climax he reserved a mood like Caesar's returning from the wars and celebrating a triumph.
>
> In the ardor of his work, he forgot the flight of time. He balked at leaving his typewriter for a meal and went to bed only when drowsiness interfered with his flow of thought.[91]

Like Cook, Libbey regarded writing thrillers as a serious vocation. In the 1870s, her romances told readers the secrets of true love, and in the 1920s they helped immigrants adjust to their new land. She described her original audience as being as ample as the wheat blowing in the breeze. By the early twentieth century, that audience had disappeared so completely that not even the stubble remained, but a new audience had replaced the old. When Street and Smith reduced their list of 3,700 titles to 1,500 after World War I, they retained Libbey, Southworth, Agnes Fleming, and numerous domestic romance writers. Detective and adventure stories also survived the pruning. Horatio Alger "found a new public among the little boys of the East Side. Again it is Americanization; Alger writes always of success."[92]

Keep the Pot Boiling

With song collections and how-to booklets, Petersons and Beadle and Adams rallied their customers to pursue self-improvement and success. The Reverend Washington Gladden explained that the Roman games had made mayhem and murder into sporting events; thus Christians had become suspicious of amusements. "The frightful debaucheries and cruelties, which constituted the sports of the Romans, merited the holy indignation with which the disciples of the early days denounced them."[93] He thought sports had evolved, however, into positive, innocent diversions that revived the spirit and refreshed the weary.

Many writers considered producing stories in the fiction factory diverting and personally rewarding as well as financially expedient. However, the satisfaction of creating plots did not compel them to justify their labor in lofty tones. Indeed, one of the most successful of the "scribbling women," Southworth, refused to claim literary status for her serials. Although her fans asked her to expound upon the universal themes in her romances, she referred to her stories as "potboilers" written to please audiences and not critics.

C. Hugh Holman defines *potboiler* as "a slang term" describing a book or article written to make money: "It is writing that will 'keep the author's pot boiling' and, thus, supply sustenance, it is hoped, for work more worthy."[94] Some famous authors, including Theodore Dreiser, who supported himself by editing *Smith's Magazine* for Street and Smith, relied upon the fiction factory to support their novel writing.

Many other authors had no intention of producing masterpieces, but instead avidly developed formula plots emphasizing the power of righteousness. For example, Adeline Whitney praised hearth and home in the familiar terms her audience appreciated. Her "Real Folks Series" contained *A Summer in Leslie Goldthwaite's Life* (1866), *We Girls* (1870), *Real Folks* (1871), and *The Other Girls* (1873). Each of these books sold ten thousand volumes in the first printing. Besides describing "simple, lovely perfect homes peopled by nice, agreeable, natural young people," Whitney validated American values. In her first book, *Mother Goose for Grown Folks* (1859), she composed this verse, which Alger could have written:[95]

> Minding the lesson he received,
>   In boyhood, from his mother,
> Whose cheery word, for many a bump,
>   Was Up and take another!

The title suggests that adults enjoyed recalling childhood stories and verses. Moreover, the messages imparted in nursery rhymes and tales deepened through lifelong repetition. Perhaps, like Whitney, the formula writers ransacked their childhood memories for inspiration. Among the beloved fairy tales of their youth, they rediscovered Cinderella and adapted it to reflect modern conditions.

Indeed, Smith and Street survived for over a century by publishing plots that appealed to readers emotionally in the same way fairy tales satisfy listeners—by defying reality to make good triumph over evil. The title of Quentin Reynolds's history of Smith and Street, *The Fiction Factory: Or From Pulp Row to Quality Street,* assumes the firm improved its product by shifting its focus from "pulp" thrillers to special-interest magazines like *Mademoiselle, Modern Living,* and *Astounding Science-Fiction.* Reynolds offers insights into the publishing business and thoroughly records the events that made Smith and Street a legend. However, the title expresses a common but mistaken value judgment, an assumption that, in the twentieth century, aesthetically superior periodicals have displaced formula literature. It is often assumed that writing thousands of words in a short time automatically damages compositions. Nevertheless, some authors of classics produced stories at an astounding pace. For instance, Bret Harte claimed to write his best stories between bedtime and breakfast, after an evening of smoking cigars and drinking. Justin Kaplan repeats one of Mark Twain's favorite anecdotes about Harte:

> One Friday night in December he [Harte] came to dinner with a double deadline to meet: He was scheduled the following morning to read a story to the Saturday Morning Club, a select circle of Hartford young ladies, and Dana of the *New York Sun* was counting on this story and had promised a bonus of $100 if Harte delivered it on time. Harte had until morning to write it. Instead of rushing to his room after dinner, he sat up in the library talking and drinking whiskey.
>
> By one o'clock Clemens was ready for bed. Harte was ready for work and for more whiskey. He went up to his room and worked and drank steadily through the night, although Clemens' estimate that Harte consumed two quarts of whiskey between one and nine in the morning is clearly a heroic embellishment of the facts.
>
> Harte came down to breakfast alert, sober and with a finished story called "Thankful Blossom." The young ladies were delighted, Dana got his story, Harte got his bonus, and thirty years later Clemens was still awed by Harte's ability to work under pressure and by the story

itself: "It is my conviction that it belongs at the very top of Harte's literature."[96]

The difference between formula writers and authors who follow a private muse into uncharted creative territory clearly is not simply a matter of speed. In fact, some aspiring novelists may spend a long time polishing their copy but still unconsciously repeat the success archetype. Narrative roots reach to one's earliest socialization. Not even venerated authors can erase the myths of their culture from their brains to avoid entering the fiction factory.

The factory metaphor had positive as well as negative connotations. Cook invoked it in 1912 to emphasize the dignity of writing for a living. Most Americans respected practical and useful arts like steel making. Conceiving of books as a commodity suggests a tension between aesthetics and pragmatism. The fiction factory, rather than producing cheap, throwaway stories on an assembly line, might have applied Frederick Taylor's theories of efficiency to publishing. Those ideas prevailed in the community long before Taylor codified them.

Readers in fact may have respected the diligent writers who could rapidly transform raw words into finished adventures. This passage from the *New York Times* obituary of Harlan Page Halsey, the creator of "Old Sleuth," suggests that people admired authors who could produce plots quickly. "He wrote sometimes two books in a week, dashing them off at a marvelous rate of speed, and in a hand that could only be deciphered by experts. When necessary he could write a novel in a day's time. As he finished a page, he would throw it on the floor and begin the next. When the story was finished, a family member picked the sheets up and put them in order, and 'Old Sleuth' used to say, jokingly, that this was the hardest part of the job."[97]

Public awe at the astounding rate at which Halsey, who came to be identified with his character "Old Sleuth," and his colleagues produced stories reflected a popular fascination with speed and the technological implosion. The world moved more quickly in 1870 than it ever had before. The telegraph, the trans-Atlantic cable, and the telephone had freed communication from geographical constraints. Improvements in railroads, electric trolleys, and shipping methods, as well as the construction of bridges and roads, shrank the physical world by making it possible to travel easily and quickly in a few hours over distances that once had required a week to cross. Newspapers and periodicals brought the outside world into the home and routinely relayed the misfortunes of remote places within hours of their occurrence.

Maybe the producers of formula plots simply marched in step with the larger society, waving the banners of capitalism and modernity. The great writers may have been those who followed their own instincts as realists and naturalists. Nevertheless, greatness rarely receives public approval, because most people spend their lives goose-stepping to the drumbeat of economic necessity. A blown fuse commands more attention than a literary masterpiece because, while most cannot do without electricity, no one feels compelled to read classics. In fact, today, in a media-saturated world, the act of reading for pleasure requires planning.

The tendency to label everything as either good or bad reflects the persistence of the success formula, which promised that virtue would vanquish villainy. The trademark "Book Soap" figuratively encapsulated commercial attempts to justify reading as a practical and useful endeavor guaranteeing clean thoughts. The designation of certain books as classics and others as trash attached a didactic justification to the activity of reading. Perhaps critics' denigration of the formula plots arose from their assumption that *cheap* meant *base*. Moreover, highbrows believed themselves superior to people who had less education; the former felt compelled to set the standards for their neighborhoods. Many hoped identifying evil would prevent the public from harming itself. Despite vociferous warnings against succumbing to temptation and the proliferation of paperbacks, which made it possible for everyone who wanted to do so to commune with Dickens, James, and other literary stars, the multitude often preferred bardic tales.

Perhaps readers felt safer with the popular bards than with the classic novelists. Perhaps the small themes and petty concerns of the popularizers expressed both the frustrations and the joys of ordinary people. Perhaps, regardless of income or social status, a cheap but big chuckle appealed to the human instinct for play. Perhaps the need to reinforce social mores made people love the simple tales that repeated fundamental archetypes in moral formulas and so validated their world view. And, during the Gilded Age in the United States, the success paradigm powerfully justified the status quo. Simultaneously it provided an arena in which people could experiment with change.

Chapter 4

The Fear of Sinking

There are two times in a man's life when he should not speculate: when he can't afford it and when he can.
—Mark Twain, 1897

Long ago, bards sang ballads celebrating the heroic deeds of individuals worthy of emulation. The songs provided continuity with
the past and gave listeners a sense of their place in history. The bards
set to music the cherished tales that once had been told around the
family hearth. As technology changed the world, lute-strumming
bards were superseded by mechanical storytellers. The printing press
enabled people to read stories rather than merely hear them. Television lets audiences see bardic tales in the seclusion of their homes,
thus melding private and public experience:

> Television, according to our analysis of its message, function, and
> mode, communicates a metonymic "contact with others," in which all
> Levi-Strauss's lost storytellers, priests, wise men, or elders are re-
> stored to cultural visibility and to oral primacy: often indeed in the
> convincing guise of highly literate specialists, from news readers to
> scientific and artistic experts. This selective communication is what
> we have termed television's bardic function, and it restores much of
> the personal autonomy to the viewer in the sense that he supplies the
> conditions, both semiotic and social, under which any specific mes-
> sage becomes meaningful.[1]

The bardic function that John Fiske and John Hartley ascribe to television also applies to the stories created by the cheap press to entertain the masses. The bardic tales, being social narratives, enable the
individual to derive a sense of self in relationship to the rest of society: "Through its recitation, a story is incorporated into a community,
which it gathers together."[2] The text creates a public composed of
readers who seek the tale because it repeats an essential social paradigm. Narratives with traditional motifs reinforce the values that distinguish one culture from another.

The cardinal American bardic tale during the Gilded Age passed on the success archetype. Regardless of genre, the core message of the narrative remains the same: in order to succeed, one must attain spiritual riches as well as material wealth. Besides this often unarticulated moral, bardic tales have these features: a hero or heroine of uncommon virtue, a plot built around the struggles of the protagonist to overcome adversity, a happy ending, lucky coincidences, a reptilian or deceased father, and, usually, a benefactor. Success tract writers invoked old bromides about clouds with silver linings. By analyzing the success prototype as it appears in late-nineteenth-century formula plots, this chapter clarifies how bardic tales differ from literary masterpieces.

Why Bardic Tales Are Not Novels
Authors such as the Reverend E. P. Roe, General Lew Wallace, Owen Wister, Anna Katharine Green, and Mary Roberts Rinehart named their characters plausibly and created credible environments for them. Regardless of how many characteristics of the novel such bards borrowed, however, affectively their plots continued to be expanded versions of fairy tales. As Michael Denning noted in *Mechanic Accents,* the dime novels functioned as allegories, not novels.[3] The pervasiveness of the success archetype suggests that many popular authors, in passing on paradigms that earlier bards had codified in folk tales and folk songs, deliberately wrote one plot containing several story lines.

Oppressive living conditions made formula fantasies appealing. Unlike novels purporting to deal with reality, bardic tales unveiled a dream world. While indulging the reader's expectations, the repetitive plots reinforced the individual's personal sense of being valuable as a member of a large, significant group. Moreover, belonging to the family, church, nation, or other collective entity entailed making sacrifices for the sake of that community.

The bardic tales often fade away after a generation because, to remind a particular community of its links to its narrative and moral past, they are embedded in a specific time. A few such works, including Edward Eggleston's *The Hoosier School-Master* (1871), succeed so completely in glorifying the prime capitalist myth that they become Americana classics. Others, like *Mrs. Wiggs of the Cabbage Patch* (1901), remain charming pieces of children's literature. Bardic tales celebrate the noble struggles of ordinary people to find meaning in their lives by converting hardships into magic carpet rides through stormy skies to higher economic and social status.

The same theme—diligence as the route to prosperity for impoverished but honorable youths—saturated the media. Newspapers, magazines, and pamphlets urged readers to rise above destitution through perseverance. The internationally acclaimed impresario P. T. Barnum; steel tycoon Andrew Carnegie; the Reverend Russell Conwell, the founder of Temple University; and others who wrote success tracts believed that industrious Americans prosper while the lazy languish. Romantic views of the open land in the West and of the inventions making settlement possible in areas once uninhabitable fired the imaginations of opinion shapers in the clergy, the press, and business. The popular bards and the Prophets of Profit encouraged plain folks to join the cult of success. Their words sound hollow to modern readers. But a century ago, Conwell's anecdotes about ambitious go-getters who had struck it rich right in their own back yards thrilled those who packed the lecture halls to hear him recite *Acres of Diamonds* (1887).

Besides lectures about leaps from poverty to prosperity, newspapers and magazines retold amazing success stories of leaders in business, science, and politics. Indeed, Carnegie, Cornelius Vanderbilt, Jay Gould, and scores of moguls had risen to the top just as handily as Horatio Alger's lucky, plucky heroes. Concern for maintaining moral standards permeated the commercial, social, and political arenas. Despite the perception of the era as a time of Robber Barons, the Gilded Age was not dominated by graft or decadence. According to historian John Garraty, who wrote *The New Commonwealth, 1877–1890,* those decades defy simplistic characterization as either degenerate or progressive.[4]

The combined forces of progress (industrialization, immigration, and innovation) reshaped thoughts as well as environments. Americans expanded their world views to accommodate vast changes. Ready-made products, department stores, apartment houses, electricity, and elevators, as well as such ideas as the Social Gospel, spiritualism, and labor unionism, transformed society. The popular press bridged the gap between inventions and belief systems. The trappings of progress provided convenient props for the popular bards.

Characters rode street cars, dialed telephones, and wore the latest fashions. Contemporary details grounded the plot in the present. Moreover, the bards built their narratives around the success prototype, exploring emotions rather than reality. Perhaps because real workers frequently rose to supervisory positions, while fewer than ten in every one hundred millionaires had grown up in lower-class families, writers and readers created a world that rewarded hard workers and penalized money-grabbers.[5] Optimism and fellowship enriched common people. Their hopes remained fluid because the success archetype promised the deserving magical rescue from tribulation.

Perhaps blind faith in magic exists in all epochs. Today, despite laser surgery, space shuttles to the moon, and telecommunications, those with inquiring minds believe Granny Ice smuggled a fortune in gems in her hollowed-out dentures and the patriotic Loch Ness Monster sank a German submarine during World War II.

Modern success seekers expect to make "earnings unlimited" by responding to advertisements for burglar alarms, to stash away fifty to a hundred thousand dollars next year by joining a circular mailing club or to win at the bingo table by mastering Clark's secret. Others ask "Sister Flossie [to] solve all problems [and] call enemies by name" or take comfort in "Jeanine, God-gifted psychic [who] is here to help with love, marriage, business, weight problems. Restores lost nature, falling hair, reunites lovers. Removes evil influences. Results, 45 minutes. Card Readings by phone."[6] But today's believers in success schemes break the Alger formula by expecting to get rich without working. Breathing should be enough. Indeed, one needs only to send $24.95 to Papa Propper in Cleveland, Ohio, to receive a fortune:

"MONEY TO BURN"

Is that your dream? Almost everyone we know has wished for **"money to burn"!** . . . You will receive the **"Money to Burn"** along with the Triple Strength Money Drawing Oil set and **complete instructions.** It's almost unbelievable—it works so well! Everyone who has used this "kit" has declared that they have received plenty of money since they finished the ritual. **Now, it's your turn.**[7]

In the nineteenth century, people hoped to receive plenty of money, but they expected to earn it. They struggled to reconcile their dreams of getting rich with their knowledge that piling up earthly treasures jeopardized one's soul. Preoccupation with the nature of morality and the role of the church in the community overshadowed all the *isms* more frequently associated with the Gilded Age. Indeed, the vast wealth of the few contrasted dramatically with the enormous poverty of the multitude, impelling even backsliders to ponder the social consequences of such economic disparity.

Although belief in God was universal, many did not attend church, and some defied the gloomy constraints of fundamental Protestantism. Nevertheless, most viewed faith, family, and patriotism as holy.[8]

In lecture halls across the country, even the "American Infidel," "Pope Bob" Ingersoll, who denounced the hypocrisy of religion, affirmed the tenets of the success creed. His "Gospels of Cheerfulness, of Good Health, of Liberty, of Intelligence" reflected the mores of his generation. These latter were evident in the movements to expand education, enfranchise women, reform prisons, build sanitary systems, humanely treat the insane, and establish settlement houses for the urban poor.[9] Some popular bards described rare instances in which the righteous amassed material goods in the course of responding to the call of stewardship and attempting to inspire the poor to self-improvement.

"Sinking in the World"

During his visit to the United States in 1830, Alexis de Tocqueville noticed that, regardless of class or situation, all Americans worried that they would lose face simply by staying in the same place economically. Acquisition of wealth constituted the standard by which personal worth was measured: "In democratic countries, however opulent a man is supposed to be, he is almost always discontented with his fortune because he finds that he is less rich than his father was, and he fears that his sons will be less rich than himself. . . . In this respect they share the instincts of the poor without feeling the same necessities; say, rather, they feel the most imperious of all necessities, that of not sinking in the world."[10]

This obsession with increasing one's self-esteem by advancing economically doomed the masses, author Edward Bellamy argued. In *Looking Backward* (1888), utopian leaders motivated the citizenry with solidarity rather than with hunger. Bellamy balanced spiritual and physical needs. This proponent of the Social Gospel understood that justice could not prevail without economic as well as political equality. Ironically, the key to the spiritual life, which rejuvenated the hero, Julian West, was "more materialism, a generally diffused access to wealth in the real sense, with a consequent recognition of the true valuation of things."[11] In fact, many popular authors struggled with two key questions, even while telling an exciting or funny story. The first issue was the methods by which wealth was accumulated. The second was the proper uses of financial gain. Although some writers examined both issues concurrently, to avoid confusion each idea will be treated separately in this chapter.

Conwell walked the tightrope of respectability by giving away most of his fortune. His biography sounds like pages from a dime thriller. Conwell's parents hid runaways in their home and guided them to the next station on the Underground Railroad. Like many breadwinners in cliff-hangers, his father barely earned enough money to pay the bills. Despite his humble origins, Conwell studied law at Yale. He marched off to fight with the Union Army. After the Civil War, he wrote for newspapers and lectured for organizations devoted to reforming society. Then Conwell turned to religion.

The minister followed his own advice about attaining wealth by giving the people what they wanted. In addition to publishing his book, *Acres of Diamonds* (1887), he delivered its message in over six thousand lectures between 1861 and his death in 1925, using some of the proceeds to found Temple University in Philadelphia. Conwell's biography proved that getting rich quickly required determination and luck. Moreover, to be happy it was necessary to relinquish the money. The minister kept only a small percentage of his earnings and invested the rest of his fortune in philanthropy, just as Carnegie had recommended in his *Gospel of Wealth* (1889).

Conwell would open his *Acres of Diamonds* lecture with an anecdote he had heard during his travels down the Tigris and the Euphrates rivers. In that faraway land, a sage had taught him an ironic lesson concerning a man who missed his chance for success by forsaking his own home town to seek the fabled City of Gold. "That old Arab guide then took off his cap and swung it in the air to get my attention to the moral of his story. . . . Had Ali Hafed remained at home and dug in his own cellar or underneath his own wheat fields or in his own garden, instead of wretchedness, starvation and death by suicide in a strange land, he would have had 'acres of diamonds.'"[12]

Evidently the impatient farmer had left his homestead to search for a foreign river between white sandbanks, not realizing his own fields contained the Golconda—"the most magnificent diamond mine in all the history of mankind."[13] Conwell's guide shared this story only with particular friends because its message revealed the secret to getting rich that evades most people. Instead of selling their property to fund journeys to distant El Dorados, the wise invest their savings in neighborhood enterprises.

Later in his address, Conwell would tell how a fool polished a shiny stone on his land with his sleeve until he could see his reflection in it and then sold the estate to obtain money to seek copper ore along the banks of Lake Superior. Of course, the steadfast farmer who bought the property dug up the potatoes planted by the soldier of fortune. Pausing to rest on his way back to his house, the old man noticed "a block of native silver, eight inches square."[14] The humble but observant farmer got rich overnight, while the educated wanderer died destitute after devoting his life to futile schemes in the Midwest. The moral warns that going to college will not replace common sense or guarantee prosperity: "That professor of mines, mining and mineralogy, who knew so much about the subject that he would not work for $45 a week, when he sold that homestead in Massachusetts sat right on that silver to make the bargain."[15] Thus, the know-it-all lost it all by being preoccupied with dreams of distant mother lodes.

P. T. Barnum dreamed about bringing the impossible onto the stage. His American Museum invited spectators to laugh as well as to think. Indeed, when Barnum lectured, he took his text from his experiences in finding "acres of diamonds" right in his own back yard. *Harper's Weekly* proposed adding a new word to the dictionary in honor of the "Great American Showman" who had turned novelty and humor into millions of dollars. Although Barnum had died on 7 April 1891, *Harper's* predicted that his flamboyant business techniques would endure so that soon the word *Barnum* would be synonymous with "harmless humbug, amusement enterprise and unfailing invention."[16]

Barnum tried a dozen occupations before discovering his true calling, being an impresario. After turning twenty-five, Barnum borrowed money to purchase Joice Heth—an old black woman who claimed to have been George Washington's nurse—from her manager. Barnum quit clerking in the grocery store and spent the next five decades astounding audiences.

Although skeptics claimed that Joice Heth was a humbug, Barnum explained in his biography, *Struggles and Triumphs* (1883), that the bill of sale from George's father, Augustus Washington, dated 5 February 1727, seemed genuine. Newspaper ads run prior to his interest in Heth declared that the crone had remained undiscovered for over a century because her Virginia owners had sold her to Kentucky planters. (A recent audit had accidentally revealed her true identity.) The debate over Heth's authenticity attracted huge crowds. Heth "was pert and sociable and would talk as long as people would converse with her. She was quite garrulous about her protégé 'dear little George' . . . and she claimed to have 'raised him.'"[17] She also sang very old Baptist hymns upon request, reflecting the interest in morality that was manifested in many ways during the Gilded Age.

Barnum's life illustrates the social tug-of-war between religious and secular concerns. He shared his contemporaries' respect for morality and saw no inconsistency between showing Joice Heth and expressing religious sentiment. The *Trumpet and Universalist Magazine* called Barnum a sinner who was brazen enough to brag about defrauding the public.[18] Nevertheless, many ministers read his essay, "Why I Am a Universalist," to their congregations, and Dr. George L.

Perin, a missionary, translated it into Japanese.[19] Barnum gave audiences wholesome entertainment worth their nickel; still, "many God-fearing people were uncomfortable in his presence—almost as though he wore 'horns and hoofs.'"[20]

Critics overlooked the fun Joice Heth generated. Patrons did not care whether she really was George Washington's nurse. Those who wanted to believe her could. Those who delighted in exposing a humbug could do that. Joining the public conversation swirling around the identity and talents of a very old black woman was worth five cents. The afternoon's amusement gave folks something to think about as they plowed fields, worked on an assembly line, or washed clothes. Barnum's gift for filling his audiences' need for whimsy endeared him to all classes and ages. He milked the Heth debate for comic relief in his biography, noting that a post-mortem examination had suggested a lack of ossification and hence had convinced some medical students the sideshow star was not a centenarian. "But the doctors disagreed, and this 'dark subject' will probably always continue to be shrouded in mystery."[21]

Barnum declared that God's world needed entertainers just as much as it needed physicians or farmers: "Men, women and children, who cannot live on gravity alone, need something to satisfy their gayer, lighter moods and hours, and he who ministers to this want is in a business established by the Author of our nature. If he worthily fulfills his mission and amuses without corrupting, he need never feel that he has lived in vain."[22] Throughout his life, Barnum was accused of cheating the public by offering them spectacles like the FeFe Mermaid, which was nothing but a monkey's head sewn onto a fish tail. The skeptics ignored how such displays appealed to the imagination. Moreover, Barnum always interspersed the ridiculous exhibits in the American Museum among the wonders of the world his agents had collected.

Despite his fascination with distant wonders and outrageous claims, Barnum nevertheless respected the practical and useful arts. He brought "the Swedish songbird," Jenny Lind, to the United States and discovered Tom Thumb; both were talented individuals worthy of public attention. Moreover, in addition to preaching on behalf of temperance, he refused to serve alcohol at his shows. Barnum invested much of his income in schemes to provide jobs for the citizens of Bridgeport, Connecticut. Despite his success, the impresario declared, "I have been indebted to Christianity for the most serene happiness of my life, and I would not part with its consolations for all things else in the world."[23]

Biographer Arthur Saxon concluded Barnum had devoted much of his life to practicing Christianity both on the lecture platform and in good deeds.[24] Moreover, the showman had backed up his eloquent words with hard cash. Saxon estimated Barnum had contributed six times more than generous members of the congregation each month. He restored Bridgeport's First Universalist Society after fire had destroyed it and purchased a furnace, stained-glass windows, and an organ as well as paying off the church's debts and mortgages. Later, the impresario built Sunday-school rooms and a parsonage. Barnum donated specimens and cash to Universalist schools. Tufts University Museum in Medford, Massachusetts, became his pet project during the last ten years of his life.

Heavenly Vistas in Fiction and Success Tracts

To Barnum, paradise was "a museum in which all the varieties of human curiosities lived in harmony with no embarrassing attempt to delineate good from bad and in which there was no willful segregation of types on the part of the creator, who in His everlasting mercy made them all in His own image."[25] The "Great Director" of this ethereal collection of natural history valued all souls, regardless of their earthly propensities.

Like Barnum, Elizabeth Stuart Phelps believed in a benevolent despot who shaped mortal clay into the glowing penumbra of the spirit. She supplied the details, which the circus promoter chose to leave to the viewers' imagination. In *The Gates Ajar* (1868), *The Gates Between* (1887), and *Beyond the Gates* (1883), protagonists passed over into a heaven resplendent with rainbows, abloom with mignonette, and interspersed with bungalows, pianos, and orphanages. The shades, as Phelps called the residents, ate berries and wild fruit. A cookie jar filled with gingersnaps comforted travelers in the strange land above the clouds.

Phelps envisioned a Blue Book for heaven from which miscreants such as artists, scholars, doctors and speculators—who had fretted about things rather than people—would be excluded. Such obsessed, "soul sick" sinners would be trapped between heaven and earth and forced to walk the byways of their earthly existence. Intellectuals would stay in libraries reading musty books, speculators hover at their broker's offices, artists paint in their garrets, and drunkards slump at the bar of their favorite tavern until closing time when they would be forced into the alleys, just like their mortal brethren.

However, no matter how materialistic individuals had been, celestial social workers eventually inspired them to redeem themselves.

Through the compassion of the shades, who had spent their lives ministering to others, the fallen experienced grace. After repenting of their selfish compulsions, the broken souls ascended to heaven, where physicians at the hospital for the spiritually ill cured them of their deficiencies in faith. This merging of science and religion reflected the optimism many in the Gilded Age felt about finding panaceas in the laboratory to heal social dysfunctions.

Phelps's books focus on mortals who have attained worldly success but have remained wanting spiritually. In *The Gates Ajar* (1868), the heroine records her adventures in her journal. The protagonist in the utopian novel, *Beyond the Gates* (1883), describes her experiences— which turn out to be a dream—in the first person. *The Gates Between* (1887), because it ripples with conflict and humor, tells the most satisfying story. In all three works, Phelps concentrates more on the idea of heaven than on the characters.

Although many writers ascribed the flaw of overly zealous materialism to villains who persecuted the innocent, Phelps altered the motif by compelling protagonists to overcome their own inner vices instead of vanquishing external enemies. For example, in her most engaging plot, *The Gates Between* (1887), Dr. Emerald Thorn refuses to take the cure at the hospital for skeptics. Instead, he works as a janitor to pay for his son's food and lodging. Even in heaven, the Protestant Work Ethic prevails, at least among the newly dead. Dr. Thorn is afraid to confess to his saintly neighbors that he has yelled at his wife. He regrets his cruel words, realizing too late that speech as well as fists can injure loved ones. Ironically, his remorse for his mistake qualifies him for heaven. Of course, he cannot walk on water, visit distant planets, or receive the Lord. Only the spiritually whole may enjoy these rewards. Earthly poverty matters little. "Spiritual character form[s] the sole scale of social position."[26]

Like Phelps, many authors of cheap paperbacks alluded to a forgiving creator who valued character more than possessions or power. Even the most secular writers showed respect for the mores of the times by having their characters acknowledge God. For example, in E. L. Wheeler's dime novel, *Deadwood Dick on Deck; Or, Calamity Jane, the Heroine of Whoop-Up* (1885), Calamity Jane asks for only this remembrance: "If you ever kneel to pray to the All-Wise Ruler above, just give me a favorable mention."[27] This religiosity blends with the success themes of these books. Sandy, the hero who drinks nothing stronger than sarsaparilla and milk, finds a hunk of gold bigger than his fist while strolling down the ravine near the campsite he and Colorado Joe had built. Sandy, one could argue, has had to leave home to find his wealth and so has ignored Conwell's advice to seek riches in his own back yard. However, Sandy has been driven away from his home by crooks. He longs to settle down. His virtue is rewarded by the discovery of the nugget in his new back yard.

Besides respecting religion and denouncing hypocrites, the popular bards reiterated these motifs: the lucky appearance of strangers, orphans, intergenerational conflicts, class barriers, adolescence, and coincidences. In their works, the adolescent protagonist often must leave home to seek employment and thus must become a stranger. Once established in a new community, the hero or heroine witnesses or participates in intergenerational clashes. Life is repeatedly disrupted by luck.

The coincidences may simply move the story line along to the next juncture or change a character's existence. Sometimes fortune intercedes unexpectedly. In other instances, bad luck dashes someone's hopes. Eventually, however, benefactors reward the deserving and occasionally punish miscreants. Always, the question of class as an indicator of self-worth arises somewhere in the story. The authors praise those whose nobility stems from integrity rather than from birth. Moreover, many protagonists renounce European titles for the sake of love or prestige in the New World. Authors ransacked history and current events for situations in which they could apply the motifs of the success archetype.

"Strangers and Orphans Everywhere!"

Adversity compels many bardic heroes or heroines to relocate. Nevertheless, the desire to establish a new family motivates the diligent and often nauseatingly moral youth to participate in the community. Sometimes, as in *The Hoosier School-Master* (1871), coming of age requires moving several times. In Opie Read's novel, *The Jucklins* (1895), Bill Hawes also must leave home to find acceptance. After taking a teaching job, he lives with the Jucklins, who show him what it means to belong to a family. He proves himself worthy of his adopted family's love, and, then, while digging for fishing worms, he uncovers deposits of mica—"acres of diamonds"—right in his own back yard. Read and Eggleston created teachers who fit the Alger success formula. Through their hard work and a few well-placed breaks, the protagonists prevail, against astounding odds. *Fly-Away Ned* (1895), Old Sleuth's assistant in Halsey's fictional world, also prospers, because he perseveres and appears in the right place at the right moment.

New York is the right place for Phemie Frost, Ann Stephens's heroine, who leaves her aunt and uncle to minister to urban sinners. Ultimately, she finds true love in the city. Stephens ridiculed the penchant for having adolescent protagonists in romances by having Phemie imagine herself to be a maiden, when in fact she is at least forty years old. Heroic teenagers were popular in the decades following the Civil War. "[In] the works of Twain and Crane, at least, the emphasis remained on the viable possibility of initiation into the adult world."[28]

The discovery of psychology and especially the canonization of Freud by the press inspired bards to scrutinize the years between late childhood and adulthood. Writers exaggerated the trials of adolescence, much as they intensified good and evil. Moreover, publishing firms at this time first recognized different age levels of juvenile readers as educators realized that children are not miniature adults. According to the parlance of the popular plots, even General Lew Wallace made Ben-Hur, his twenty-year-old biblical hero, an adopted orphan who later must pass through a series of initiation rites, culminating in the famous chariot race against his rival.

Children as well as young adults must leave their homes to find happiness. Rebecca of Sunnybrook Farm goes to live with her maiden aunts to be educated. James Otis's [Kaler's] Toby Tyler must learn this sad lesson: life at home, if one is fortunate enough to have a home, proffers love while the circus brings only deceit and despair. Little Dorothy and Toto in *The Wizard of Oz* (1900) confront the Wicked Witch of the West in order to return to Aunty Em. Even the splendor of Emerald City cannot induce Dorothy to forsake her kin, who live on the dreary, gray Great Plains of Kansas. Polly Pepper moves out of the dear little Brown House to study music in the city. Pollyanna, the brainless "Glad Girl," checks into a metropolitan hospital for miracle surgery to cure her leg paralysis.

Frank Merriwell, Patten's hero, never stays home. If he is not setting athletic records and defeating bullies at Fardale Academy or Yale, he is off to "the West," "Down South," on a "Hunting Tour," or traipsing through Europe. Carol Bird and Jimmy Wiggs in *Mrs. Wiggs of the Cabbage Patch* fly to heaven. To heal her husband who has contracted jungle fever on a tropical island halfway around the world, Captain June's mother leaves him in Japan with his governess. The Little Princess, Sara Crewe, enrolls at Miss Minchin's Seminary for Young Ladies in London but longs to return with her father to their home in India.

As the success formula prescribed, all these protagonists were either abandoned orphans or the sole breadwinner available to support a dear mother. Characters like Luke Walton sought opportunities in the city only after misfortune had destroyed their tranquillity. *Five Little Peppers and How They Grew* (1880), the classic about father-less orphans struggling cheerfully against overwhelming odds, was "one of the most popular juveniles ever written." By 1944, the series of twelve Pepper stories had sold "more than 2,000,000 copies and the demand for them [remained] undiminished."[29] Margaret Sidney [Harriet Mulford Stone Lothrop] had sacrificed Papa Pepper solely to strengthen the plot: "Now my judgment told me I must eliminate Mr. Pepper because the whole *motif* 'to help mother' would be lost, if the father lived. It hurt me dreadfully. He was a most estimable man, and I loved my own father so much, it seemed the most wicked thing to do. I went around for days, feeling droopy and guilty. But it had to be done."[30]

Technically, the Pepper brood qualified only marginally as orphans since the dictionary defines an orphan as "a child who has lost both parents through death, or, less commonly, one parent."[31] The roster of characters whose mothers and fathers had died included Freckles; Pollyanna; Toby Tyler; Dorothy in *The Wizard of Oz;* Michael, the good-hearted simpleton in *Jan Vedder's Wife;* the match girl (a cou-pon from the Fresh Air Fund) adopted by Josiah Strong's family; Polly Oliver; the children of Brainerd, the brave Revolutionary War hero in *Wyoming;* Shocky, the Hoosier school-master's favorite pupil; and many acquaintances of Alger's plucky, lucky lad, Luke Walton. Attor-ney Gifford, in Margaret Deland's domestic tale about the austere preacher John Ward, lives with his maiden aunts until starting his law practice.

In *The Gilded Age* (1873), Squire Hawkins and his wife adopt Clay, whose mother had just died, because none of the villagers want the boy. A few days later, thinking her parents have perished with twenty-one others in the crash of two racing steamboats, they adopt Laura. After the Squire dies, Laura learns from letters in the attic that her natural father may be alive somewhere in the East. However, she never finds him.

The orphans who vow to emulate Christ make sacrifices to follow *In His Steps* (1897). Loreen, a "child of the streets," conquers the de-mon rum and dies saving her benefactor from an intoxicated mob an-gry over the closing of saloons in the nefarious Rectangle district of town. In that same plot, Cousin Rose reaps spiritual rewards by open-ing a cooking school near a settlement house in Chicago. Her vain sister, on the other hand, cannot adjust to the financial ruin that has driven their father to commit suicide and killed their feeble mother. Perhaps the most "orphaned" character in this literature is Julian

West, the narrator of Bellamy's utopian fairy tale *Looking Backward* (1888), who loses not only his parents but his entire world when he awakens after being mesmerized for 130 years!

Of all these books, E. D. E. N. Southworth's romance, *The Beautiful Fiend or Through the Fire* (1873), and its sequel, *Victor's Triumph* (1875), contain the most orphans. Among them are Victor Hartman, the framed dupe; Alden and Laura Lytton, who lose both parents and then their grandfather; Gov. Charles Cavendish, who has a fatal heart attack upon discovering the treachery of his prospective child bride; Emma Cavendish, his daughter; Mabel Taylor, the lighthouse lass; the Reverend Stephen Lyle; the mysterious Italian beauty, Electra; and Craven Kyte, possibly Alden and Laura Lytton's illegitimate half-brother. The most vicious orphan is "Mrs. Mary Grey," who at sixteen claims to be both an orphan and a widow but in actuality is Emma Cavendish's cousin, Ivy Fanning, the daughter of the proprietors of the White Perch Point Inn. Ivy's transgressions compel her father to die of shame after fatally clubbing an innocent man.

Amelia Barr, in *Jan Vedder's Wife* (1885), deals with dozens of homeless children whose fathers have died at sea and whose mothers have succumbed to fatigue and illness. The children's plight serves to redeem two selfish, greedy merchants who have never married and who have no heirs. Ironically, by dying, they do more for their island community than they ever did for it while alive. They bequeath their fortunes to a charity that builds homes and hires women to care for the orphans.

All these plots center on protagonists who have lost at least one parent. Sometimes a courageous mother whose improvident or saintly but poor husband has died must provide for her brood. The dependency of mothers and siblings compounds the ambitious orphan's responsibilities and inevitably intensifies her or his hardships. For instance, to support his mother and two little sisters, penniless, fatherless Dennis Fleet overcomes formidable obstacles in Roe's *Barriers Burned Away* (1872). Following the advice of a tipsy acquaintance whom he has tried unsuccessfully to reform the evening before, he buys a snow shovel. Then the lad spends the day cleaning off sidewalks. At the last place Dennis stops, he not only earns a quarter but is hired to replace a worthless Irish laborer whose priest cannot keep him sober.

Dennis, swallowing his pride long enough to polish boots, discovers that the mark of a gentleman is honest labor. Next, he rescues a German family by inspiring the father to put aside his whiskey long enough to give him painting lessons. Then Dennis wins several thousand dollars in a contest for Chicago painters. But these material gains do not bring him happiness. Finally, the class barriers collapse when the Chicago Fire consumes the wicked, leaving Dennis free to marry Christine, the rich snob whose icy heart melts only after the conflagration incinerates her father, her mansion, and other elements of her decadent lifestyle.

Another extremely popular character, the protagonist of *Ben-Hur* (1880), also fits the Alger stereotype. Although the son of Hur is born wealthy, he loses everything—even his mother and sister—after a freak accident implicates him in a plot to kill a Roman official. Of course, his father is dead. Ben-Hur (Juda) suffers horribly, but through inner strength and cunning, he perseveres. Through quick thinking, Juda avoids the occupational hazard inherent in prolonged service as a galley slave—having one arm stretched until it is longer than the other. He sits on the right side of the vessel on even-numbered days and on the left side on odd-numbered days.

Not only does the pure-hearted victim of cruel circumstances avoid being deformed, but his initiative catches the captain's attention. The officer asks to hear his story. Inspired by this crumb of kindness, Juda pours all his energy into his job. Then, lucky calamity strikes once again. While hundreds die in an attack on the ship, Ben-Hur pulls the captain onto a beam from the sinking vessel. He is so grateful he gives the slave his seal ring to prove to even the most venomous Roman the boy is his heir. When his new benefactor asks Juda to drown him if the pirates approach, Hur throws the ring into the waves and thus sacrifices financial security rather than compromise his honor. Soon an imperial galley arrives, and the captain proclaims that Ben-Hur will be his son. Conveniently, this Roman citizen, Arrius, has no children or wife.

Ben-Hur spends seven years with Arrius, learning to be a Roman citizen. He masters the arts of waging war and chariot racing. Then, after his foster father dies, he returns to his family home, only to find that his sister and mother have vanished. The second half of the book indicates what a boy in a Horatio Alger story might have been like as an adult.

Coincidence and luck enable Ben-Hur and the heroes of many other popular stories to prove themselves worthy to a benefactor. For example, the protagonist of *Luke Walton* (1889), one of Alger's boys, just happens to be in the street at the moment when a wealthy matron freezes in front of a trolley. Of course, Luke jerks her off the tracks just in time, and she is so impressed by his politeness and his quick thinking that she immediately befriends him. His financial woes are over.

Abundant Coincidences

Like Alger, other popular bards relied upon fortuitous encounters and random happenings to advance their plots. Indeed, Old Sleuth muses, "accident, as a rule, usually suggests pointers, which oft times lead to great results."[32] In Holmes's romance, *Edith Lyle's Secret* (1874–78?), a lucky boating mishap that almost drowns two people helps the lovers find their destined partners, despite class barriers and the dictates of conventional wisdom. Hoping to murder her new husband, whom she has wed solely to get revenge upon her benefactor, Southworth's "beautiful fiend," Mary Grey, stages a fake rowing accident; but the victim escapes.

Some accidents prove tragic. For example, characters in *John Ward, Preacher* (1888) and *The Gates Between* (1887) die in carriage crashes. Pollyanna suffers paralysis after being struck by a car. But not all accidents entail grim results. In *The Wizard of Oz* (1900), Dorothy inadvertently melts the Wicked Witch of the West by throwing water on her to protest the hag's theft of one of the silver slippers. Certainly, finding a mica mine, as the hero of *The Jucklins* (1895) does while fishing, qualifies as a lucky coincidence. The frequency with which the main character of *John March, Southerner* (1894), unexpectedly meets his neighbors on trains and even in Europe strains credulity.

Often in these works, unlikely coincidences generate humorous scenes. For instance, Alden Lytton, the hero of *Victor's Triumph* (1875), arrives at the train station before the black servant Jerome has sent a message urging him to come home because the ninety-year-old grandmother of Alden's wife is dying. Alden explains his timely appearance as merely a coincidence, but the superstitious coach driver believes that Alden's prompt return, along with Lucifer matches, telegraph wires, and steam engines, is magic.

To accommodate the plot of *The Circular Staircase* (1908), people perish conveniently. For instance, a minister drops dead before the murder of the stranger transpires, and the evening train removes a key witness who could have solved the crime seventy-five pages sooner than Rinehart was ready for it to end. Jan Vedder's career changes after his reconciliation with his wife, so that he can be home regularly instead of once every two years, as his service in the British Navy prescribed. Aunt Polly needs a sweater at just the moment when Pollyanna is enjoying the view of the tree from her barren attic room. The ten-year-old, who is about as alert as a hibernating possum, thinks Aunt Polly has come upstairs to visit her. The routine errand turns into a pivotal moment in their relationship, and the stern guardian orders a maid to help Pollyanna carry her things to the pretty chamber directly below the desolate garret.

Dorothy just happens to bump into the Scarecrow, the Tin Man, and the Cowardly Lion on the Yellow Brick Road. Mrs. William Westbrooke's baby dies from the croup just at the moment when her maid has taken in "Gertrude," in *Edith Lyle's Secret* (1874–78?). Of course, the wealthy couple adopts the foundling to replace their own lost babe. Years later, after Mrs. Westbrooke has died from a malady akin to consumption, Edith Lyle, who has just married Colonel Schulyer, and Gertie, who has lived with her guardian because her stepmother could not tolerate children, fortuitously board the same ship headed for the United States. Religious idea novels also relied on chance. In *In His Steps* (1897), Felicia unknowingly opens her cooking school in the block where the ministers have located their settlement house.

Even Bellamy's idea novel, *Looking Backward* (1888), which rejected free enterprise and competition, relied upon chance. Julian bumbles into the future when his house burns down on the very evening his physician moves away. No one but the faithful servant who dies in the blaze and that doctor know he lies mesmerized underneath the mansion in a fireproof vault. "Julian West felt alienated from society and divided against himself."[33] He is a cross between Rip Van Winkle and Sleeping Beauty. His insomnia symbolizes his emotional turmoil and his long, deep sleep simulates death. It takes Edith's kiss to induce him to fall asleep naturally without the benefit of music or stories. Sleep represents psychic peace. The humane scientists enable Julian to be reborn from the womb of the underground vault. Elements of chance in plots like *Looking Backward* may have reflected a cultural attitude toward risk that de Tocqueville suggests permeates all democracies: "Those who live in the midst of democratic fluctuations have always before their eyes the image of chance, and they end by liking all undertakings in which chance plays a part."[34]

Holmes wrote a tour de force of coincidence, *Edith Lyle's Secret.* Edith's "secret" is a "bouncing, blue-eyed babe" born after the righteous father has died and Heloise (Edith) unwittingly has burned the wedding certificate with the trash. To avoid gossip, Heloise flees with her mother to England. Shortly after giving birth, Heloise changes her name to Edith. As a result of her mother's chicanery, Edith believes her child is dead. Twenty years later, the bonny lass (very much alive!) steals the heart of Edith's stepson, who owes his life to Edith's first husband. Then the tangled web of the romance starts to unravel.

Edith confesses her first marriage, and Gertrude discovers she is Edith's daughter, Heloise Lyle, and not Gertie Westbrooke. Edith has met her second husband, Col. Howard Schulyer, because he was her wealthy companion's half-brother. Gertie meets the Schulyers, including Edith, when her guardian rents rooms from Edith's mother.

Edith's rise from obscurity to respectability through marriage epitomizes the plot of the romantic fairy tale. Phelps, too, although she sympathized with the women's rights movement, (1883) depicted marriage as the natural state. In *Beyond the Gates* (1883), once dead, one who never wed on earth would find a spiritual mate, who might drop a spouse who was still living, to be united with the ideal consort.

A fascinating split concerning the importance of birth and social status is evident in the plots of these success stories, especially the romances and children's serials. Many authors contrasted the stuffy conventions of the Old World with the bracing customs of the New World. For instance, Owen Wister's protagonist in *The Virginian* (1902) embodies Thomas Jefferson's image of the natural aristocrat. Besides mastering ranching skills, he reads books to educate himself so he may be worthy of Molly Stark, the pretty schoolteacher from the East. "A Cowboy's tenderness is usually revealed through his kindness to horses, and in this sense, the Eastern Belle's role is that of a glorified horse."[35] Wister wove the love theme into the story to amplify the Virginian's social potential. "Along with the Western environment, she serves to throw a stronger light on the hero, to make him stand out in relief, to complete the picture of an ideal."[36]

Although horses may exhibit blind allegiance, women tend to demand proof of a suitor's credentials. Molly, feeling obligated to maintain her family's social position, refuses the Virginian's marriage proposal for three years. She traces her ancestors back to the Revolutionary War era; and since the Virginian lacks upper-class status, she initially rejects him. Recalling that her family had thwarted her engagement to a genuine but poor sailor who just a few months later was swallowed by the sea, her Grand Aunt urges Molly to abandon hollow social conventions for the sake of true love. The matron declares that the only criteria necessary for the nuptials should have been that "he was brave and handsome, and I loved him."[37]

Intergenerational Conflicts and Class Barriers

Through the Grand Aunt, Wister colorfully varies the often threadbare motif of the tension between generations that mirrors the conflict between old and new technologies. Sometimes the protagonists benefit from the wisdom of their elders. For instance, Captain January raises Star Bright. Fly-Away Ned learns to be a detective from Old Sleuth. The Bird Woman teaches the Swamp Angel, Freckles, and other young people to appreciate the Limberlost marsh. The wise grandmother in Southworth's romance helps her granddaughter adjust to being orphaned. However, inevitable differences sometimes alienate youths from their elders. For example, Pollyanna's peppy outlook contrasts sharply with Aunt Polly's lethargic world view. Rebecca of Sunnybrook Farm represents modernity while stern Aunt Miranda embodies tradition.

In *John Ward, Preacher* (1888), intergenerational differences divide the characters. Two elderly maiden sisters consider it a scandal when Helen returns to her father's house after her marriage. Eventually, Helen's father and uncle accept her unorthodox behavior. The battle between the old and the new amounts to a struggle for spiritual holism. John Ward cannot tolerate Helen's soft views of heaven and her sympathy for sinners. His absolute practice of the tenets of Calvinism leads to grief and death. Since he cannot change with the rest of the world, he, like all dinosaurs, perishes.

Ideal romantic love takes its toll. Everyone has just one chance to find the perfect mate. In a subplot of *John Ward, Preacher*, Denner's inability to choose one of the Forsythe sisters for his bride finally slays him. Instead of making his own decision, he looks for signs from heaven. When he spots a runaway buggy, he assumes that rescuing the women will reveal which sister he should wed. Unfortunately, a newspaper and not fate has startled the horses. Neither Forsythe sister is in the carriage, and Denner sustains fatal injuries when he stops the vehicle. He dies holding Ruth's hand but giving Deborah a miniature picture and thinking she would have been his choice.

Like Denner, many protagonists suffered while pursuing true love. Often they struggled to overcome class biases. In *The American Myth of Success*, Richard Weiss points out that Christian writers often blended the motif of genetically transmitted goodness with the promise of upward mobility.[38] For example, in *Freckles* (1904), Gene Stratton-Porter's hero must display integrity as well as excel in the workforce before discovering his parents' nobility. Although Stratton-Porter emphasizes the gulf between European and American concepts of a gentlemen and a lady, Freckles nevertheless will not marry the rich banker's daughter so long as he lacks a pedigree. The lad almost dies saving her life, but he believes himself her inferior since he is merely the adopted son of the Limberlost Lumber Baron.

The Swamp Angel, as the heroine is called throughout the story, sets out to prove to Freckles his parents did not beat, maim, or forsake him. She discovers that his mother and father died in the fire that cost Freckles his hand and left him bruised. Moreover, through lucky timing, she meets an Irish noble and his wife who are Freckles's kin. They want to take the lad back to the Old Country to expedite his securing his inheritance. He turns down their offer because, without his Swamp Angel, life would be hell. Besides, having learned from his benefactor to value hard work, Freckles decides he must earn his own fortune.

Despite the biblical warning about camels and needles, Phelps reflected the Darwinism of her time. In *The Gates Ajar* (1868), she suggests that low birth usually insures that an infant will be limited by a crude sensibility and a simple, dogmatic faith to a bleak life and, after death, to the lower depths of heaven. On the other hand, being born into a family of proper standing endows one with a true heart that encourages the acquisition of faith and the aspiration to know God.[39] However, Phelps allows those born into infamy to enter heaven if they place others before themselves or if the spiritually attuned should intercede. Nevertheless, social classes exist even in paradise. The upper echelon in the Holy Grove pursues altruism rather than materialism. Those spirits who have renounced the empty distinctions of European titles or commercial and political fame to serve the community are the ones most respected.

In *The Virginian* (1902), Wister Americanizes the clash between Old and New World traditions by recasting that rivalry to make the East synonymous with decadent civilization and the West represent frontier purity. The Virginian leads a posse to hang cattle rustlers because the eastern institution of the jury trial has been corrupted by unscrupulous judges who accept bribes from outlaws and politicians. The eastern missionary, Dr. Alexander McBride, decries as lies the tall tales the cowboys tell. The wily Virginian keeps the pompous holy man up all night in a vigil to "let loose his [the cowboy's] wolf" and, thus, drive the sin from his belly. McBride dwells in "the black cellar of his theology" and cannot speak of love or hope. In contrast, the Bishop speaks the cowboy's language. To Wister, the cowboys exhibit their purity in their openness to new ideas.

By 1902, when Wister's novel appeared, many Christians and popular writers, too, had lost interest in hell. The irony that self-righteous fools could not see the plank in their own eyes recurred in the fiction. For example, the Ladies Aid Society in *Pollyanna* (1913) shipped barrels of used clothes abroad and, occasionally, arranged adoptions for heathen waifs but refused to help a local orphan, Jimmy Bean, find "regular folks."

In *Phemie Frost's Experiences* (1874), Stephens satirized the preoccupation of many social climbers with class and titles by letting Phemie aspire to be the wife of a Russian prince. Phemie's cousin, Emily Elizabeth, vexes Phemie by insisting that the monarch lifted his hat to the hundreds of women who waved their hankies at him and not just to Phemie. Thousands had greeted him as he paraded from the railroad station to the hotel. Without appreciating the irony of her observation, Phemie gushes, "He must have been dazzled; he must have been impressed by this proof that republics scorn monarchies and trample them under foot."[40]

Phemie, who supports herself by writing news items about her adventures among the heathen in New York City's fashionable centers, considers herself a member of Jefferson's natural aristocracy. The real goods—genius—and not paltry gems will capture the prince's heart, she feels, since royalty cannot resist the allure of a pure spirit and a gifted sensibility. In her eyewitness report to her sisters in Vermont, she confesses: "I have been on the same steamboat with the great Grand Duke; his splendid blue eyes have looked into mine, and in that glance we grappled each other soul to soul. He has smiled upon me through the yellow glory of that yellow mustache, under which his plump, red lips shone like cherries, ripe enough to swallow whole, stones and all. He speaks English; reveres genius and knows that it can never grow old."[41]

Few flesh-and-blood lovers had the opportunities to demonstrate fidelity that were available to characters in romances. For example, while Phemie flirted with European princes, most women had to settle for grocers, lawyers, doctors, or other respectably employed escorts. And most living swains could not afford to turn down a title and a million dollars to avoid losing a sweetheart. Yet many of them admired Freckles for listening to his heart rather than to the jangle of loose change in his pockets because it reassured them that a loving wife was more precious than a treasure chest full of rubies. Most might marry a good woman, but few would hoard precious jewels. Authors concocted coincidences to ensure protagonists success in both love and the marketplace.

The notion that God's chosen people would receive material rewards in consequence of their inner value can be traced to the Puritans, who nevertheless worried about the temptations inherent in acquiring gold. Prosperity (the agent of Providence), in their view, would guarantee advancement to the deserving. In the romances, this platitude frequently was garbed in labyrinthine circumstances demonstrating the fatal flaws of laziness, dishonesty, crime, drinking, smoking, cursing, and child or wife abuse. The plots twisted through scenarios leading to the inevitable conclusion that home and love mattered more than money or prestige.

Naturally, Gilded Age readers enjoyed stories about the lessons of materialism learned in the quest for well-being. Long after rising to respectable heights in the business world, Luke Walton admits he once was a Chicago newspaper boy; however, an individual who had pursued such an occupation for a lifetime would have been ashamed of having failed to improve his status. In the 1830s, de Tocqueville had noted the American propensity for gratifying physical needs.[42] This scurrying after a larger orchard, another cornfield, a new porch, and other comforts led those who were successful in reaching their modest goals to look down upon the less fortunate.

The prosperous preferred to apply rather than to create arts and sciences; consequently they depended upon Europeans for theories.[43] *McGuffey's Readers*, newspapers, periodicals, and the popular plots all championed the ambitious who thrived while the lazy wasted away. In keeping with the harsh moral spirit of the times, Fly-Away Ned concludes that shirkers often fail to provide for their families because they are too proud to do physical labor:

> I am so smart my father turned me out of the house. He claimed to be the smartest man in the world and wouldn't stand no rivals; he feared I'd eclipse him—see—and yet he hadn't a cent in the world. He knew more than all the generals in the world on the theory of conducting a campaign, and when it came to statesmanship, why all the statesmen in the country were fools. In mechanics he couldn't be beat; he could build a bridge against all the engineers in the land. He knew all about the export and import of goods to and from all parts of the world. He knew more about medicine than the druggist in our . town; more about diseases than the doctor; more about theology than the clergyman. Yes, Sir, he knew it all, and yet didn't know enough to support his family. There are lots of such fellows in the world—they know everything, to let themselves tell it.[44]

In the formula stories under consideration, many characters who lose their jobs or refuse to work develop destructive habits, such as smoking or drinking. For instance, in Amelia Barr's romance, *Jan Vedder's Wife* (1885), Jan Vedder loses his summer's profit when he rescues the crew of a floundering ship rather than collect his own nets and hooks. His father-in-law, Peter, withholds one-third of Jan's share of the earnings because Jan has broken the unwritten law of the sea:

each captain must worry first about his own ship and equipment. Jan's cycle of bad luck begins with that storm. The dispute costs him his job at the store. He cannot buy food for himself and his wife. His clothing becomes shabby. He quarrels with his wife and in-laws. To pass the hours, Jan drinks with smugglers at the saloon, and they make him the captain of a vessel. Jan collects a lot of money until his boss stabs him in the side one night during a fight over loot. The wound leads to Jan's redemption. After saving the fallen man, a minister introduces him to Lord Lynne, who takes him away from the vices induced by chronic unemployment and despair.

However, not all these characters benefit from their suffering. Vices usually destroy scoundrels. Jan Vedder is one of the few protagonists who fall from grace prior to the appearance of a benefactor. Usually, diligence rather than injuries prepares characters for redemption. Poverty often kills. In Deland's domestic tale, *John Ward, Preacher* (1888), a pauper who beats his wife and drinks excessively drops a match while attempting to light a cigarette in the lumberyard where the drunkards meet to gamble and gossip. The blaze guts the town's only source of employment. As the tosspot pulls a tot from the flames, he dies. His sin, nevertheless, costs him salvation, according to Preacher Ward, who believes that, regardless of the good deeds they commit, those who do not repent suffer everlasting damnation worse than any earthly fire.

Roe depicted the Chicago Fire as burning up the vices and artificial class distinctions that led to drinking port with dinner and admiring paintings of nudes. Of course, it was mostly the depraved and unworthy who perished in the conflagration. In *Barriers Burned Away* (1872), boozehounds break into grog shops instead of fleeing the fire: "Finding some kindred spirits sacking a liquor-store not far off, he joined the orgy, seeking to drown his feelings in rum, and succeeded so effectually that he lay in the gutter soon after, and the escaping multitude trampled over him, and soon the fire blotted out his miserable existence, as it did that of so many who rendered themselves helpless by drink."[45] Apparently, only the tipsy butterflies who fly upside down after guzzling fermented nectar in the swamp in Gene Stratton-Porter's Cinderfella tale, *Freckles* (1904), flit away from hell's maw.

After drawing his courage from a bottle on the night before the Virginian's wedding, Trampas—"an evil to the country"—challenges the groom to a shoot-out.[46] Trampas drinks whiskey to drum up the nerve to carry out his rash threat. He cannot back down. The code of the West decrees that he either face the Virginian in a fair fight or be labeled a coward for the rest of his life. The duel ends with the outlaw dead and the Virginian vindicated because he did not shoot until after Trampas had fired. The bartender had warned Trampas that guzzling drinks might affect his aim, but the villain could not control his thirst.

The authors of the success tracts (Carnegie, Barnum, and Conwell) agreed with the popular bards that many people wasted money on alcohol and tobacco. These Prophets of Profit shared the fiction writers' conviction that employment provided the means of salvation. In fact, Carnegie advocated building state-run workhouses to force labor from the "social lepers" whose idleness arose from innate flaws so grievous that they would never master "the virtues necessary for improvement."[47] Barnum advised, "Do your part of the work, or you cannot succeed." While lecturing on "The Art of Money-Getting," he admonished audiences that "idleness breeds bad habits and clothes a man in rags."[48]

Wister demonstrated Barnum's ideas about work by contrasting boyhood friends, the Virginian and Steve. While Steve organizes a gang of rustlers, the honest southerner rises to become foreman of Judge Henry's crew. Steve's dreams of "getting rich quick and being a big man in the Territory" get him hanged as a thief.[49] The noble knight in chaps, in contrast, marries the eastern schoolteacher, becomes the judge's partner, and lives happily ever after, surrounded by his children and the material rewards of diligence.

Even Dorothy and her companions in *The Wizard of Oz* (1900) must pay as they go for the services they receive. Benefactors—the Queen of the Field Mice and the Good Fairies—assist them once the characters have proven their worthiness. Only the stork gives his labor away freely, snatching the Scarecrow from the river. Ironically, the mighty Wizard turns out to be a frail old humbug who can help the group only if they have faith in his powers. It is only by promising to help them get what they want that good, innocent Dorothy is able to enlist comrades in her project of going to Emerald City; no one makes the journey out of altruistic sentiment. The Scarecrow desires a brain, the Tin Man seeks a heart, and the Cowardly Lion hopes to acquire courage. The Munchkins treat Dorothy royally because they credit her with executing the Wicked Witch by dropping a house on the hag. To pay Dorothy for dispatching the Wicked Witch of the East, the Good Witch of the South gives her the deceased's silver shoes as well as a kiss on the forehead that will dispel evil.

The travelers' quest teaches them that, while material things disintegrate, love endures. Moreover, they realize that attaining happiness involves earning the respect of one's peers and finding a true home. Their concern for one another inspires them to draw upon resources they did not know they possessed. Dorothy discovers she is not a helpless little girl but indeed can outwit witches as well as save Toto from lions. The brainless Scarecrow proves to be the most ingenious of the pilgrims. The heartless Tin Man cries when he steps on a beetle and beheads a wild cat to save a field mouse who happens to be the rodents' Queen.

The Queen remembers this kindness later when the lion falls asleep in the deadly poppy field. Following the Scarecrow's directions, they construct a sled and pull the snoring fat cat to safety. The Cowardly Lion tries to protect Dorothy from the deadly Kalidahs; and, although he is terrified, he leaps over the chasm carrying his friends on his back. Emerald City is appropriately green. Oz will not grant wishes unless the petitioners compensate him. He orders Dorothy and the others to bring him the Wicked Witch of the West's broomstick. Even Glinda, before helping Dorothy go home, appropriates the Golden Cap, which grants the bearer three wishes from the winged monkeys. Leaving Oz costs Dorothy the friendship of her three comrades, whom she has grown to love. Not beauty, not magic, not even the fidelity of marvelous soulmates can stop Dorothy from returning to the place where she belongs—in Kansas with Aunty Em and Uncle Harry (who seems to be an afterthought). The moral of the tale is either "Pay as you go" or "There's no place like home." Both mottoes echo the success archetype.

To cultural historian Henry M. Littlefield, however, *The Wizard of Oz* (1900) is a "parable on Populism."[50] Dorothy represents Miss Everybody; the Scarecrow, the farmers; and the Tin Man, exploited eastern labor. Like the Cowardly Lion, many politicians failed to appreciate the possibilities that silver presented to those headed down the Yellow Brick (gold) Road. "Baum makes these Winged Monkeys into an Oz substitute for Plains Indians."[51] The Banker Boss or Mark Hanna inspired the Wicked Witch of the West. The Wizard could be any of the United States presidents, from Grant to McKinley. In the end, Dorothy and her comrades understand that the Wizard is just an ordinary human being with no supernatural powers. "Like any good politician, he gives the people what they want. Throughout the story, Baum poses a central thought: the American desire for symbols of fulfillment is illusory."[52]

The populist tale celebrated the same values (hard work, honesty, loyalty, faith) that other writers, including Carnegie, Barnum, and Conwell, emphasized. In fact, these seers of success would have admired Nick Carter's diligence. By conducting "a fatiguing search no one not possessed of the wonderful patience of an expert and thorough detective" would have undertaken, Carter uncovers evidence overlooked by the police.[53] Despite the odds against finding relevant clues on the busy highway in front of the roadhouse, Nick, disguised as Old Thunderbolt, reconstructs the murderer's route by collecting horse hairs. This Herculean deductive feat illustrates the power of persistence.

Carnegie and Conwell both proclaimed that those worthy of success got it. Carnegie cautioned listeners against unrestrained charity, saying it would be better to throw millions of dollars "into the sea than so spend it as to encourage the slothful, the drunken, the unworthy."[54] Only those willing to help themselves merited aid: "Those worthy of assistance, except in rare cases, seldom require assistance."[55] Moreover, in *Acres of Diamonds* (1887), Conwell suggests that charity displeases God, because the scourge of poverty chastises sinners: "To sympathize with a man whom God has punished for his sins, thus to help him when God would still continue a just punishment, is to do wrong, no doubt about it. . . . While we should sympathize with God's poor—that is, those who cannot help themselves—let us remember there is not a poor person in the United States who was not made poor by his own shortcomings, or by the shortcomings of someone else. It is all wrong to be poor, anyway."[56]

To emphasize how wretches made themselves poor, Conwell denounces a husband who smokes up the wages his wife has earned. He declares that too many sluggards pour their paychecks down the neck of a rum bottle. Mrs. Ruggles and the heroine of *Mrs. Wiggs of the Cabbage Patch* (1901) raise large families despite their drunken husbands and their poverty. Although Mrs. Ruggles disowns her dead spouse, who perpetually had been out to sea anyway, Mrs. Wiggs forgives her partner: "When Mr. Wiggs traveled to eternity by the alcohol route, she buried his faults with him, and for want of better virtues to extol she always laid stress on the fine hand he wrote."[57]

Although Eggleston, in *The Hoosier School-Master* (1871), portrays the poorhouse sympathetically, he conforms to the prejudices of his day concerning the connection between spiritual worth and the ability to make money. Eggleston's hero helps a regal old Englishwoman who has spent two years confined with the cursing, blaspheming Old Moe in a cellar of the county poor-farm. Despite being nearly blind, the virtuous crone knit almost enough stockings there to support herself. Eggleston mentions this accomplishment twice.

Since the success paradigm promised middle-class respectability to the worthy, being poor indicated God's wrath. Being rich did not guarantee happiness, however. Some millionaires in the Gilded Age recognized the truth of a twentieth-century advertising platitude: "If you've got your health, you've got next to everything." For example, *The Birds' Christmas Carol* (1886; the Birds' daughter was born on December 25) showed everyone the meaning of Christ's birthday. As his child wasted away with a terminal disease, Mr. Bird "felt like throwing [his fortune] into the ocean, since it could not buy a strong body for his little girl."[58]

Why the Rich Choke on the Silver Spoon

De Tocqueville observed in 1831 that Americans embrace virtues associated with commerce, praising the procurement of fortune and decrying the dissipation of earned capital.[59] A half-century later, orators were lamenting the debilitating effects of gold upon unsuspecting upper-class children. Being born wealthy limited a child's prospects, according to the success prototype. Carnegie warned, "Great sums bequeathed often work more for the injury than for the good of the recipients."[60] Conwell urged his audiences to leave their sons and daughters the pristine legacy of "education, . . . Christian and noble character, honorable name [and] a wide circle of friends," rather than money. He warned youths: "Oh, young man, if you have inherited money, don't regard it as a help. It will curse you through your years and deprive you of the very best things of human life. There is no class of people to be pitied so much as the inexperienced sons and daughters of the rich of our generation."[61]

This theme of rich children impoverished spiritually by their wealth interested writers of popular fiction. For example, Rose, the speculator's daughter in *In His Steps* (1897), is unable to adjust to life without riches after her father's suicide. On the other hand, her sister, Felicia, converts her sorrow into an opportunity to serve others. Just as Conwell and Carnegie predicted, "For the first time in her life, she had the delight of doing something of value for the happiness of others."[62] This girl would "do anything honorable to make [her] living and that of Rose."[63] She works as a domestic and attends cooking school until opening a school of her own near a settlement house in the tenement district. While teaching nutrition classes to the city's poor, she meets a carpenter. They marry and live happily ever after. On the other hand, Rose, to reclaim her social position, weds a rich man much older than herself, and her life is overcast with "certain dark and awful shadows."[64]

Of course, Horatio Alger also repeats this popular motif of the devastating effects of money upon progeny. Luke Walton works hard and, through luck and gumption, rises in the world. Harold Tracy is not fortunate enough to be destitute. Although the fathers of both boys have died, Harold does not benefit from the invigorating squalor that frequently accompanies partial orphanhood in these books. Without the incentive of hard times, the pampered lad succumbs to temptations—the theater, billiards, fancy eateries, cigarettes, and, ultimately, theft. At the end of the adventure, Alger notes Harold's indolence: "Harold seems unwilling to settle down to business, but has developed a taste for dress and amusements of a young man about town. He thinks he will eventually be provided for by Mrs. Merton, but in this he is mistaken, as she has decided to leave much the larger part of her wealth to charitable institutions after remembering her nephew, Warner Powell, handsomely."[65] Mrs. Merton leaves only a token remembrance to her selfish, sluggish daughter, who has married a rich, intemperate brute and taught her grandson Harold to lust after money.

The generous Mrs. Merton practices the "gospel of wealth" by rewarding the deserving, who would invest the money wisely in ventures to enhance the community as well as to enrich themselves. Just as the success writers like Carnegie and Conwell dictated, Mrs. Merton and other fictional benefactors endow public institutions that serve large numbers of the poor. Even the detective stories contain instances of philanthropy organized in accord with Carnegie's guidelines.

For example, in Rinehart's *The Circular Staircase* (1908), Rachel promises the local pastor a new carpet for his church. The whole village appreciates this gift. Rachel's attitude about her generosity echoes Carnegie's belief that, through giving, the rich received their real treasures and grew "poor, very poor, indeed, in money, but rich, very rich twenty times a millionaire still, in the affection, gratitude and admiration of [their] fellow-men."[66] After handing the Methodist minister a bouquet of roses to take to his wife and sending him home in the Dragon Fly (her car), Rachel considers her motivation on that hot afternoon: "As for me, I had a generous glow that was cheap at the price of a church carpet. I received less gratification—and less gratitude—when I presented the new silver communion set to St. Barnabas."[67]

Just as her heroine epitomizes the responsible upper-class woman who invests her money wisely, Rinehart's villain in *The Circular Staircase* exudes the moral corruption induced by aristocratic birth in the fictive realm of the Gilded Age—where fathers and sons alike forgot that shrouds have no pockets. Paul Armstrong, president of the Traders' Bank, is a lousy role model for his son Arnold. Arnold perfectly typifies the coddled parasite who inherits riches. He fits Conwell's description of "a millionaire's son . . . an indescribable specimen of anthropologic impotency . . . [who] dressed like a grasshopper . . . [and was a] poor, miserable, contemptible, American monkey . . . [a] travesty upon human nature."[68] Certainly, to deserve such harsh words, Rinehart's scoundrel emanated rottenness. Not even massive doses of "common sense rather than copper cents"—Conwell's curative for lisping dandies—would have redeemed this cad.[69]

Arnold's dastardly deeds sound like a summary of a modern television soap opera. His first public crime, embezzling from his father's bank, prompts his family to disown him. Next, he carouses until he meets a sweet young girl who convinces him to put aside his bottle. Unfortunately for her, he marries her. They move to Chicago, where he abuses his new bride and abandons her after she becomes pregnant. What a blackguard!

But Arnold's treachery has just begun. He eventually blackmails his mother-in-law. She supports herself and Arnold's son by serving as the housekeeper for Arnold's parents. Arnold extorts every possible cent from the terrified grandmother by threatening to take custody of the child away from his ex-wife and send his son to a distant boarding school. He spends the money on fancy cigars, liquor, playing billiards, and cavorting at his country club. True to his bestial nature, one lovely spring evening, he clobbers his mother-in-law with a "golf-stick." The justly enraged woman shoots him dead. But the good, loving grandmother dies tragically from blood poisoning, contracted from the fatal wound inflicted by the destroyer of her daughter and the bane of her grandson's existence.

Not all mothers in these stories act in their children's best interest. In fact, in *Edith Lyle's Secret* (1874–78), one, Mrs. Fordham, takes her pregnant daughter, Edith, to England, drugs the new mother long enough to snatch the fatherless newborn, pens a note proclaiming the child's noble lineage onto her blanket, and then abandons the infant on a hospital doorstep. Edith's sorrow culminates in brain fever, and her cunning mother convinces her the baby has died of a heart condition. As arthritis twists her face and body, this monstrous lie erodes Mrs. Fordham's spirit. Obsessed by her desire to place her daughter in high society, Mrs. Fordham ultimately drives away everyone whom she loves, including her daughter Edith.

Despite the delicious possibilities for melodramatic incident provided by mother love gone sour, some authors chose to focus on the sins of coddled children who could not be counted among Conwell's honest "ninety-eight out of one hundred of the rich men of America" who prospered by behaving morally.[70] Indeed, greed literally kills Arnold Armstrong's father, when the latter breaks his neck trying to recover the fortune he has embezzled from his own bank. Nick Carter confronts a diabolical heiress whose gangster father has bequeathed her instructions for recovering thirty thousand dollars he had stolen. His confession of crimes inspires new horrors: to recover the illicit booty, the cunning criminal attempts to blame the murder of her lover on her doltish brother.

Revenge as well as avarice motivates some rogues in the American bardic tales. In Green's mystery, *The Circular Study* (1900), Amos Cadwalader nurtures his son Felix's obsession with avenging the wrong done to his sister Evelyn, who died of shame after being "ruined" by John Poindexter. The widower had arranged for Felix and Evelyn to stay with his lifelong friend, Poindexter. The father returns home from serving in the Union Army just in time to see his daughter's funeral procession. Poindexter shows no remorse.

Cadwalader remarries, and his wife bears a son, Thomas. Cadwalader sends the infant to England to be educated. Thomas's French guardian advises the lad to read every romance he can find, because, compared with his own family history, these thrilling stories of betrayal and despair look pallid. Felix and Amos call Thomas home when Cadwalader contracts a fatal malady similar to consumption. They compel him to swear an oath of vengeance against John and Eva Poindexter. Thomas cringes, but their passion overwhelms him. He agrees to ruin the daughter born to Poindexter's second wife. Inevitably, the obsessed brother Felix and the confused Thomas both fall in love with the blonde, fragile Eva. Despite her father's cupidity, the girl has become a good person.

Thomas's malevolent older brother Felix realizes that, once Thomas has married Eva, he will not betray her. Felix builds an elaborate circular study with an "ironclad-steel door" that, when snapped shut, will entomb him along with the newlyweds. By the time Poindexter answers the telegram summoning him to Felix's study, the trio will be dead. Cadwalader and Felix want revenge more than life. They would die to hurt their enemy. They would sacrifice a maiden as innocent as their own beloved Evelyn to spite her cold father, who had told them that "when a man cares for nothing or nobody, it is useless to curse him."[71] Eva thwarts Felix's evil scheme by stabbing him in the heart, because she and Thomas are too young and too happy to die. The police decide that she acted in self-defense. Thomas has offered to give up his share of the family fortune to marry Eva, and she was willing to give up luxuries to be his wife. With Felix's death, they are spared the trauma of losing their money.

Gilded Age authors repeatedly demonstrate the truth of Christ's assertion that a camel could pass through the eye of a needle more readily than a rich person could enter heaven. Even Colorado Joe in *Deadwood Dick on Deck* (1885) warns that "gold is p'izen." Moreover, when his "pard" Sandy returns with a massive nugget, Colorado's resolve to "bid farewell to tarant'ler juice forever" melts. The sudden wealth entices him to drink to celebrate their good fortune. Sandy remains cool enough to "freeze ice in fly time" because he realizes that the chance discovery of the gold is a mixed blessing. The righteous cowboy names the spot "Satan's Bend," anticipating the influx of rogues who will trample the serene valley once news of the pay dirt has spread like wildfire.[72]

Sandy's nemesis, a speculator from Washington, D.C., hauls a cavernous Saratoga trunk full of champagne with him to Satan's Bend and hires Arkansas Alf the Ghoul to kill his two former wives, who just happen to live in the boom town. The speculator thrives on meanness and gold, though not necessarily in that order. He belongs to a legion of swindlers who slink through the popular plots. For instance, in *Luke Walton* (1873), the nasty Mr. Brown, who has a wart on his upper cheek and no scruples, squanders his savings on land deals after Luke generously accepts restitution of his father's money and refrains from prosecuting the scoundrel. The title character of *John March, Southerner* (1894) loses his inheritance in schemes involving northern capital.

In Twain and Warner's *The Gilded Age* (1873), the dream of making a fortune through selling the Tennessee land impoverishes rather than enriches the heirs. Some bards reversed the motif of ruinous dreams of sudden riches developed by Twain and Warner. Indeed, these plots reinforced the caveat against speculation while illustrating the wisdom of being satisfied with modest gains. For example, since the Jucklins, in the novel named for them, and their roomer Bill Hawes do not fritter their money away on get-rich-quick schemes, they prosper.

In religious stories like *Ben-Hur* (1880), money tarnishes the soul. For example, to gain power and worldly possessions, Iris, the exotic Egyptian temptress, plots with the Romans against Ben-Hur. Christine must have her *Barriers Burned Away* (1872) by the Chicago Fire to be redeemed from the foul influences of mammon. Her father has filled her head with visions of a royal estate in Germany purchased with profits from selling foreign art in the United States to amoral social climbers. She rejects religion and her country until the conflagration warms her cold heart. Then, Christine rises from a toasty grave in a dilapidated Catholic cemetery to declare herself a simple, American, Christian girl.

Two other American girls also find themselves entangled in a web of despair as a result of money misused. Green's mystery, *The Leavenworth Case* (1878), opens with the murder of a rich man whose two nieces share his mansion. One, Mary, inherits most of the estate. The other, Eleanor, receives a modest bequest. The girls' characters reveal the pathology produced by wealth. Proud Mary has grown accustomed to being indulged. She cannot bear to join the middle class. In contrast, humble Eleanor practices the homespun virtues she acquired by serving as her uncle's private secretary. Eleanor dresses plainly and accepts her spoiled sister without jealousy. Green herself condemned passing fortunes from one generation to the next. Refusing "to accept property so stained by guilt," her heroines give the city their inheritances to build a charitable institution for the poor.[73] Then, they marry diligent youths with promising prospects.

Millionaires—Shepherds or Wolves?

News of real belles eagerly moving from a mansion to an ivy-covered cottage doubtless would have made Carnegie and Conwell break out in hives. No such parable graces *The Gospel of Wealth* (1889). No such heresy mars *Acres of Diamonds* (1887). The success tract writers believed that individual salvation lay in amassing property. Only competition and shrewd investment proffered solutions to social problems. The poor did not have to be poor. They could work for the rich and so pull themselves up by their bootstraps. Carnegie declares that wealth enables wise philanthropists to supervise the maintenance of God's perpetual motion machine—Earth—for the childlike lower classes. Conwell agrees:

> Money is power, and you ought to have it because you can do more good with it than you could without it. Money printed your Bible, money builds your churches, money sends your missionaries, and money pays your preachers, and you would not have many of them, either, if you did not pay them. . . .
>
> I say, then, you ought to have money. If you can honestly attain unto riches in Philadelphia, it is your Christian and godly duty to do so. It is an awful mistake of these pious people to think you must be awfully poor in order to be pious.[74]

Like Conwell and Carnegie, Bellamy preached respect for property. Although the author denounced capitalism, John A. Garraty, in *The New Commonwealth,* explains that Bellamy was only "superficially radical."[75] While the utopia in *Looking Backward* (1888) eliminates class distinctions, it retains an oligarchy. Only those past retirement age vote. Indeed, all enlightened citizens "were as concerned with material things and creature comforts, as interested in gadgets and as worshipful of technology as any American capitalist of his own day."[76] The Social-Gospel novelist resembled a minister who expected his flock to transform society simply through goodness and empathy. Characters discuss religion and the importance of reconciling old visions of morality with new exigencies.

In *The Brown Decades,* Lewis Mumford calls *Looking Backward* "a real looking forward: it showed both the promise and the threat of actual conditions."[77] Although Mumford praises Bellamy for predicting telephonic broadcasting, the banishment of the corset, and the role of modern women, Bellamy himself said he had intended to write "a mere literary fantasy, a fairy tale of social felicity," not a blueprint for reformers.[78] The plot does not unfold until the end of the book, when Julian falls in love with Edith, who (coincidentally) is the granddaughter of his former fiancee. The latter, fourteen years after the fire supposedly had killed Julian, had married at last. In fairy-tale fashion, after undergoing the ordeal of time travel and the loss of his world, Julian marries the princess. This fractured fairy tale resembles *Barriers Burned Away* (1872); in both stories lovers overcome incredible odds to be together. On the other hand, while wise investment guarantees morality in *Looking Backward,* Roe's stark moral imperative decrees that gaining spiritual riches requires surrendering all material possessions.

Looking Backward and *Barriers Burned Away* both call fervently for the creation of a new order out of the ashes of the old. Fire leads to salvation in both stories. The Chicago Fire of 1871 purifies the city by annihilating the wicked and rekindling respect for God in the hearts of the weak. In *Looking Backward,* the conflagration lifts Julian West from his benighted existence in the nineteenth century and into a heavenly future. His friend Edith several times compares her society to paradise. Julian reads a "romance in which there should, indeed, be love galore, but love unfettered by artificial barriers created by differences of station or possessions, owning no other law but that of the heart."[79] Roe illustrates that same altruistic state in his grim morality tale.

Both books reflect a cardinal characteristic of the Gilded Age, the obsession with success. Perhaps the shift from a farming to an industrial society, the respect for technology that made people as well as machines more efficient, and the arrival of multitudes of immigrants all combined to impel tremendous social changes. The popular plots eased the anxieties of readers confused by the mandate to succeed materially without damaging their souls.

Like ballads, legends, and fairy tales, the bardic tales filled emotional needs and reinforced values. Through the deliberate repetition of the sacred success archetype, the writers recast old scenarios to monitor changing conditions. Bardic tales blended elements from novels and fairy tales into a new hybrid that evolved as the shell for the success paradigm. Bardic tales were not novels. They did not impart universal insights into life, explore new literary territory, or endure for centuries. Bards wrote for the moment. They tailored the cherished sequence into plots their audiences could relate to their own lives. Newspaper clippings supplied a wealth of detail for applying the success prototype in the present.

The success archetype mirrored the cultural fear of sinking rather than rising in life. Money opened a Pandora's box of temptations. The bards praised prudent advances from poverty to the middle class and castigated rash ascents into the upper class. The esteem of peers and the love of one's family—not power and wealth—brought contentment. Ironically, although silver and gold could not purchase salvation, many authors depicted heaven as a physical utopia similar to earth. The success prototype resolved the dilemma of how to acquire material possessions without losing one's soul.

Through repeated examples, the success archetype warned that those most susceptible to greed were the children of wealthy parents. In bardic tales, having everything that money could buy on earth led to losing everything heaven had to offer. Their position at the acme of society doomed upper-crust youths to a parasitic existence serving nobody but themselves and, in consequence, withering spiritually. On the other hand, children who had to toil to survive developed integrity. In the serials, romances, mysteries, cowboy stories, and other bardic tales, strangers and orphans alike work their way up from the gutter to respectability. They turn poverty into an elevator, and, upon reaching the top floor of opportunity, these former urchins assume their rightful places in the community. Then they remember their pasts and become benefactors of worthy orphans.

Chance kept the success paradigm fluid. Although the anticipation of key events increased the power of the tale, unexpected coincidences that ironically or fortuitously pushed the plot ahead enlivened the story. Moreover, the coincidences invoked magic. No one could predict exactly how the protagonist would prevail over crushing circumstances. Omnipotent coincidence guaranteed the timely invocation of the fairy-tale convention that justice must triumph over evil. In the complex world of the late nineteenth century, uncertainty in the form of unemployment, technology, and catastrophe threatened common people's lives. The success prototype, lying at the heart of the bardic tale, filled the emotional demand for closure that reality denied.

The success archetype reiterated the cherished values that had preserved community for millennia—the bond with others created in the individual by belonging to something greater than the self. The story provided a stage for experimenting with social changes and reforms. Fictive intergenerational conflicts often revealed that artificial class barriers are cemented with false notions of worth, based solely on material possessions. Some plots suggested that millionaires might redeem themselves by becoming wise benefactors. Other stories insisted that the wealthy destroyed everyone around them, including their own families. Indeed, the rich human had as much chance of entering the Kingdom of Heaven as a camel had of passing through the eye of a needle.

Here is the Gospel of Success, according to Brother Russell Conwell: "Look ye in your back yard, and ye shall prosper." According to Brother Andrew Carnegie: "Respect the rich, for they already have inherited the earth." According to Brother Phineas Barnum: "Let ye who have not humbugged throw the first tomato." And according to Brother Horatio Alger: "If ye have faith so as to move mountains but have not pluck and luck, then ye shall be as nothing."

Chapter 5

Why Children Read Success Tales

First through nursery rhymes and later through fairy tales, adults teach children values. Popular bards of every generation in every community recreate a body of lore that recycles cherished archetypes to perpetuate mores. Part of the process of socializing children or immigrants involves educating them, whether through popular culture or in classrooms, about society's hidden agenda. In the United States in the Gilded Age, the unspoken rules often involved learning to reconcile a desire for material wealth with a need to feel spiritually whole.

As the trend toward secular purposes and escapist fare prevailed, people feared amusement would jeopardize children's spiritual well-being by glorifying materialism rather than diligence and altruism. This fear made *McGuffey's Readers* remain ubiquitous in schools. William H. McGuffey's Scotch-Irish, Presbyterian roots molded his optimistic but stern world view and compelled him to warn children to be wary of those who thought ambition could replace idealism: "The economic opportunities America offered could be its nemesis unless they were pursued with conscience and restraint."[1] Serials written for children reinforced values while showing readers how to cope with hardship.

The narratives written for juveniles during the eighteenth and nineteenth centuries were published during three phases that coincided with the emergence of the success prototype and the evolution of the American publishing industry. First, stories reinforced spiritual teaching. Next, as the country grew and society changed, popular writers blended features of novels and archetypal motifs, creating hybrids that retained the stock characters of didactic narratives, including the angelic child.

Finally, as the number of millionaires increased during the late nineteenth century and the living standard improved for most citizens, traditional strictures on amassing fortunes underwent revision. *Literary Digest* reported that, between 1814 and 1914, the nation's wealth multiplied nearly ninetyfold. Moreover, "those who emigrated were inconceivably poor and destitute, but in general they have attained incomes and wealth much greater, on the average, than persons who elected to remain" in Europe.[2] These social changes inspired the popular bards to pose alternatives to justify secular pleasures that would have shocked the earlier angelic characters.

Pious Prigs Teach Adults What's Important

In the colonial era, angelic prigs chastised materialists, including parents and ministers, and even died to remind survivors that piety, not gold or power, entitled the righteous to enter God's kingdom. Saintly children persisted even into the twentieth century. For example, in *The Birds' Christmas Carol,* a little girl named Carol Bird saves a boisterous family from destitution. Kate Douglas Wiggin wrote this tale of innocence and sacrifice in 1886, but it was available in paperback as recently as 1995.

Like Carol, Little Eva, the pious daughter of the kind but foolish planter in *Uncle Tom's Cabin* (1855) exemplifies the child who is too good for earthly life.[3] The *National Era* printed Harriet Beecher Stowe's melodramatic abolition parable in 1851–52. During 1852, readers bought three hundred thousand copies of the book. C. B. Tillinghast noted in the *Forum* on 16 September 1893: "The most popular book in our libraries today is that thrilling story of the days that, happily, are past—'Uncle Tom's Cabin.' It is still read in all our communities by people of all ages and classes and all nationalities. Wherever lists of books are kept, this book usually heads them."[4] Unlike the title character of *Pollyanna* (1913), who inflicts her "glad game" relentlessly, Little Eva teaches others by example rather than nagging.[5] Stowe wrote her indictment of slavery for adults, but children still read it.[6]

Perversely, in didactic literature, the good children, like Little Eva and Carol Bird, die young. The titles of early stories, including *Mary Lothrop Who Died in Boston in 1831,* indicate the moral common to these works. The book named opens with an illustration of the pious heroine and her little brother kneeling.[7] After he kicks her, Mary prays him into a state of repentance. Apparently the effort proves too taxing, and Mary falls ill. Three-fourths of the plot describes her decline and joyous preparation for heaven. The story ends gloomily, by modern standards, admonishing the living and glorifying death as the route to eternal life.

Puritans believed that sober tales would show youngsters how to merit salvation.[8] James Janeway's *A Token for Children: Being an Exact Account of the Conversion, Holy and Exemplary Lives and Joyful Deaths of Several Children. To Which Is Now Added, Prayers and Graces, Fitted for the Use of Little Children* (1671–72) may seem morbid to later generations, but during the colonial era, devout families discussed the fates of the thirteen good little boys and girls who converted sinners as well as brooded about the torments of hell and the purity of their souls. The Pilgrims brought these tracts with them from the Old World.[9]

In "The Pap We Have Been Fed On: The Old Time Books for Children," Edna Kenton satirizes a didactic story, *Little Dot*.[10] "*Little Dot* is a cheerful *tour de force* [*sic*] of many years ago. It opens gaily with a bright spring morning and the cemetery looking more peaceful than usual." Little Dot and her grave-digging best friend, Old Solomon, ponder the destiny of drunkards, the machinations of misers, and other great mysteries of the universe. Alas, one day the perceptive tot notices the hole is much smaller than usual. Old Sol explains that a baby will be buried on the morrow, and Little Dot "decorated the grave with elaborate hysteria." The shock triggers a fatal neurosis. Little Dot pines away "until that sad day came when she lay 'at rest,' and Old Sol faced the saddest work of his life.'"[11] But he cheers up when he realizes he will soon join his Little Dot.

Such bleak plots as *Little Dot* reflected the grim realities of the high mortality rate among infants. Religion comforted the bereaved. Many authors in that neoclassical generation invoked faith as a means of coping with earthly responsibilities and losses. For instance, Martha Mary Butt Sherwood recalled learning the value of discipline while mastering speech. She was born at Stanford, Worcestershire, England, on 6 May 1775. In *The History of the Fairchild Family* (1818), she recalls that her father, a minister, educated his children at home rigorously. "Life at the paternal rectory was strict. When she was in the presence of her parents she was not allowed to sit, nor approach the fire, nor take any part in conversation. She wore daily an iron collar about her neck to which a back-board was attached. Yet, she herself says she was a happy, healthy child!"[12]

In 1790, her father sent her to the school at Reading, France, which soon moved to London due to the political climate of the French Revolution. While Martha Mary danced with displaced nobles, her cousin and future husband, Capt. Henry Sherwood, fought on the side of the rabble, much to his parents' horror. After their marriage in the early 1790s, the couple went to India, where they had five children and adopted three more. Martha Mary founded the first orphanage there, as well as writing juvenile books.[13] Her prosy stories drip with heavy-handed piety and sugar-coated didacticism. On the other hand, "she did have a sympathetic insight into the child mind." Nevertheless, "it is hard to believe that Mrs. Sherwood's *Little Henry and His Bearer* went through a hundred editions up to 1884 and was translated into a dozen languages."[14] Even after her death at Twickenham, Middlesex, England, on 22 September 1851, her stories remained popular.

Didactic stories dominated children's fiction on both sides of the Atlantic. By 1870, even *Hours at Home*, a magazine that scolded parents for giving children too much opportunity to read, nevertheless admitted that priggish children offered unhealthy role models. Such "self-conscious goodishness" encouraged "morbid precocity" and a "dreary fascination of the horrible." Moreover, infants who were taught to admire death grew up to be "buzzard-like persons whose constant and keen joy" becomes attending funerals and "who . . . would count themselves defrauded of their lawful right and of their choicest privilege if they failed to see the corpse."[15] While fragile heroines like Mary Lothrop and Little Eva embodied perfection, the protagonists in subsequent plots displayed flaws and survived the rigors of righteousness, which often forced them to defy their parents to obey God.

Martha Finley's parables show obedient girls—courageous enough to defy authority figures who tempt them to sin—prospering, while unruly youths perish amid chaos and shame. Her plots marked a transition from didactic to child-centered narratives. Finley started writing by contributing to Sunday-school newspapers. Although she usually avoided publicity, in 1893 Finley granted Florence Wilson an interview for the *Ladies Home Journal*. Wilson praised Finley's determination to support herself despite illness: "In her simple womanliness and Christianity she is a type of the best in American spinsterhood."[16]

In the late 1860s, Finley created Elsie Dinsmore—an angelic child prone to jags of crying and fainting spells, who searched for virtue in the depraved world. Although *St. Nicholas* and *Youth's Companion* magazines never ran Finley's austere prescriptions for domestic felicity, between 1867 and 1909 Finley earned $250,000 from her twenty-eight Elsie books. Her semi-realistic tales for adults sold briskly in the "Do-Good Library." Finley repeated the traditional tale of purity conquering adversity. Readers living in a complex society fixated on progress found her work reassuring. "[Her] books abound in the stuff of romance: the fairy-tale trappings of scores of engagements and weddings more than balanced for female readers the leaden movements of her heroine."[17]

Many of her characters, including Elsie, live in "an imitation fairy tale world, peopled by wealthy white folks and contented, servile blacks."[18] Fantasy, not reality, prevails. Later critics called Elsie "a nauseous little prig" whose exploits were a "compound of sentimentality and masochism."[19] The Philadelphia humorist Agnes Repplier parodied the "tear soaked . . . Little Pharisee" and warned that Finley's stories exhibit "an abundance of ignorance and a lack of charity . . . hurtful to a child."[20]

Nevertheless, Finley understood what girls wanted to read. Although she never enjoyed the luxuries she allowed Elsie, she never complained about her childhood. The creator of Elsie Dinsmore was born in 1828 into a family that for generations had followed the tenets of Calvinism. Her grandfather, Michael Finley, was a major in the Virginia Cavalry and was one of George Washington's friends. Her father, James Brown Finley, who was a physician, served as a lieutenant under his father's command in the War of 1812. After Martha's mother died, her father married his first cousin, Maria Theresa Brown. They attended the Presbyterian church, and Martha taught Sunday school in Chillicothe, Ohio, until a scandal forced them to move to South Bend, Indiana.

Finley respected her Scottish-Irish roots so much that she selected the Finley clan name in Gaelic, "Farquharson," for her *nom de plume*. After her parents died in 1853, she moved to Pennsylvania. When poor health forced her to quit teaching, the inspiration for Elsie Dinsmore came to her as "the answer to a prayer for something, which would yield income."[21] Finley never married. Writing, first for the Presbyterian Publication Committee and later for herself, kept her busy.

Although critics found "no excuse for the immense and long-continuing sale of the Elsie Books," the English novelist G. B. Stern appreciated Finley's penchant for suspense and grandeur.[22] Sometimes Elsie planned trips to the Roselands Plantation in the Deep South and other exotic places. "Martha Finley had never been below the Mason-Dixon Line when she began her famous series, and, consequently, she was not hampered by any factual considerations in describing life on the various estates, which Elsie, who was as rich as she was good, owned in various parts of the South."[23] Wherever her travels took her, Elsie went yachting. Frequently the heroine faced danger. For example, a scorned suitor tries to shoot Elsie and her groom on their wedding day.

Finley's other heroines also felt threatened. In one story, the plight of four orphan girls hangs unresolved until the last page. "Her enormous popularity resulted largely from a workable formula of flaws whose chemistry appealed to a particular people at a favorable time."[24] In *All the Happy Endings,* Helen Waite Papashvily concluded that only Mark Twain's Huckleberry Finn competed with Elsie Dinsmore for the title of "probably the best known character ever to appear in American fiction."[25] As late as the 1940s, children found the stories engaging. "Her readers, too, enjoyed finding in book after book the same characters that made up Elsie's large circle of friends and relations."[26]

The Elsie books "were a great advance over other pious tales for girls."[27] Modern critics laugh at Elsie, but Elsie does the unthinkable and succeeds against overwhelming odds. In fact, Elsie resembles an Alger hero by persevering and, thus, proving her worthiness despite the temptations that surround her. She differs from the rags-to-riches lads mostly by being rich instead of poor. In a male-dominated world, Elsie dares to defy her father. Perhaps girls avidly followed Elsie's adventures because they too lived under paternal tyranny.

Moreover, Elsie embodied the stock character in fairy tales who overcomes being small and powerless by being intelligent and moral. Her readers may have "[considered] themselves martyrs to parental cruelty."[28] Many of them had been punished for disobeying their fathers. No doubt they reasoned that, if Elsie did not deserve to suffer, then maybe they too were innocent and even noble for following the dictates of their consciences despite the consequences. The *Ladies Home Journal* writer exclaimed that not even "the dogs of criticism" could destroy Martha Farquharson's fame as the creator of Elsie.[29] Indeed, while experts ridiculed Elsie, millions of readers over the decades escaped mundane reality by fleeing into the fantasy world of the rich girl's incredible adventures in balancing sumptuous pleasure with duty.

In one episode, when Elsie refuses to play ditties on Sunday, her worldly father makes her sit at the piano until she faints and cuts her forehead. Although he felt sorry for Elsie, he would not relent. In a sequel, the strain of trying to compel his virtuous child to sin triggers a life-threatening illness. Then the motherless nine-year-old endures not only the censure of her aunts and uncles, who blame her for her father's sickness, but also the guilt of having to choose between a parent and God. Only her black mammy, Chloe, understands her. Although Elsie is Christian, Jewish girls also read about the brave heroine whose conscience forces her to oppose her father.[30]

Upon recovering, Elsie's father travels north on business without resolving the quarrel with his daughter. Then Elsie languishes until he repents. In the Calvinist stories, the heroines die, and their erring parents do penance, fulfilling the biblical prophecy that the child will lead the way to heaven. However, Finley steps into the nineteenth-century stream of thought by having Elsie live. Together, Elsie and her father conquer the daily temptations inherent in being rich. The tension between spiritual and material well-being forms the backdrop for all of Finley's plots just as this same dilemma demands resolution in innumerable Gilded Age books. The glamour of Elsie's wealth fascinated readers: "Miss Finley probably liked to shower on her book-children luxuries unknown to the fourteen of her parent's brood."[31]

Finley the Calvinist, who believed in the virtues of simplicity, waffled on the question of money. She could not decide which was worse—too much or too little. That stumbling block tripped scores of popular bards who predicted the meek would inherit the earth. Some wrote for both young and old. For many, *St. Nicholas* magazine opened an exciting channel for serials, poetry, and short stories aimed at boys and girls. In fact, since most publishers refused manuscripts until the writer had established a track record, beginners proved themselves in children's magazines and Sunday-school newspapers.

Backsliders as well as churchgoers read Finley's books. The Judeo-Christian tradition permeated society so thoroughly that tale spinners reflexively endorsed cultural mores. Since families read aloud together, the distinction between adults' and children's fare remained fuzzy. Sometimes kids appropriated books aimed at adults, like Mark Twain's *Huckleberry Finn* (1885). Many adults enjoyed Francis H. Burnett's *Little Lord Fauntleroy* (1886) and Eleanor H. Porter's *Pollyanna* (1913). Some novels, including Louisa May Alcott's *Little Women* (1868), *Little Men* (1871), and *Eight Cousins* (1875), appealed to everyone.

The Old-Fashioned Precedent Breaker

Scholars have compared Mrs. Adeline Dutton Train Whitney's domestic novels to Louisa May Alcott's classic, *Little Women* (1868). Whitney's work represented a transition between popular bards like Finley, who created angelic heroines, and authors like Alcott, whose earthy protagonists still charm readers. Once her children had started school, Whitney sent newspapers instructional pieces preaching the gospel of homemaking.[32] Elm Corner, her residence in Boston, was "a home above all things, with old-fashioned furniture, and an old-fashioned garden and the voices of children mingling with those of the birds."[33] Whitney defended the sanctity of motherhood against the inroads of suffrage and careers. Her message—that doing one's duty leads to happiness—resembles fairy tales about good individuals who endure a sequence of trials but ultimately triumph over evil. Thus love transforms ordinary women into princesses worthy of their domestic kingdoms.

Whitney set values to verse in *Mother Goose for Grown Folks. The Dial's* critic noted her "subtle deduction and . . . gift for moralizing. . . . The book can beguile an hour at any season with the mere ingenuity the author has shown in discovering ethical lessons in what all the world has heretofore regarded as the senseless jingle of favorite nursery rhymes. . . . The sermons they spring upon us in a playful style are many of them deeply impressive."[34]

Whitney broke away from the grim precedent of didactic literature by balancing the preaching with droll New England humor. The *Eclectic Review* called *The Gayworthys: A Story of Threads and Thrums*: "The most helpful and purposeful story we remember for a long time . . . full of radiant and kindly humor." Moreover, "now and then the author shows that the teeth of wit might not be wanting."[35] Whitney emulated Dickens by naming her characters "to fit the part they were to play."[36]

Harriet Beecher Stowe and John Greenleaf Whittier admired both her writing and her social graces. Adeline learned the mores of Boston society early. She was born on 25 September 1824 to Adeline Dutton and Enoch Train. After her mother died, her father, who was a ship owner and merchant, remarried in 1836, and the family left Lyman Beecher's Congregational church to attend Unitarian services. Later, Adeline became an Episcopalian. Upon graduating from Emerson's private school for girls at the age of nineteen, Adeline wed Seth Dunbar Whitney, who was forty. They set up housekeeping in Milton, Massachusetts, and had three children—Marie Adeline, Caroline Leslie, and Marie Caroline (who died in infancy)—in addition to raising Theodore Train.[37] Heeding the gospel of domesticity, after turning forty Whitney designed her own white grandmother's caps.

Although A. K. Loring issued twenty editions of *Faith Gartney's Girlhood* (1863), Whitney valued her domestic life more than fame. She warned girls not to trade their home for a career, because she believed "the dear fireside places" were the natural sphere of feminine influence.[38] Although Whitney wrote stories for girls until she was eighty, her second book, *Faith Gartney's Girlhood* (1863), established her reputation and launched Loring. Sunday-school libraries circulated stories by

Whitney, "Pansy" (Mrs. Isabella MacDonald Alden), and other Christian writers.

Street orphans and working children preferred tougher plots than Whitney and "Pansy" produced. They bought dime novels that promoted a chivalrous code of honor and respect for mother, country, and God. The exuberant plots and flamboyant characters pleased juveniles but distressed adults. "Oliver Optic" (William Taylor Adams) and Louisa May Alcott wrote wholesome fiction but usually were considered too exciting for Sabbath meditation. The Methodist Episcopal Church's Sunday-school paper, *Golden Hours: A Magazine for Boys and Girls,* noted: "Louisa May Alcott is a very sprightly and fascinating writer, and her sister, Mary Alcott, always makes beautiful pictures to illustrate the books. Their books and stories are always very interesting and instructive about every-day life. They are not religious books, should not be read on Sunday and are not appropriate for the Sunday School. This is the character of the book before us [*Little Women*]. It is lively, entertaining and not harmful."[39]

"Civilizing the Ignorant and Vicious"

Although Alcott's novels usually received conditional approval, ministers often banned Alger's tales, arguing that his plots prompted youths to adopt slang, shirk responsibilities, and indulge in vices. Thousands of Sunday-school librarians had ordered Alger's rags-to-riches adventures until public libraries in the 1870s launched a cleanup crusade against the dumpy philanthropist. In 1880, some condemned "bloody and very exciting dime novels" and feared not only that "a great deal of time [was] wasted" in devouring "Oliver Optic's" books, but also that "boys occasionally ran away from home [after] reading them."[40] *Hours at Home* rebuked Sunday-school libraries for creating a market for religious dime novels and other twaddle aimed at amusing rather than enlightening the young. Newspapers in Boston chastised Mark Twain for vulgarity, and in 1885 the Free Library of Concord removed *The Adventures of Huckleberry Finn* from its collection.[41]

Nevertheless, a few librarians argued, "a boy begins by reading Alger's books but later outgrows them."[42] They believed that boisterous tales nurtured a love for reading. Youths who invested their pennies in Alger and "Optic" did not buy the *Police Gazette* or other highly sensational fare sold at railroad stations. Alger and "Optic" had religious roots and "meant well"; moreover, they civilized "the vicious and ignorant" by exposing ruffians to a more elevated moral code than they were likely to encounter in their neighborhoods. Reading "saved" children "from idleness and vice," inspiring them to advance modestly.

"They . . . will naturally . . . read such books as correspond to [their] grade of culture and [their] stage of intellectual development."[43]

According to John Falk, Alger celebrated the Protestant work ethic by casting virtuous, obedient heroes in roles demanding persistence at humble tasks. These offer hope and ultimately salvation to those who are deserving.[44] Although Alger kept track of money in his plots, boys proved their innate worthiness by impressing a benefactor with selfless acts. Readers knew to the penny how much money "Ragged Dick" had to earn to buy "Mark the Match Boy" medicine. Nevertheless, it was Dick's character that won him middle-class respectability.

In fact, Alger's heroes sought contentment and social acceptance rather than wealth. Perhaps the charge that he promoted materialism by exhorting children to "get rich quick" more accurately reflects a twentieth-century mania for immediate gratification than Alger's intent.

By the late 1870s, public libraries considered themselves "Cultural Custodians of the Gilded Age" and, in shielding young readers from corruption, condemned the popular bards.[45] Alger's stories came to serve as emblems of the flaws of the late nineteenth century.[46] Herbert Mayes fabricated Alger's biography, casting Alger as an effeminate failure who was too childlike to do anything but romanticize the brutal economic and social system that forced an army of waifs to support themselves.[47] Henry Steele Commager and Stewart Holbrook accused Alger of espousing Social Darwinism.[48]

Some historians blamed Alger for the resistance to reform that intermittently frustrated philanthropists during the late nineteenth century. They concluded that Alger had spoon-fed the syrup of fantasy to the masses, blunting their appetites just enough to keep them satisfied. The balding teetotaler became a dispenser of opiates. Although Alger adopted three street urchins and helped his niece financially, some Marxists cast him as a cunning opportunist whose treachery paralleled the vices of the villains in the melodramatic cliff-hangers he wrote. On the other hand, John Seelye surmised that Alger saw himself as a benefactor who rescued deserving newsboys and sparked interest in the plight of street children. Garrison, Cowley, Scharnhorst, and Bales, as well as Cawelti, concluded Alger had opposed Social Darwinism as a perversion of the Protestant work ethic.[49]

Ironically, after Alger's death, searches for the "real" Horatio generated a new cycle of success stories. This time he served as the protagonist for historians and critics who were eager to explain why a Harvard graduate had devoted himself to telling such simple stories. One claimed Alger had clandestine trysts in China Town. Another insisted his hair had turned white after his Chinese ward, Wing, was kicked to death by a runaway horse. Several blamed "Holy Horatio's" domineering father for his alleged homosexuality. Others declared the pudgy *artiste* had lost his heart to married women and had indulged in a flaming affair with a French cafe singer. Many clucked over his inability to write *Tomorrow*, the serious novel worthy of his genius. The critics' fanciful scenarios ignored the quiet life Alger led as an author of boys' books.[50] Indeed, Alger's name still remains an icon for both the myths he perpetuated and the legends he inspired. It is no wonder the *Library Journal* worried about the influence of thrill peddlers and the impact of books on morality.[51]

The Triangle—Library, Church, School

Many considered the public library to be an adjunct of the church and the school. John Dewey pointed out that the Pilgrims had believed the public library, the meeting-house, and the school functioned equally as three sides in the triangle of "great educational work" essential for maintaining public felicity.[52] Debates over the role of the library in the community flared around these issues: opening libraries on Sunday, sensationalism in fiction, the deleterious effect of too much reading on children, and the possibility that fiction might distract students or disrupt the Sabbath. Many churches established libraries.

Besides offering a natural place for membership recruitment, Sunday-school libraries acted as agents of social improvement. Long before public schools had produced a literate populace, each library emerged within a locality to meet the needs of its patrons. The earliest Sunday schools promoted literacy as part of religious responsibility. Sunday-school libraries gave settlers access to the same books citizens everywhere in the country borrowed from their local churches. Reading kept the old archetypes alive. Sunday-school libraries encouraged a national respect for reading that led to the construction of public libraries.[53]

Free libraries had existed for less than fifty years in 1898. By then the United States contained eight thousand public, society, and school libraries, with thirty-five million volumes. Thirty-four million dollars had been invested in buildings and seventeen million in endowments. Annual income amounted to over six million dollars. The number of libraries was increasing "with disproportionate and amazing rapidity." For example, all but 10 of the 353 Massachusetts cities and towns had built libraries. Only 75 percent of the residents of that state, where individuals had donated 110 library buildings by 1890, lived in areas without book-lending institutions. Many wealthy families bequeathed facilities, and municipalities across the nation erected libraries: "No form of private memorial is now more popular; no form of municipal expenditure meets with readier assent. . . . Chicago . . . considers its million and a half of people entitled to a municipal library, with a $2 million building, studded with costly mosaics and aided by 40 branches and stations in bringing the books nearer each home."[54]

In the early nineteenth century, collections contained mostly biblical tracts and periodicals from denominational offices. Later, librarians added popular and classical works tinged with morality. However, some churches banned Alger's rowdy heroes and tales, which were set in the wicked metropolis. Many otherwise sensible souls declared that the Republic's salvation lay in rural life. "Sermons, popular verse and tales of country lasses corrupted on a Saturday night taught small-town Americans to think of the city as fundamentally different and thoroughly dangerous."[55] Provincial residents rejected writers who depicted urban neighborhoods as anything less than decadent. *Hours at Home* excused missionaries who used sleazy publications as a tool for saving the souls of "the young savages of the street . . . who, before their time, have grown old in sorrow, . . . wise in sin and blunted to all commonplace experiences."[56]

Sunday-school libraries encouraged country as well as city people to read. The selections varied. Kate Douglas Wiggin's heroine, *Rebecca of Sunnybrook Farm* (1903), tells the stagecoach driver that she has read many Sunday-school library books, including *The Lamplighter, Ivanhoe, Cora: The Doctor's Wife, The Gold of Chickaree, Plutarch's Lives,* and *Pilgrim's Progress.*[57] Rural youths borrowed books more often than adults, who preferred agricultural periodicals over novels.[58] These libraries introduced fiction to some children who, like Samuel Clemens, later became authors.

By the turn of the century, Sunday-school libraries were offering histories, travelogues, biographies, historical romances, and best sellers celebrating the righteous, like the novels of General Lew Wallace and E. P. Roe. Of course, *Pansy, Elsie Dinsmore, Little Lord Fauntleroy,* and other works about perfect children found a home on the churches' bookshelves.

Under the pseudonym "Pansy" (her father's pet name for her), Isabella MacDonald Alden created dozens of ideal protagonists. When she was ten years old, a local newspaper ran her first story, an item about "an accident that befell the family clock" by "Pansy." She had been born to Isaac and Myra Spafford MacDonald on 3 November 1841, in Rochester, New York.[59] "Pansy" and her five older siblings studied at home with their father, a devout Presbyterian. She kept a diary of criticism and stories and attended three boarding schools while a teenager. "Pansy" married the Reverend Gustavus R. Alden in 1866. The couple published *Pansy,* a nondenominational magazine, from 1874 to 1896.

During her writing career of almost eight decades, "Pansy" produced seventy-five books. Church libraries purchased over 100,000 copies of her children's books. "Pansy" Societies inspired youths to "root out besetting sins" and learn "right conduct."[60] Besides writing books and an annual winter serial for the *Herald and Presbyter,* Isabella helped organize the Chautauqua movement and shared its podiums with other educators. After her husband and son died, she lived with her daughter-in-law and grandchildren in Palo Alto, California. The romance writer Grace Livingston Hill finished an autobiography of her aunt "Pansy" after the author died of cancer on 5 August 1930. "Pansy's" books were published abroad in France, Armenia, and Scandinavia. In an editorial published on 6 August 1930, the *New York Times* concluded: "Known to thousands of readers all over the world, 'Pansy' was ignored by the critics who flourished when she was most popular. Nor should Charles Monroe Sheldon, whose *In His Steps* has sold even more widely than 'Pansy's' publication for children, be overlooked. At the same time, it would be useful to find out if an author unknown to book-of-the-month clubs is today occupying the hearts of the vast majority."[61]

Most Sunday-school boards appreciated "Pansy's" *Helen Lester,* which won a prize in 1866 for effectively explaining salvation to children. The book condemns adventure stories written for boys, noting that *Father Brighthopes* and *Neighbor Jackwood,* by J. T. Trowbridge, "for some mysterious reason were admitted to Sunday-school libraries and yet were 'really novels.'"[62] She also rejected works by Mayne Reid, "Harry Castlemon" (Charles Austin Fosdick, who also published stories as "the Gunboat Boy"), and "Oliver Optic" although their heroes scrupulously obeyed the code of honor inherent in the success archetype. Therefore, youngsters could have read any of these authors "without injury to . . . morals."[63]

While Reid, "Castlemon," and "Optic" did not equal Trowbridge in literary ability, they matched and sometimes exceeded him in sales. Boys and girls bought dime novels and story papers from news vendors or the general store. They traded with friends and kept their dime novels hidden from adults. Children's author Samuel Scoville, Jr., a minister's son, read Harry Castlemon after falling from a balm of Gilead tree onto a picket fence. Normally, Castlemon's thrillers were on the parsonage index of forbidden books, but after a parishioner brought the boy a basket full of dime novels, "in view of [his] parlous state the bars were let down."[64] Despite the appeal of the orange-jacketed paperbacks, children borrowed books from Sunday-school libraries, which were occasionally dull but always free.

Writers embedded the success paradigm in library books as well as in dime novels. Until World War I, many Sunday-school libraries existed in tandem with public libraries and lent out many of the same books. "The United States Census of 1870 reported 33,580 Sunday-school libraries with an aggregate of 8,346,153 volumes (exclusive of Connecticut)." By 1876, when some towns as well as cities supported public libraries, the Sunday-school libraries were "almost as numerous as the churches in the country."[65]

Martha Finley's series of didactic family stories, collectively titled "The Do-Good Library," remained in Sunday-school libraries for generations. She headed a platoon of popular writers whose stories depicted the differences between right and wrong. Although later generations tended to assume that stories with a moral were for young audiences, during the nineteenth century authors wrote parables and fairy tales for readers of all ages. These works were set in industrial locations and featured characters who, outwardly at least, resembled modern people. "The Victorian Age was . . . the Age of the Family, a family far more self-contained, self-sufficient in its interests, its amusements, its aspirations, than families today."[66] After supper, families sometimes read magazine stories and articles aloud.

St. Nicholas, **the Child's Friend**

During the Gilded Age, publishers began experimenting with a new type of journal, one aimed at specific age groups rather than at such amorphous audiences as "the family" or "children." In 1873, Scribner's launched the most popular and influential juvenile publication of the nineteenth century, *St. Nicholas,* with Mrs. Mary (Lizzie) Mapes Dodge as editor. Critics and professors have praised *St. Nicholas* for its innovations, its lively spirit, and its literary excellence.

Both the great and the popular writers sent Dodge material. For example, Brander Matthews contributed an essay in which he asserted that "Franklin [represented] the prose of American life, Emerson the poetry. . . . Self-reliance was at the core of the doctrine of each of them, but one urged self-help in the spiritual world and the other in the material." According to Matthews, *St. Nicholas's* "nonfictional contents [argue] for personal knowledge of the material world; its fiction [argues] for a moral world, and both genres advance the message of individual competence and self-reliance."[67] *St. Nicholas* gave readers the information and the emotional ballast they needed to understand and cope with their complex world. Dodge included educational and entertaining features in *St. Nicholas.*

Dodge's own life story rivaled the plots of the popular bards. She met William, her attorney husband, when he lent her father the down payment for a farm at Waverly. He was fifteen years older than she. They were married on 13 September 1851, and had two sons, James (Jamie) and Harry. The Dodges lived happily with three generations of William's family in a town house in New York City until William mysteriously drowned on 28 October 1858. He may have committed suicide; his oldest son was critically ill, and the loan to his father-in-law had brought on financial difficulties.

Lizzie went home to Mapleridge, her family's farm near Newark, New Jersey. There she made up *Hans Brinker, or The Silver Skates* (1865) as a "good-night" story for her boys.[68] She planned to sell this work (which eventually won the French Academy's Montyon Prize) to the *Independent,* whose editor had admired her *Irvington Stories* (1864).[69] The manuscript was too long for serial publication, however. The story of family life in Holland attained its "greatest popularity when republished by Scribners in the next decade [the 1870s]. During the next 15 years, it received more reviews than any other children's book in America."[70] Dodge turned to literature to pay for her sons' education.

The author of *Hans Brinker* wanted her sons to have a childhood as happy as her own had been. Dodge, who was born on 26 January 1831, may have learned storytelling and the art of witty conversation from her father, the "universal genius" James J. Mapes—a scholar, scientist, inventor, and author. Her grandfather Jonas Mapes told her lively stories about fighting in the Revolutionary War beside his friend, the Marquis de Lafayette. Horace Greeley, William Cullen Bryant, Capt. John Ericsson, and other celebrities visited the Mapeses' home regularly.

Lizzie and her three sisters studied English, French, drawing, music, and Latin at home with governesses. While a teenager, Lizzie wrote pamphlets and essays with her father. Although she sold adult pieces to *Harper's Magazine,* the *Atlantic Monthly,* and the *Century Magazine,* Lizzie's forte was children's writing. Her interest in juvenile literature blossomed into a thirty-two-year career as the editor of *St. Nicholas.* Dodge wrote poetry, stories, sketches, and short items such as the "Jack-in-the-Pulpit" advice column. Her serial that was later published as a book, *Donald and Dorothy* (1882), impressed parents as well as children. "So alluringly were the brother and sister depicted that in many families throughout the land there are living Donalds and Dorothys who were named after the hero and heroine of Mrs. Dodge's noble story."[71]

When Dodge died in 1905, the neighborhood children dressed in white and put garlands in their hair to escort her coffin. She had listened to boys and girls for over three decades. The letters of condolence reflected the grief felt by youngsters all over the world. Editors praised Dodge for making *St. Nicholas* "every child's best friend." The *Century Magazine* declared, "*St. Nicholas* has proved a gift of inestimable value to generations of children." The *New York Times* explained: "Right from the start the magazine was successful, and it soon was regarded as one of the best for children that has ever been published in this country."[72]

After the Civil War, dozens of journals, including *Pansy* and the Baptist Church's *The Young Reaper,* catered to youth. These magazines often bored children with priggish parables. Therefore, innovative publishers tried to satisfy parents and teachers while simultaneously entertaining boys and girls with stories about role models who learned from their mistakes. Excitement, too, made its way into plots. *Oliver Optic's Magazine,* Frank Leslie's *Boys of America* and *Boys and Girls,* Demorest's *Young America,* and Mayne Reid's *Onward* all thrived. Most of the publishers of juvenile magazines had written dime novels or newspaper copy and so knew how to court the public. Some discovered budding literary talent. For example, *Wide Awake,* which was "almost but not quite in *St. Nicholas*'s class," ran Margaret Sidney's serial, *Five Little Peppers and How They Grew* (1881).[73]

Wide Awake and other enterprising magazines preceded *St. Nicholas.* For example, in 1827, Nathaniel Willis established *The Youth's Companion,* the oldest continuing publication for children. Families subscribed to both the *Companion* and *St. Nicholas.* The *Companion's* editors banned tobacco, alcohol, and love. "So excellent were the contributions, so normal and happy the characters in the stories that readers were unconscious of any restrictions in editorial policy."[74] Both the best and the most popular writers contributed to the two publications. *St. Nicholas* viewed its audience in singular rather than plural terms. Dodge became "the most important influence of the time on children's literature," and Scribners gave her the budget to hire gifted illustrators and constantly improve *St. Nicholas.*[75]

Nearly three decades after "Good Old *St. Nicholas*" had come to town for the last time, *The Horn Book* and the *Saturday Review of Literature* agreed that, in happy times, *St. Nicholas* went everywhere.[76] Children all over the English-speaking world waited for the red and black volumes. *St. Nicholas* conveyed "a light-hearted quality, a gaiety [in] its appearance, which could not have been achieved in the earlier magazines."[77]

Eventually, *St. Nicholas* absorbed competitors, including *Our Folks.*

But artistic rather than commercial triumphs earned Dodge's opus a place in history. The "children's symphony of a magazine" featured the best writing of its day, introducing Louisa May Alcott's *Eight Cousins* (1874), Howard Pyle's *Tales of King Arthur,* and serials destined to become classics. Science articles nestled amid the poetry, serials, and games, encouraging children to learn. In the 1880s, Harlan H. Ballard launched the junior Agassiz Association in the magazine to nurture budding interest in fossils and natural wonders. Experts wrote how-to articles.

While serving with Harriet Beecher Stowe and Donald Mitchell as associate editor of *Hearth and Home,* Dodge had sensed the need for a child-centered magazine and set out to create one. She named *St. Nicholas* after the true friend of boys and girls. In an unsigned article in *Scribner's Monthly,* she explained:

> We edit for . . . fathers and mothers and endeavor to make the child's monthly a milk-and-water variety of the adult's periodical. But, in fact, [it] needs to be stronger, truer, bolder, more uncompromising than the other. Its cheer must be the cheer of the bird-song, not of condescending editorial babble. If it *mean* freshness, heartiness, life and joy, and its words are simply, directly and musically put together, it will trill its own way.
>
> Most children . . . attend school. Their little heads are . . . taxed with the day's lessons. They do not want to be bothered nor amused nor taught nor petted. They just want to have their own way over their own magazine.[78]

She expected readers to browse, but correspondents from as far away as India indicated that they read each page of *St. Nicholas,* even the advertisements. Children appreciated her ban on "editorial grimacing . . . halt and lame old jokes . . . sermonizing . . . [the] spinning out of facts," and "the rattling of the dry bones of history."[79] Eventually, some who had read the journal as children contributed to *St. Nicholas.* When the British author Rudyard Kipling volunteered to write for the magazine, Dodge asked him if he felt up to it. "Oh, but I must and shall! For my sister and I used to scramble for *St. Nicholas* every month, when I was a kid," he replied.[80] Kipling's "Toomai of the Elephants" and "Rikki-Tikki-Tavi," later published as part of the *Jungle Book,* debuted in *St. Nicholas.*

Besides Kipling, Mark Twain, Jack London, Thomas Bailey Aldrich, Frances Hodgson Burnett, Edward Everett Hale, Lucretia P. Hale, Sarah Orne Jewett, and Laura E. Richards were among its list of distinguished contributors. *St. Nicholas* also introduced Bennett Cerf, Norman Bel Geddes, Joel Chandler Harris, Ring Lardner, Cornelia

Otis Skinner, E. B. White, and Edmund Wilson to the literary world. Moreover, scores of popular bards who have been forgotten wrote stories and poems.

A century ago, nearly everyone appreciated *St. Nicholas.* Although Dodge rejected the didactic approach of early children's magazines, she nonetheless selected material that engagingly presented the values essential to maintaining democracy. Few children's magazines survive the death of their founding editors, and *St. Nicholas* faded until, by the 1940s, its glory had melted into memory. Today scholars rather than boys and girls salute *St. Nicholas*: "Through articles in the volumes of *St. Nicholas* can be traced the changing American scene of the late nineteenth century, the effect of inventions and industrial development, the shifting of emphasis in social life."[81]

The Installment Plan

During the Gilded Age, people bought adventure and romance, rather than appliances, on the installment plan. Each month or week, a new episode with a cliff-hanger ending appeared in the story paper or magazine. Authors ended every episode dramatically in order to entice readers to buy the next issue. Newspapers also ran fiction. In fact, many books began as continuing stories. Some dime novelists, including Col. Prentiss Ingraham and Buffalo Bill Cody, based their plots on their own adventures. However, many authors relied upon their imaginations to write thrillers because their work, church, and family responsibilities precluded taking sojourns to the Far West or fighting in revolutionary wars in foreign countries. Many "free lances" led quiet lives. Mrs. Mary Jane Crowell sang in the Baptist choir and raised three children with her husband, Joseph E. Crowell, who was the editor of the *Morning Call* in Patterson, New Jersey.

William Taylor Adams taught school in Boston for two decades and served as a Sunday-school superintendent most of his life.[82] Even after retiring, he kept abreast of educational issues. Adams served as a representative to the Massachusetts State Legislature for one year but declined renomination.[83] His writing consumed his time.

Adams occasionally used aliases: Irving Brown; Clingham Hunter, M.D.; Gale Winterton; Brooks McCormick; and "Old Stager." But after 1865, he preferred "Oliver Optic." The author of more than a thousand short stories, 126 books, and many features edited *Oliver Optic's Magazine for Boys and Girls, Student and Schoolmate,* and *Our Little Ones and the Nursery.* In 1867, Adams published Alger's "Ragged Dick" in *Student and Schoolmate* and thus "discovered" the famous architect of the era's success paradigm.[84] "Alger and 'Oliver Optic' . . .

did their best to sell virtue to American youth." In the 1890s, when Ormond Smith launched *Good News* for boys, "Optic" was "perhaps the most popular writer of boys' stories in the country," but Alger quickly caught up.[85]

While "Optic" and Alger both described boys struggling to succeed, the two emphasized different things. "His heroes, like Alger's, were rather priggish, but Adams's were more concerned with patriotism and adventure than with rising in the business world."[86] "Oliver Optic's" adventure series provided the model for *The Rover Boys* and *The Hardy Boys*. "Optic" was the master of the formula boy's story, which featured manly deeds, exciting escapades, practical jokes, and, of course, danger.[87] The hero conquered adversity through a blend of bravado, athletic prowess, courage, and innate goodness.

The Boston firm, Lee and Shepard, owed its prosperity in part to selling at least 100,000 copies a year of "Optic's" books.[88] Like many authors, Adams started humbly and rose slowly but steadily to prominence. Under the alias of Warren T. Ashton, he received $37.50 from a Boston publisher in 1853 for his first book, *Hatchie, the Guardian Slave; Or, The Heiress of Bellevue, A Tale of the Mississippi and the South-West* (1853). Adams borrowed his favorite pen name from "Doctor Optic," a central character in a burlesque playing in Boston in 1851.[89] He added "Oliver" for euphony.

The future "Oliver Optic" was born to Captain Taban and Catherine (Johnson) Adams on 30 July 1822, in Medway, Massachusetts. His father owned a tavern in Boston until moving his family to a farm in West Roxbury in 1838. Adams went to school briefly in Boston but did most of his studying behind the plow. After helping his father rebuild the "Adams House" on the site of the family's former tavern, he served as the principal of a primary school in Dorchester. In 1846, "Optic" married Sarah Jenkins.

Although the couple had two daughters, the author never understood girls as well as boys. Nevertheless, both boys and girls read his stories about active heroes whose homebody sisters pray for their success. He wrote mostly boy's stories in six related but nonconsecutive volumes. "His style was so pleasing, his plots so interesting and the action so lively that he was very successful and had a very large following of youthful readers."[90] His fiction commanded top prices. In fact, the *Fireside Companion* paid him five thousand dollars for two tales in 1873.

One reviewer referred to "Oliver Optic" as "the Prince of Story-Tellers." However, Alcott denounced "Optical delusions" in *Eight Cousins*, accusing him of sensationalism. In "Sensational Books for Boys," an article in *Oliver Optic's Magazine*, "Optic" repeated the routine criticisms of Alcott's work—that she loaded her dialogues with slang and diluted her plots with improbable occurrences. Optic claimed that "she said enough to identify his books and then charged them with the faults of all the juvenile books published, her own included."[91] Skeptics accused popular bards of committing the offenses Alcott found in "Optic's" work.

Alcott's quarrel with "Optic" may have reflected the resentment felt by many literary figures at the fact that thrillers sold more briskly than classics. In fact, just as Alcott was starting *Little Women* (1868), her publisher suggested she "do something like 'Oliver Optic.'"[92] The pressure to please the multitude affected gifted novelists who, like Alcott, relied upon manuscript sales for their livelihood. Commercial demands stunted Alcott's development:

> She never expressed fully the great talents she possessed; she learned too early that writing is a way to earn a living. But what richness nevertheless is in her work! If there be an immortal American story, *Little Women* surely has a claim to that title, and *Little Men* and *An Old-Fashioned Girl* are not too far behind it. The tomboy who grew up into the tall girl with chestnut hair and dark flashing eyes had the spark of genius in her, and all she needed was a happier life, some respite from care and responsibility to have brought it all out for the world's good.[93]

Sunday schools handed out "Optic's" books for prizes despite the criticism of Alcott and of powerful religious and civic leaders, including the Reverend Henry Ward Beecher, who denounced his plots as coarse.[94] Some libraries banned both Alger and "Optic." The editor of the *Nation* warned, "They ["Optic's" heroes] encourage youthful impudence and 'smartness' and do nothing at all to take the average New England boy away from the *Boston Herald,* from a Young American's belief in his foolish self and from general insufferableness."[95]

Critics disagreed about Adams's literary merit. One said that "Optic" wove morality into his tales without damaging his "lively, well-told stories." But another declared the only redeeming feature of "Optic's" stereotypes to be "the sheer absurdity of their remarks."[96] "Optic's" plots delineated the strict moral code of the success archetype. No protagonist swore, drank, or smoked. Moreover, readers never sympathized with his villains.

Although "Optic" never shot buffalo with William Cody or faced a lynch mob like Mayne Reid, he visited Europe twenty times, stopping in Africa, Asia, and the Mediterranean. The prolific writer taught himself to read Spanish, French, German, and Italian. The globetrotter filled notebooks with observations that later added authenticity and color to his plots. "Optic" spent five hours a day writing. Several generations of young people read his works, including *A Millionaire at Sixteen,* the *Boat Club* series, and the *Onward and Upward* series.

However, "Oliver Optic's" success tales succumbed to time, which makes one decade's best seller another era's curio. His heroes persevered despite incredible odds in at least possible if not always probable scenarios: "[The] man had a real gift for vivid narrative; he could convey a feeling of excitement and curiosity to his readers, and no critic who once wandered breathlessly in an open boat over the submerged tree-tops of the flooded Amazon basin with 'Oliver Optic' could ever have the heart to deny him his meed of well-deserved praise."[97] Indeed, in the 1880s, a critic said that young people contracted "Oliver Optic fever" and recovered only upon reading the last page.[98]

Perhaps children contracted "Oliver Optic fever" as a curative for the "McGuffey vapors." *McGuffey's First Eclectic Reader* (revised edition, 1879) mixes platitudes with condescending images of children playing. The girls put their dolls to bed while the boys alternate between driving goat carts and hoisting flags on their tents. When big brothers go skating, they pull their little sisters on sleds. Children pick up shells at the beach and watch grandfather stare at the waves. The McGuffey's readers magnified the success archetype. For example, Mother hens feed only the chicks "who try hard." This is the most exciting tale in the *First Reader*:

Lesson XXX

"Kate, I wish we had a boat to put the dolls in. Don't you?"

"I know what we can do. We can get the little tub, and tie a rope to it, and drag it to the pond. This will float with the dolls in it, and we can get a pole to push it from the shore."

"What a funny boat, Kate! A tub for a boat and a pole for an oar! Won't it upset?"

"We can try it, Nell, and see."

"Well, you get the tub, and I will get a pole and a rope. We will put both dolls in the tub and give them a ride."

Slate Work

The dolls had a nice ride to the pond. A soft wind made the tub float out. Nell let the pole fall on the tub and upset it.

Lesson XXXI

"Here, Ponto!" Kate called to her dog. "Come and get the dolls out of the pond."

Rose went under, but she did not drown. Bess was still on the top of the water.

Ponto came with a bound and jumped into the pond. He swam around, and got Bess in his mouth, and brought her to the shore.

Ponto then found Rose, and brought her out, too.

Kate said, "Good, old Ponto! Brave old dog!"

"What do you think of Ponto?"[99]

Readers may have wondered if "good, old Ponto" wrote the book since the story glorifies dogs. When trouble strikes, the heroines cannot help themselves. They have to rely upon "Brave old dog!" to rescue them from their own foolishness. Is it any wonder that some students hid dime novels inside the covers of the required texts? They learned by reciting the lists of words printed at the top of each lesson. Then, after reading the passage aloud, they copied the whole thing onto their slates. Finally, the readers tested their skills:

We have come to the last lesson in this book. We have finished the First Reader.

You can now read all the lessons in it and can write them on your slates.

Have you taken good care of your book? Children should always keep their books neat and clean.

Are you not glad to be ready for a new book?

Your parents are very kind to send you to school. If you are good, and if you try to learn, your teacher will love you, and you will please your parents.

Be kind to all, and do not waste your time in school.

When you go home, you may ask your parents to get you a Second Reader.[100]

Most children probably would have preferred an "Optical delusion" or an Alger adventure over the avalanche of McGuffey moralism dumped upon them at school. But eminent teachers and scholars who contributed suggestions based on their work in the schoolroom endorsed this approach to education.[101]

McGuffey's Readers contradicted the laissez-faire mindset of the time by reminding children of their moral responsibilities to the community.[102] These primers emphasized education as a route to character development and spiritual fulfillment, much as authors had during the first two stages in the development of American children's literature. During the colonial era, books prepared the young for heaven by introducing them to pious role models. In the early to mid-nineteenth century, authors like Finley and Whitney incorporated humor and bits of worldliness into family stories. Then, around 1870, publishers divided the old category of "children" into specific age groups and sought writers to entertain as well as to inform these newly defined audiences. In all three phases, authors embedded in their plots archetypes that preserved values. By the end of the nineteenth century, popular bards were experimenting with new interpretations of the Cinderella paradigm to make it relevant to the rapidly changing, risky world.

In the Gilded Age, children often fit into one of two categories: middle-class youths who went to school, and orphans who worked to help support a family or who lived in the streets. Authors of the popular serials and success tracts found inspiration in both. The street children offered models for rags-to-riches heroes. The pupils made up an audience bored enough to read anything forbidden, as well as occasional prototypes for precocious protagonists like "Little Lord Fauntleroy," "Polly Pepper," or "Jo March," who charmed adults into buying a story for their children. Parents and teachers constantly heeded the biblical adage about the wealthy and hoped to push students through the eye of the needle by ignoring the harmless if essential material needs inherent in childhood.

McGuffey's Readers, textbooks, cliff-hangers in periodicals, and children's paperbacks taught young readers to share the same value system and to appreciate the traditions that had been handed down orally for generations. The printing press enabled nineteenth-century seers to engage multitudes instead of crowds in town squares. The old plots were frozen in words on pages. The bards borrowed techniques from novelists to make the transition from the oral mode palatable to their anonymous readers. Pupils, as they learned to read, acquired the mores essential for participating in the adult world. The success archetype promised the young a bright future if they earned respectability through diligence and faith.

Chapter 6

Biography—Truth or Legend?

Biographies tell life stories patched together from records, anecdotes, and interviews. The distorting lens of time foils the historian's quest accurately to reconstruct the significant person's experiences. Even those who write their own life stories cannot describe exactly what happened to them. Memory, like fog wafting off a bay, masks perceptions, revealing only the most dramatic and the most personally relevant incidents. Moreover, individuals remember their own pasts in terms of images they have absorbed from hearing stories and learning language. Of course, to teach the next generation traditional values, every community immerses its children in bardic tales.

Unconsciously, United States citizens interpret their experiences in terms of the success archetype because Americans struggle to attain inner peace and material wealth simultaneously. This Cinderella prototype is stored in the subconscious narrative pool that binds communities. Jung's collective unconscious, the world mind, preserves archetypes across generations, often through folklore.

The bardic tales supplied a stage upon which new scenarios could be tried and different interpretations of the old messages gradually introduced. Groups rely upon fantasy to supply a safe terrain for imagining different relationships and, thus, for creating options for restructuring their members' everyday lives.[1] "Narration in community does not only mirror events; it opens the possibilities for events to actually take place," according to Ronald C. Arnett, author of *Communication and Community*.[2]

Life resembles fiction because individuals apply the same set of narrative conventions both in constructing plots and in understanding how personal existence fits into the panorama of history. Unconsciously, they model themselves after stock characters inherited from their ancestors. For instance, during the Gilded Age, women became Cinderellas—not necessarily passive and certainly not helpless, but truly princesses whose hard work and integrity entitled them to happiness. Men became Prince Charming in search of the maiden who would wear the slipper. Those who view Cinderella as a rescue story miss the point. Cinderella earned her chance at greatness by persevering. Her diligence and faith impressed a benefactor—the fairy godmother—who endowed Cinderella with worldly goods that allowed her to claim her place in the kingdom. Without her inner beauty, Cinderella would have remained in obscurity on her ash heap; her external loveliness would have dazzled fools but not the true-hearted. The Prince also had to prove himself. His quest to find her revealed his willingness to work hard despite his privileged background. In the realm of fairy tales as in life, nothing worth having came easily.

The success archetype conveyed in modern fairy tales provided categories for organizing experiences into meaningful patterns. To define self in relationship to others, humans drew upon the symbols, metaphors, and myths that distinguished their particular communities from all other places. The popular bards perpetuated traditional narratives by recasting them into contemporary scenarios. A hundred years ago, potboilers connected the predictable past to the unpredictable present, just as television programs, movies, supermarket tabloids, and steamy romance novels today ground an individual's fragmented encounters in popular culture.

In the biographical sketches of the forty-one bards upon whom this study focuses, we see the same contrivances they built into their stories; writers and biographers automatically selected incidents that fit reality into the reliable success prototype. The prototype contained these motifs: worthy protagonists, triumphant rise into the middle class, demonstrations of good conquering evil, many characters overcoming adversities, coincidences, benefactors, clever disguises, and pseudonyms. Sometimes an internal struggle between old ethics and new opportunities threatened to destroy the protagonist. Always, divine forces rewarded hard work and honesty.

Even the news followed the fairy tale rags-to-riches plot format. For example, numerous articles about Andrew Carnegie reminded readers that at the age of thirteen the Scottish immigrant had ridden a bicycle to work. For over three decades, feature writers described Carnegie as if they were writing potboilers. In 1896, Carnegie explained "How I Became a Millionaire" in *Cassell's Family Magazine*. Twelve years later, the *Century Magazine* retold the tale: "Andrew Carnegie placed his foot upon the first rung of the ladder of success, when in 1849, he went to work in a cotton factory in Allegheny City where he served as a bobbin boy, his wage being $1.20 a week." The *New York Times* emphasized the same theme in its obituary when the steel king died of pneumonia on 12 August 1919.[3]

The obituary and most of the other articles repeated the crucial success prototype. First, Carnegie had advanced through a sequence of humble jobs. Then, when he least expected it, he accidentally met the designer whose visions inspired him to invest wisely in comfortable railroad passenger cars. Eventually the reporters mentioned King Andrew's wealth, his castle in Scotland, and his philanthropy. Some quoted him. The steel monarch, who "always wore a sprig of sweet verbena in the buttonhole of his homespun sack suit," had pointed out that poverty taught youth the value of a dollar as well as the importance of integrity.[4] Moreover, according to this apostle of "The Gospel of Wealth," anyone who died rich, died in disgrace. By his own definition, Carnegie died in disgrace.

The story and not the facts appealed to people. Simultaneously, Carnegie fit the stereotype of the generous benefactor and that of the ruthless speculator. His perorations concerning money's corrupting influence indicated the success archetype's hold over the imagination of the day. Although those who could joined the upper class as soon as possible, Carnegie proclaimed the misery inherent in hoarding wealth, reinforcing the message that diligence paid off while speculation and "big" business led to spiritual bankruptcy. By founding public institutions across the nation to serve the poor, Carnegie showed millionaires how to save their souls. His *Gospel of Wealth* reflected the popular bards' favorite narrative pattern for achieving prosperity without sacrificing spiritual wholeness. Those writers told reporters details about themselves that were reminiscent of the Cinderella prototype.

Many bards remembered their humble roots. Indeed, the "Prince of Humbugs," P. T. Barnum, recalled driving cows from the pasture, weeding the kitchen garden, shelling corn, and saving his pennies when he was only six years old. Although denied the stimulus of destitution, he rose from being a poor farmer's son to occupy the pinnacle of the world of show business. Since I.O.U.s rather than change filled the Hodgson orphan's cookie jar, plucky Frances sold wild grapes to pay for the postage on her first short story. Eventually, Frances Hodgson Burnett's homespun tales added a new word to the English language: *Fauntleroy*, denoting an affected fop. George Childs blacked boots and sold newspapers until finally turning his dreams of success into reality by purchasing the *Philadelphia Ledger*. Somebody else made a killing on the kewpie doll.

The myth of the cool million waiting under some cabbage leaf, hidden within an uncanny assemblage of hardware, or wriggling out of the pages of a thriller seeped across the nation as swiftly and indelibly as beet juice stains the tablecloth where diners mine the vegetables too aggressively. Making money was easy for those who seized opportunities. Clichés sprinkled newspapers and other public conversations as randomly as watermelon juice dripped off the chins of seed-spitting contestants at a county fair. Moreover, bromides salved the disappointments sustained by those who sought success. While politicians resented being cast as public violators of Mark Twain's aphorism that after three days fish and guests begin to smell, popular authors snacked on the sour grapes of recognition without critical acclaim.

Years of fleshing out the same archetype tended to give the bards a vision of fiction that limited their view of reality. The unconscious narrative pool that inspired their plots also provided these authors with schemas for organizing their memories. Even Mark Twain referred to himself as "Little Sammy in Fairy Land" after receiving a mansion from his father-in-law shortly following his wedding.

Through anecdote, autobiographers blended fiction and reality. Childhood memories proved that the storytellers could be loved despite their foolishness and sloth. Most American children, of whatever era, sympathize with the grasshopper long before appreciating the sobriety of the ant. However, while growing up, they absorb so completely the moral that diligence brings rewards that, as adults, most aspire to be efficient and fear that frivolity will destroy them. During the Gilded Age, many flesh-and-blood writers, as well as their protagonists, rose modestly by working hard. For instance, both the Reverend Edward Payson Roe and General Lew Wallace constantly revised their manuscripts. Wallace rewrote his sentences on a slate and edited them even after copying them onto paper.

Opie Read set type on the undergraduate newspaper to pay his expenses at Neophogen College in Nashville. To learn how to minister to his flock, the Reverend Charles M. Sheldon rode on the engines with firefighters, spent a week at Washburn College, and lived with the Negro residents of the "Tennessee Town" slum for three weeks, before writing the sermon stories that made him famous. Although ill and destined to die less than a year later, Edward Bellamy finished *Equality*, the sequel to *Looking Backward*. The godmother of modern mystery writers, Anna Katharine Green, toiled from 9 A.M. to 5 P.M. daily and revised *The Leavenworth Case* (1878) twelve times before submitting it to Putnam's.

Despite the widespread respect for diligence, people worried that making money could become an obsession. Owen Wister, who like Green revised his works extensively, "said Americans were too busy chasing wealth to be interested in spiritual things."[5] This same concern inspired Sheldon's *In His Steps* (1897). He ended each installment at an exciting point so his parishioners would attend Sunday night Congregational services to hear the next episode.

Roe, too, appreciated the power of narrative to rouse dormant consciences. He tried to make his plots interesting and plausible. He commented on "The Elements of Life in Fiction" in *Forum* magazine in 1888: "Even the reader who is not at all religious is fair enough to remember that faith is a general and potent factor in life, and therefore as legitimate a theme for the novelist as fighting, gambling, or love-making."[6] The Chicago Fire in 1871 so moved the young pastor that he gave up his country parish to write *Barriers Burned Away* (1872). Roe's parables dispelled fears that fiction might introduce the righteous to temptations.

Soul Wars

Like their protagonists, some authors struggled to resolve conflicting values. These soul wars took a toll on even the most stalwart individuals. Ironically, for many material success exacerbated inner discord. For example, George Cable's sensitivity and artistic aptitude left him torn between two opposing moral impulses—the need to feel righteous and the desire to write fiction. Like many stern Protestants, Cable initially disapproved of "the devil's tools" (novels). His budding passion for the forbidden pursuit of literature compelled him to seek the reconciliation of religion and art by proclaiming that fiction revealed truths hidden behind social facades.

George Cable seems a flesh-and-blood embodiment of the clash between the North and the South. His father's family had owned slaves in Virginia for generations, but his mother, Rebecca Boardman, was a descendent of New England Puritans. George inhaled the genteel atmosphere of New Orleans under his mother's stark Presbyterian wing. Although he served with distinction in the Confederate Army, he later alienated many neighbors by writing editorials demanding justice for Negroes. He also advocated revising election laws, reforming prisons, and eliminating the contract labor system.

Just as many southerners objected to Cable's descriptions of Creole life, Opie Read's humorous sketches about Arkansas offended readers. Both writers went north. After helping his brother-in-law launch a weekly humor paper, the *Arkansas Traveler,* Read moved to Chicago with his family in 1887; while Cable built "Tarryawhile" in Northampton, Massachusetts, in 1885. No matter where Read lived, he saw himself as a storyteller destined to introduce the rest of the world to southern lore. Cable, on the other hand, "was . . . not quite a Northerner, nor yet quite a Southerner, and the resultant inner conflict may well have been the source and inspiration of his creative work."[7]

Certainly, Cable's writing reflected his internal tug-of-war. The southerner honored his homeland by recreating the complex Creole world. The northerner—driven by commitment to the Presbyterian tenets he had absorbed as a boy—felt compelled to fight Satan through social reform activity. Early in his career, he lost his job at the *New Orleans Picayune* for refusing to review plays because strict Presbyterians considered such performances immoral. Ironically, the drive for self-education, which his mother had instilled in him as a means of pursuing his faith, convinced him that some Presbyterian rules concerning the arts were perhaps too harsh. In fact, later Cable enlivened his lectures by performing Creole slave songs and telling anecdotes in patois.

Like Cable, Edward Eggleston struggled most of his life to reconcile the "two manner of men, the lover of literary art and the religionist," inside himself.[8] Finally, Eggleston attained equilibrium between the two sides of his personality by, first, establishing the nondenominational, ecumenical Church of Christian Endeavor in Brooklyn to assist the poor, and, second, a few years later, by writing social histories. His duality of purpose arose from his respect for his two fathers. His father, a popular lawyer who served in the Indiana Senate, instilled within Eggleston a love of books. His father died of tuberculosis when Eggleston was nine. His stern stepfather taught him to revere the Lord.

Since pulmonary illness kept the lad from attending school regularly, Eggleston's mother, hoping the change would improve his health, sent him to live with his father's relatives in Virginia. He turned down a scholarship to the University of Virginia because he opposed slavery. While he became a staunch abolitionist, his younger brother, George Cary Eggleston, defended the Confederacy. The political differences between the two boys reflected differing relationships with their father's kin. However, after the Civil War, the brothers reconciled and engaged in business together.

Politics were not as important as spiritual life to the Eggleston brothers' stepfather, Williamson Terrell. That hard-shell Methodist preacher thought fantasy led to sin. Opie Read's practical parents considered the stories their son told other children in Nashville, Tennessee, to be falsehoods. Terrell, too, warned his stepsons that fiction spread deceit and led to perdition. "I had fits of religious ardor in which my literary pursuits seemed a sort of idolatry," recalled Eggleston, the author of *The*

Hoosier School-Master (1871), in an interview in the *Forum* in 1890.[9] Once he burned all his compositions.

All Midwestern young men who exuded the slightest bit of charisma were "foredoomed to the ministry" if they were surrounded by Methodism, according to Eggleston.[10] After avoiding bestsellers and other frivolities that might erode his holy resolve, Eggleston felt the call. Simultaneously, however, he sought recognition as a fiction writer. "For the greater part of my life there has been an enduring struggle between the lover of literary art and the religionist, the reformer, the philanthropist, the man with a mission. This duality survives even today," he admitted in an essay on "Formative Influences."[11]

Perhaps these competing allegiances inspired him to ride the Methodist circuit in Minnesota and Indiana as well as to edit a newspaper for Sunday-school teachers. The lecturer on practical methods of teaching morality conducted institutes for church youth leaders. He also sold Bibles before becoming a western correspondent to *The Independent*. The author of juvenile fiction helped to establish the American Historical Association. Even after broadening his religious views, Eggleston remained sympathetic toward pioneer preachers and described their strengths as well as their foibles.

Elizabeth Stuart Phelps Ward experienced an interior struggle between colliding ideals similar to the moral dilemma with which Eggleston and Cable wrestled. "She was pulled in opposite directions by a woman's movement urging the self-fulfillment for which her mother yearned and a conservative Calvinist tradition of advocating the 'feudal views' of women her father held."[12] Her father, the Reverend Austin Phelps, accepted a position at the theological seminary in Andover, Massachusetts, shortly after his daughter was born. He and his wife, Elizabeth Stuart, baptized the newborn Mary Gray. When her mother died eight years later, Mary took her name, Elizabeth Stuart. Both she and her mother published stories in Sunday-school periodicals. However, while her mother had described dutiful children and strong, restless women, Elizabeth Stuart Phelps Ward wrote about heaven.

Phelps's most famous book, *The Gates Ajar* (1868), filled a public need for consolation in the hour of national grief for dead fathers, brothers, husbands, and sweethearts. Her metaphor of heaven as a housing project managed by a gentle, omniscient landlord comforted the relatives of the army of cadavers left in the wake of the Civil War. *The Outlook* explained in 1911: "It was in no sense a speculation, nor was it a discussion of the evidence of immortality; it was a translation of the great hope and faith into terms which were comprehensible in every household."[13] She based her image of the afterlife on the religious training she had received from her father, who equated God with love and hope. Of course, hell-fire preachers denounced her book, and newspapers wrangled about the literary as well as the spiritual merits of her idea novel.

Her interest in heaven and "life on the other side" grew out of the strange experiences of her grandfather, a strict Congregational minister, who recorded the weird phenomena observed during seven months of what he called "house possession." The Reverend Eliakim Phelps described the thumps, raps, and shuffling of furniture. Turnips would bounce from the study table to the ceiling without human intervention.[14] His grandchildren destroyed his copious notes, but throughout her life, Elizabeth remained interested in psychic phenomena and the spirit world. Her mother also had written about angels, ghosts, and the supernatural.

Other popular authors dabbled in spiritualism and psychic phenomena. In 1883, romance writer E. D. E. N. Southworth dropped her affiliation with the Episcopal Church to pursue Swedenborgianism, a faith concerned with illuminating the mystical revelations of the spirit world. She dedicated *The Haunted Homestead* (1860), a collection of short stories that included "The Bottled Demon" and "The Maniac Curse," to Mrs. Ellen H. Burnette of New York. The inscription read: "My Dearest Ellen: In memory of the BRIDE's GHOST, that so troubled our Christmas and New Year's festivities, at Prospect Cottage three years since,—and that we afterwards saw 'exorcised' in the presence of some hundred persons in the city, last Spring—I beg to inscribe to you, with my sincere esteem and affection, this volume of Novelettes."[15]

Popular bards appropriated science and speculated about the supernatural. For example, the creator of Sherlock Holmes, Sir Arthur Conan Doyle, took pictures of fairies flitting in his yard. The death of her son Vivian made Burnett very interested in mediums and "crossing over." Amelia Barr believed that her dreams forecast the future and mentions the spirit world often in her autobiography. Mary Roberts Rinehart told *Life* magazine reporter Geoffrey T. Hellman that she had seen or heard ghosts nearly everywhere she had ever lived. In fact, "spooks harassed" her in her apartment in Wardman Park Hotel, where Boies Penman had died, and then returned to ring bells at odd hours, crash about, and compel potted plants to "meander, unescorted from the conservatory to the living room."[16]

Rinehart, Burnett, Doyle, and other popular bards enlivened plots with interventions by supernatural forces, suggesting that the Almighty helped the ambitious to overcome obstacles. Such intercessions defied human economic power structures and encouraged underpaid readers to persevere and to enrich their lives with those comforts of the heart that were manifested in religion.

Home, Pious, Home?

Not all writers of popular fiction believed in ghosts and the supernatural, but most had ties to organized religion. Edward Sylvester Ellis lost count of the exact number of books, stories, and articles he wrote from 1860 to 1915, but he rarely missed Methodist church services. Harlan Page Halsey, who created "Old Sleuth," inherited his Congregational faith from his ancestors, who included the Reverend Francis Higginson, the first teacher in the church at Salem, Massachusetts; and Edmund Tapp, one of the pillars of the church at Milford, Connecticut.

Eleanor Hodgman Porter's mother was a direct descendant of Gov. William Bradford of the Plymouth Colony; Eleanor, of course, was a Congregationalist. The Reverend Russell Conwell's ancestors, too, included Puritans. His parents ran a station on the Underground Railway and frequently entertained John Brown. Conwell learned the art of oratory from the Methodist pastor of South Worthington, a hamlet in the western Massachusetts hills. From the age of seven, Conwell delivered declamations to the congregation. During the Civil War, he declared himself an atheist, but after a religious drummer boy died while fetching a sword for him, Conwell recanted. In 1879, he was ordained.

For some, ordination amounted to following in their father's footsteps. For example, Sheldon and Alger were second-generation ministers. Bellamy's father served as a Baptist preacher for thirty-five years. Gene Stratton-Porter's father combined farming with preaching Methodism. He believed in a God of duty so completely that he often thrilled his children with the story of John Maynard, who slowly roasted alive as he wheeled his flaming vessel to a safe landing. Despite a flood of such morbid tales, he equated religion with being in harmony with nature. Amelia Huddleston Barr and her husband Robert both learned to revere God from their fathers, who published their sermons widely in the United Kingdom.

Moreover, experiences in family worship influenced many authors whose parents were not pastors. Even the notoriously rowdy Edward Z. C. Judson, who wrote dime novels as Ned Buntline when he was not too busy crusading for the Know-Nothings or arguing with Buffalo

Bill Cody over the proceeds from their Wild West Show, lectured for temperance and wrote hymns that rhymed excruciatingly. Kate Douglas Wiggin's maternal family tree included the outspoken Quaker, Mary Dyer, who was hanged for preaching. The creator of *Rebecca of Sunnybrook Farm* (1903) recalled singing hymns and praying daily at home. However, she did not always behave angelically. As a tot, "The Lady of the Twinkle and the Tear," as newspapers called Wiggin when she died, embarrassed her parents by telling the "kind old rector of the Episcopal church" that she would have preferred anything else other than the prayer book he had just given her. Her punishment for this misbehavior was a feeble spanking, which "introduced [her] to the necessity of concealing one's own feelings if, thereby, one can avoid hurting the feelings of somebody else."[17]

Gilbert Patten's mother wanted him to be a minister, and, through the sterling character of the dime-novel hero Frank Merriwell, he did preach to multitudes that included Woodrow Wilson, Al Smith, Wendell Wilkie, Rudy Vallee, Jack Dempsey, and Frederic March. Childhood reading influenced famous women as well as men. For instance, Rinehart recalled discovering the allure of "Nick Carter" and "Old Sleuth" thrillers during a childhood visit to a farm where the hired hand had stashed ninety-two nickel novels in a wooden settle in the barn.[18] As Covenantors, Rinehart's parents had impressed her with the reality of God's wrath. Her "abiding sense of sin and her feeling that danger lurked in the midst of happiness became components of her work, especially her crime novels."[19]

Some writers evaded the grip of predestination, which cast a pall on many domestic circles during the Gilded Age. Mary Jane Hawes Holmes learned about the goodness germinating in the human heart from her uncle, the Reverend Joel Hawes, a Congregationalist. After marrying Daniel Holmes, she participated actively in Episcopal church work. As a boy, Wallace upset his parents by drawing the minister and members of the congregation on the hood of his rain suit during long sermons. As an adult, the author of *Ben-Hur* (1880) never joined a church but still believed in the divinity of Christ. "Almost his last utterance was, 'I am anxious to know what lies beyond.'"[20]

Carnegie too avoided formal religion. Shortly after his birth, his father walked out of the Presbyterian church during a sermon on infant damnation. Despite his estrangement from formal worship, Carnegie based his system of philanthropy on the Christian gospel: "Instead of explaining away, for example, what Christ said about the difficulty of a rich man entering the kingdom of heaven, Mr. Carnegie affirms its justice, and himself puts the same teaching in secular form by declaring that 'he who dies rich dies disgraced.'"[21] However, the leader of the steel industry cautioned that charity eliminated indigents' incentive to improve. Eggleston blamed Western Methodism, "which was almost as rigorous as Puritanism and tenfold more ardent," for spurring him to work too hard and, thus, for destroying his health. Perhaps, for those who suffered from respiratory or nervous ailments, the Protestant work ethic became deadly.[22]

Many writers, including Barr, Wister, and Eggleston, tried to improve their health by relocating. In so doing, they reinforced the popular belief that, while crowded cities festered with diseases, open country nurtured health. After languishing for weeks with ague, Barr went to a farm where she drank milk daily instead of three tumblers "full of the black, nauseous liquid" distilled from tree bark, a popular remedy prior to the invention of quinine pills. "I had a headache, and it hurt me to read, and the Jesuit's bark made every day a sickening terror."[23] A few weeks of fresh air cured her. Eggleston regained his strength by working outdoors as a jack-of-all-trades in Minnesota, where he witnessed the destructive effects of the mania to buy and sell land.

Wister went west after suffering a nervous breakdown, possibly due to a conflict between his desire to write and his father's expectation that he excel in the business world. Dr. Silas Weir Mitchell prescribed a hunting trip in Wyoming. Since Wister's kinsman himself served two masters, medicine and literature, he understood his cousin's dilemma. Mitchell had created a stir in 1898 with his bestseller, *Hugh Wynne*, which cast Washington, Lafayette, and other real historical figures as characters in a romance. Mitchell urged Wister to keep a journal during his sojourn, and those notes later supplied many details for *The Virginian* (1902). Frederic Remington, who illustrated some of Wister's stories, and Theodore Roosevelt also took rest cures in the West. Wister dedicated *The Virginian* (1902) to Roosevelt.

Reversing Adversity

Money, especially when earned through speculation, was viewed as the root of evil. Not even the historian of Oz, L. Frank Baum, could resist foolishly investing in radio plays, a series of hand-colored motion pictures, and glass slides. When his Oz Film Manufacturing Company failed, he declared bankruptcy. In 1882, Roe's brother defaulted on notes the writer had signed, so Roe declared bankruptcy. Mark Twain lost his money speculating on development of a superior printing machine. The children's friend, as some newspapers called P. T. Barnum, let the promise of quick riches for East Bridgeport cloud his otherwise shrewd business judgment. He poured most of his assets into the Jerome Clock Factory, which never opened. Even the highly respected Methodist minister William Henry Huddleston, Barr's sincere but flawed father, drove his wife Mary to an early grave by subjecting himself to financial stress and by preaching long after his health would permit.

Many writers struggled with adversities just as grim as those that confronted the uncommonly virtuous heroes or heroines of potboilers. For instance, the Panic of 1837 ruined Cable's father, who died in 1859. Cable took a job as a clerk to help support the destitute family. Although hard times and physical weakness plagued the youth, he became adept at finding opportunities amid setbacks. For example, when his sisters refused to take a loyalty oath during the Civil War, Union soldiers sent them behind the lines. They asked to take their little brother, George, with them. Since the boy looked puny, the officers consented. Once over the line, "little George," who was nineteen, joined the Confederate Army. His bravery and discipline won him respect. Moreover, to combat the boredom of camp life, he read the Bible, studied Latin grammar, and learned higher mathematics. A near-fatal wound in his armpit afforded him further opportunity for the pursuit of knowledge. When the Civil War ended, despite widespread unemployment in New Orleans, George's self-education earned him a position on a surveying expedition of the Atchalfalaya River. Unfortunately, he contracted malaria. He spent the two years it took him to recover studying the prairie and swamp communities that he later immortalized.

Rinehart's writing, too, often reflected her own harrowing experiences. She gleaned incidents for *Kings, Queens and Pawns* (1915), *The Amazing Interlude* (1917), and *Dangerous Days* (1919) from her adventures at the front during World War I. Emphasizing the contributions that women make during national emergencies, Rinehart's heroine in *Bab: A Sub-Deb* (1917) infiltrates an espionage ring. Rinehart herself ignored her husband, her sons, her physician, newspaper editors, and British officials who told her to stay home in January 1915. As the lone correspondent at the front, she dodged a German sniper's bullets to interview the King and Queen of Belgium, as well as Queen Mary of England, who, according to *The National Cyclopedia of American Biography*, never before or afterward cooperated with a reporter.[24] Once the United States had entered the fray, Rinehart toured American and European camps as the representative of the U.S. secretary of war. After the armistice, Rinehart went to Germany with the U.S. Army.

Being a war correspondent taught Rinehart to take responsibility for her own safety. However, nearly two decades after the Belgians had presented her with the Medal de la Reine Elisabeth in honor of her war service in hospitals and relief work for the American Red Cross, the random forces of chaos coincidentally struck twice in one summer. When her Filipino cook tried to shoot her, Rinehart lived through a scene rivaling any she had created. The butler and the chauffeur saved the shocked author of murder mysteries from the insane killer. Ironically, she had set a mystery, *The Yellow Room* (1945), in that same location, her home in Bar Harbor, Maine, which burned in a forest fire a few weeks later.

The traumatic events of Rinehart's summer of 1947 illustrate how hazy the line between fiction and reality sometimes became in the lives of these Gilded Age authors. Margaret Deland's father and maternal uncle both had the surname Campbell but were not related. Eggleston discovered the charm of local color when Washington Irving's *The Sketch Book* was the only volume he could reach through a broken pane in the locked glass doors of the bookshelves in his boarding school's library.

The success archetype promised that the worthy would rise because of a benefactor's kindness. By supplying Eggleston with books he could not read at home, the master of Amelia Academy in Virginia unintentionally became the pious Indiana lad's intellectual benefactor.[25] Kate Douglas Wiggin called Mrs. Carolina M. Severance her "fairy godmother" after the latter invited Wiggin to live with her in Santa Barbara so that the writer could enroll in Emma Warwedel's kindergarten training school. Just as the success paradigm predicted, Wiggin excelled. She taught in the first public kindergarten west of the Rocky Mountains and later founded a normal school for teachers. She wrote *The Story of Patsy* (1881) and *The Birds' Christmas Carol* (1887) to raise money for the Silver Street Kindergarten in a San Francisco slum. Three thousand copies of *The Story of Patsy* (1881) were sold within a few days of the first private printing. Commercial publishers accepted both novels after the initial philanthropic editions had sold out. Wiggin donated most of the royalties from her stories and novels to children's charities and gave public readings and lectures to generate public support. She did not faithfully practice the "Gospel of Wealth" espoused by Carnegie, however, because she occasionally assisted individuals.

Carnegie thought institutions and not individuals should receive assistance. Ironically, he owed much of his own success to a kind boss who offered him advice and occupational opportunities, rather than a library card! Thomas A. Scott, the superintendent of the Pennsylvania

Railroad, hired the Scottish telegraph operator to organize the Union Army's railroad operations. Besides learning about stocks and bonds, under Scott's tutelage Carnegie realized that railroads and steel would dominate the post–Civil War industrial boom. Carnegie broke his rule of not assisting individuals once to rescue Mark Twain financially.

In contrast, by 1916, the Reverend Russell Conwell helped pay college tuition for three thousand needy students. He gave away two million dollars he had earned delivering *Acres of Diamonds* (1887) over five thousand times. Through philanthropy, Conwell practiced what he preached. In an era when many boasted about their bank balances, the pastor of the Baptist Temple in Philadelphia asked the church's governing board to freeze his salary at ten thousand dollars a year. Conwell, America's middle-class millionaire, who founded Temple University and two hospitals with his own money, said that giving wealth away freed the soul from the bonds of avarice and guilt.

Like Carnegie, Conwell believed in *The Gospel of Wealth* because "the Lord doesn't like failures any more than the rest of us do." After visiting Carnegie at his home in 1916, the minister told Bruce Barton, a famous journalist who wrote for *American Magazine,* that he thought the steel mogul was unhappy because he had learned too late that "money is like fire—a good servant but a bad master. He struck me as a tired, harassed old man, whose money was a burden that he was trying to lighten—and having a hard time doing it." While Carnegie applied the tenets of *The Gospel of Wealth* by building libraries and museums to inspire the downtrodden, Conwell anonymously helped deserving individuals. For example, once he paid an elderly widow's rent for two years in advance and had the receipts delivered to her on Christmas Eve, as she was packing her possessions in anticipation of eviction.[26]

Just as real and fictional personalities relied upon benefactors, both imaginary protagonists and their creators donned disguises. Kate Wiggin dressed up as a princess crowned with a three-cornered sachet. Nora, her sister, wove quill pens into her hair to make herself look like a witch while their mother wrapped up in camel's-hair shawls to play the godmother. To entertain her kindergarten classes and her family, Wiggin often performed impromptu scenes with anyone she could cast in the requisite supporting roles.[27] After graduating from college, Anna Katharine Green often tucked up her floor-length hair, as she and her roommate at Haverstraw on the Hudson "dressed up in quaint, ugly or curious costumes [to] go to the house of a lively friend and amuse ourselves and her for hours, coming back to our room to write sometimes until the 'wee sma' hours.'"[28]

Wiggin and Green won applause for their characterizations, but Frederick Van Rensselaer Dey, who inherited John Russell Coryell's character—"Nick Carter"—and developed that sleuth in hundreds of dime-novel thrillers, was arrested in Denver on 24 August 1913 for "impersonating an officer."[29]

The act of impersonation embodied in invoking pseudonyms is easy to overlook because using pen names enabled writers to sell several manuscripts simultaneously. However, financial explanations do not consider emotional factors. Disguises appealed to unspoken notions of romance associated with mysterious masked strangers who had performed heroic feats in tales for centuries. Green and many fictional characters hid their true identities so completely that no one recognized them; most authors used pseudonyms to achieve the same anonymity. Through pseudonyms, popular bards vicariously played the roles of unnamed, universal paragons of virtue.

Perhaps Coryell, the creator of master detective Nick Carter, used the most pseudonyms when he wrote one million words in one year for the *Family Story Paper* under the names "Barbara Howard," "Julia Edwards," "Geraldine Fleming," "Lucy May Russell," "Lillian R. Drayton," and "Bertha M. Clay." In the last case, he appropriated the pseudonym of the English author, Charlotte M. Braeme. Another dime-novel author, Edward S. Ellis, helped to create the myth of the Wild West in dime novels written under so many *noms de plume* that scholars have given up trying to count them. He cranked out 467 major works and between 500 and 600 sketches, articles, and poems, as well as history texts and how-to pieces for teachers. He liked military titles, and his best-known pen name is "Lt. R. H. Jayne." Ellis's bibliographer estimated that he used ninety-eight pen names. Once he attributed a series of circus thrillers to P. T. Barnum, his friend.[30]

The Prince Who Loved "Peppers"

Harriet Mulford Stone, alias Margaret Sidney, probably had given up on Prince Charming by 1878, when she published "Polly Pepper's Chicken Pie" in *Wide Awake*. She was thirty-six when the magazine invited her to write twelve more installments chronicling the Pepper family's adventures. Amazingly, the machine responsible for the proliferation of imaginary romances became the conduit for a real love story. The spunky Five Peppers who lived "to help mother" melted the heart of the fifty-year-old publisher of *Wide Awake,* Daniel Lothrop. The widower fell under the "Pepper" spell so completely that, en route to a business engagement in New York, he took a side trip to Concord to meet the creator of the Pepper clan. Soon his business in the city became less urgent than his personal affairs in Concord. In October 1881, he married Harriet Stone. Unlike many Victorian brides, Harriet combined family life and writing. Indeed, her husband's juvenile publishing firm prospered in part because of her.

In 1883, the Lothrops moved from Cambridge to a castle called the Wayside, the former home of both Nathaniel Hawthorne and Louisa May Alcott. They raised their daughter Margaret there. The typewriter determined the social season for the Lothrops. Upon finishing her narratives, Harriet gave lavish parties and participated in the rich literary life of Concord. Ralph Waldo Emerson's daughter, Miss Ellen Emerson, led games and songs at Margaret's childhood birthday celebrations. Whittier and other authors visited the Lothrops frequently. Despite her busy writing and social schedule, Harriet always made time for Margaret. For eleven years, the Lothrop family lived happily. Then Daniel died, and Harriet took over the publishing business.

Since Daniel fit the pattern of the good father who died before his child grew up, his survivors grieved for him. In fact, to immortalize her husband, Harriet crusaded to make corn the national flower, a cause Daniel had fervently espoused. In *The Arena,* she describes Daniel transforming the dining room into a corn shrine, by placing stalks heavy with "red and golden ears" in the corners, festooning the picture frames with silky tassels, and draping the curtains with long leaves so "the light and shade gave out new tints to add to the glory of the corn." She wrote this rhyming tribute:[31]

> Hail to thee, corn!
>   For wide as the sea,
> Are the waves of thy fields
>   O'er the land of the free.

> With blessing benignant
>   Thou crownest our days
> We choose thee our emblem
>   O glorious maize!

Although Harriet Lothrop had a privileged childhood and a happy marriage, nevertheless she created the Pepper family to provide the idealized simplicity denied her in real life. Her family traced its roots to the Mayflower and the Reverend Thomas Hooker, founder of the state of Connecticut. Harriet's father was a wealthy and successful architect. Little Harriet longed to live in a brown cottage in the country, where she could run unfettered by the conventions in force at the famous Grove Hall Seminary, where she attended school. She loved her father but still "could not understand how [he] could be so foolish as to live in a big city and not in this place where I might have hens and chickens and scratch the backs of pigs."[32] When her parents took her on long drives into the country, Harriet searched for the little brown house but, alas, never found it. Then she began to imagine what such a home might look like and who would live there.

After years of amusing her friends with tales of the Pepper family, Harriet wrote her first story about the brave mother and her devoted children, who remained optimistic no matter how hard they had to struggle to survive. To prevent anyone from associating the proud Puritan name of Stone with the shady occupation of fictionalizing, she published the tale under a pseudonym. She chose her pen name, Margaret Sidney, because Margaret meant "truth," and Sidney, her father's name, symbolized chivalry and justice. As Margaret Sidney, Harriet created nearly forty juvenile books and scores of short stories. The first sequel to the *Five Little Peppers and How They Grew* did not appear for over a decade; nevertheless, the author vividly remembered her girlhood fantasy family. Her daughter Margaret recalled her mother sitting by the fire dreaming of the Peppers: "I could almost see them clustered around Mother and her chair, they seemed so real to me. The mental picture is as vivid today as it was then."[33]

Although Lothrop, Ann Stephens, and Mrs. Alice Hegan Rice found Prince Charmings through their writing, other Cinderellas rose from the ash heap only after their prince had died. Indeed, some husbands can be viewed as princes only through generous hyperbole. One of the ironies most striking in the lives of the popular women bards was their ascent to fame, after their husbands had died or disappeared, through stories featuring deceased or reptilian patriarchs. In fact, many of them wrote to support their children. The storybook princess lives happily ever after with her prince, but many flesh-and-blood Cinderellas found the road to happiness lined with black veils, pencils, and erasers. For example, both E. D. E. N. Southworth and Amelia Huddleston Barr survived matrimonial shipwreck by converting their domestic disappointments into potboilers.

When Prince Charming Died

Just as fictional good fathers die young, Emma Nevitte's beloved papa died, when she was five, from wounds he had sustained in the War of 1812. The future E. D. E. N. Southworth remembered waiting for his visits home because those happy interludes made the lonely periods when he was away bearable. His death forced her mother and grand-mother to open a boardinghouse. In *The Haunted Homestead,* she describes her formative years. Southworth either genuinely re-sembled many of the characters she created, or else she unconsciously appropriated for herself and her associates the traits she assigned to her protagonists:

> She was a child of sorrow from the first year of her life. Thin in frame and dark in complexion, with a pair of great wild eyes, she had no soft infantile beauty to attract love; and for the first three years of her life, judging from what she has since heard, she was nothing but an un-mitigated trouble to her friends. But this child was gifted by a vitality that enabled her to live not only through the illness of her infancy and childhood but also through the heavy misfortunes of her girlhood and womanhood.[34]

Emma's sister Charlotte was born beautiful—"rounded form, fair, rosy complexion, soft blue eyes and flaxen hair." The difference in temperament and physique of the two sisters resembles the potboil-ers' plot device of disparate siblings. By the age of three, Emma had alienated her parents and servants by being a "willful imp." On the other hand, her angelic sister had won everyone's love. Of course, in ugly-duckling fashion, Emma grew into a beauty.

Like many of her brooding heroines, she escaped social ostracism only by being given a second chance through her mother's remarriage. Fortunately, the good stepfather did not die as fiction would have de-creed. Instead, he taught Emma, who was ten, horseback riding, which obsessed her as thoroughly as it did the stormy heroines she created later. Emma often wore the dunce cap before her intellectual powers blossomed in her mother and stepfather's private school. She read every book. Upon graduation, Emma became a schoolteacher and married Frederick Southworth, who took her to Wisconsin, where she taught in Platteville. She left the dreary farm near Prairie du Chien three years later when her husband abandoned her. Emma took her infant son to Washington, D.C., where, shortly after relocat-ing, she gave birth to her daughter. She struggled to support her chil-dren by teaching. To supplement her income, she wrote articles for the *National Era*. Although Southworth never talked about her un-happy marriage, deserted and abused wives frequent her novels.

While Southworth knew the pain and humiliation of desertion, Amelia Barr mourned her husband off and on until her own death, de-spite his poor judgment and business failures. Most of her husband's troubles arose because he treated her "like a dog or doll" and, especially, early in their marriage, never discussed his plans with her. During the nineteenth century, many husbands considered their wives incapable of logic.

Indeed, when Anna Katharine Green published *The Leavenworth Case,* members of the Pennsylvania Legislature insisted some man had developed her mystery: "The story was manifestly beyond a woman's powers . . . that an American woman should write detective stories was preposterous. And, yet, nowadays [1901], it would seem no more preposterous than a request to Mr. Carnegie to build a library." In 1878, the book created a "fervor" because "old novel readers recognized in it a touch of power and dramatic ability rare in American fiction, and reviewers were filled with wonder that a woman could have written it."[35]

Anna's father, James Wilson Green, a prominent defense attorney in Brooklyn, introduced his daughter to criminology. Her characters always behave credibly. Although modern readers rarely ask for her stories, during the Gilded Age she won middle-class respectability for the mystery as a literary genre. Initially, after graduating from Ripley Female College in Poultney, New York, with a bachelor of arts degree in psychology, Anna aspired to be a poet. She struggled with verse for a decade before realizing that she could write powerful detective tales.

Green did not write the first mystery, but she did emphasize strong female characters who refused to be victimized. "Seeley Regester" (Metta V. Victor) had published *The Dead Letter* (1867), but it was not as tightly constructed as Green's mysteries. To the tradition of crime stories begun by Emile Gaboriau, Monsieur Lecoq, Edgar Allan Poe, and Wilkie Collins, she contributed the brilliant detective who solves the case. Conan Doyle's immortal Sherlock Holmes appeared a decade after Green's detective, Ebenezer Gryce. Her explication of cause and effect impressed a Yale professor so greatly that he added *The Leavenworth Case* (1878) to his list of texts.

The amazement critics expressed upon discovering that a woman, not a man masquerading under an alias, had written *The Leavenworth Case* reflects the pervasiveness of the notion that women could succeed only in emotional arenas presumed to require limited thought—clerking in department stores, acting, "scribbling," teaching, nursing, and, of course, homemaking. When Margaret Deland published *John Ward, Preacher* (1888), critics denounced her unladylike subject—hell. Not only did she comment upon damnation, but, in the course of four years, she and her devoted husband, Lorin Fuller, opened their home to sixty unwed mothers.

Helping these unwanted women rebuild their lives despite the stigma of illegitimate motherhood exposed Deland to facts of life unknown to the genteel. Her early plots embody insights into the sordid realities that precluded happy endings for many people. Later, to placate the reading public, she tempered the despair in her stories about unwed mothers, divorce, and similar serious social problems. Moreover, she created "Old Chester," an idyllic village where the saintly Episcopalian minister, Dr. Lavender, dispenses advice to the troubled. Because science news and lectures had taught her readers that all organisms, including human beings, must either change or perish, they found comfort in escaping to "Old Chester" where everything, ultimately, remains the same.

Certainly, scores of women besides Deland supported social change, but in the Gilded Age sexist fallacies persisted despite women's accomplishments. The assumption that women could not think logically and should not contemplate unpleasant things hurt homemakers as well as working women. They, too, remained voiceless.

Amelia Lived the Story She Wrote

As a young wife, Amelia Barr, who after her husband's death wrote best sellers, spoke for the muzzled Cinderellas. Barr unconsciously organized her autobiography around the romantic pattern she also used in fictional plots. However, she declared that, in fact, being shut out of making important decisions had frustrated her. In *All the Days of My Life: An Autobiography—The Red Leaves of a Human Heart*, she traced her dissatisfaction with the lot of women to the time of her brother's birth when a servant explained to her:

> "[Girls] are of no account . . . , and women don't signify much either. It is a pity for us both. I have been fit to drop with work ever since you went away, Amelia, and who cares? If any man had done what I have done, there would be two men holding him up by this time."
>
> "Ann, why do men get so much more praise than women, and why are they so much more thought of?"
>
> "God only knows, child," she answered. "Men have made out, that only they can run the world. It's in about as bad a state as it well can be, but they are proud of their work. What I say is, that a race of good women would have done something with the old concern by this time. Men are a poor lot."[36]

Her father confirmed that "men are a poor lot" by failing to take his wife's advice to put his money in a "reputable bank." Instead, he listened to a scoundrel who absconded to Australia. Suddenly the family was impoverished. Mary, the stoical wife, released the servants and prepared her children for sacrifices. Amelia taught school at the age of sixteen to help support the family and later was shocked to learn her maternal uncle had given his sister a row of cottages to rescue her from drudgery. Believing that poverty inspired thrift and built character, her parents had not told her about the windfall. Amelia split the twenty shillings she had saved with her mother, who gratefully accepted the gift. Her father had refused to take his daughter's money because he had recouped his losses through the rent from the cottages. Amelia's mother resented her husband's silence regarding the disposition of her money. Yet society and tradition dictated that a husband owned his wife's property. Amelia protested against this tyranny.

However, her outrage did not protect her from a similar fate. Indeed, she was to prove herself just as worthy of the Cinderella crown as any of her heroines. Like the steadfast women of romance novels, she fled with her husband Robert to escape his enemies, endured poverty because of his financial ineptitude, moved her family half a dozen times to help him realize his dreams, mourned the deaths of six children, and always sought passage through the eye of the needle. When helping Robert complete the tax rolls kept her too busy to do her daily reading and praying, she lamented in her diary on 21 September 1862: "I made a few dollars and have lost what no money can buy. Dear Christ forgive me."[37] In her autobiography, she often refers to Providence as the source of her courage to face adversity.

For example, after her husband had lost his modest savings in the collapse of the Confederacy, he and their three sons died, leaving Amelia and her three daughters penniless. Her struggle released resources that had lain dormant for years. Her hardships induced her to join the public conversation via articles in magazines and newspapers. In true formula-story fashion, Barr succeeded as an author only after proving herself worthy by opening a school for girls in New York City. She expressed her respect for God as well as her feelings on a myriad of subjects.

Amelia's romance began as smoothly as any fairy tale. She married the handsome, attentive, wealthy, Scottish executive prince. They moved into a sumptuous home in Glasgow, where Cinderella for the first time ordered mass-produced clothing. The delicacy of the lace thrilled her. Soon after their idyllic honeymoon, however, her husband began treating her badly.

In *All the Days of My Life*, Amelia recalls seeing him for the first time: "A feeling of deep sadness overcame me. I said I was sick, lay down on my bed and fell into a deep sleep."[38] Ironically, Amelia met her prince en route to see the Queen and Prince Albert, whose commonness, despite their fancy trappings, had disappointed her. Her own prince took her to the "valley of humiliation," rather than to a storybook kingdom. After indulging in a series of unwise speculations, he declared bankruptcy, which ruined him socially even more than financially. The couple's shame compelled them to leave Scotland.[39] Amelia believed their troubles in the United States arose mostly from her husband's lack of insight into human nature. For instance, during their voyage, Robert "fell under the spell of his enemy," a rich, jealous former governor with a military title.[40] Politicians, military leaders, and others with titles often betray protagonists in romances. Robert ignored Amelia's warnings to stay away from the beguiling fraud. In fact, he refused to settle in Boston, where true friends would have helped him establish a business. Instead, Robert followed the rogue to Chicago.

In Chicago, although croup constantly hovered over the nursery, Amelia successfully ran a school in which she educated her own two daughters, Mary and Lilly, as well as girls from the city's prosperous families. Meanwhile, Robert got his picture in the paper for denouncing the Know-Nothings and, thus, became a target of their anti-alien campaign. Amelia had told her husband that such antics would lead to disaster because he knew little about American politics. A few months later, the couple lost their money through the shipboard "friend's" treachery, and Robert prepared to flee to avoid killing his enemy in a duel. The foe died in a dispute with other rivals. However, to escape the thug's associates, the family fled to Memphis, leaving behind the small grave of their baby daughter Edith, who mysteriously had died in her sleep.

They left Memphis when cholera broke out in a town ten miles away. Robert next took his family to the Lone Star Republic. There they found yellow fever in every house in Harrisburg, after escaping from the same disease in Memphis and Galveston. They settled in Austin, where Robert quickly rose in the bureaucracy. Several carefree years passed. Amelia gave birth to Calvin on 2 July 1857; Alice on 16 April 1859; and Ethel on 15 April 1861. Then, during a drought in summer 1861, Robert lost his job. A violent storm ended the reign of death caused by the searing heat, but the social and political discord of the Civil War left most Texans destitute. In the fall, an epidemic of diphtheria killed Ethel and many of the Barrs' neighbors. Despite the fear of Negro uprisings and shortages of such domestic necessities as pins and coffee, Amelia and Robert persevered. Their son, Alexander Greg, was born on 13 March 1863. Then the home they were renting suddenly was sold.

They moved to a comfortable house behind the Capitol called "the Morris Place." There Archibald was born on 7 August 1864; and Lilly contracted camp measles. Soon the whole family had the disease. The tender nursing of a cavalry doctor and a captain's wife saved their lives. Unfortunately, late that summer Archibald died of a "nearly always fatal malady." An offer of employment from a cotton house in Galveston seemed to Robert to promise his mourning family members a chance to rebuild their lives. The dissolution of the Confederacy had left many Texans, including Robert, unemployed. Hard times complicated finding new jobs. Although Amelia remembered witnessing the terrors of fever in Galveston during their first days in the Lone Star Republic, Robert accepted the job.

When the train arrived in the city, Alexander and Calvin went into trances just like Baby Ethel's "vision" on the day before her death. Despite this ominous omen, the Barr family prospered for six months before yellow fever turned Galveston into a massive charnel house. During June, survivors kept tar fires burning in town and flushed the gutters with disinfectants. Afraid to live next to the meat market because many believed it infected, Robert moved his family to a cottage by the sea. When Amelia warned him their new home emanated an "unclean" aura, he laughed.

While Amelia languished in the heat and the stress of living always with death, her children experienced "spiritual terror." They refused to sleep in their bedrooms because objects moved, drawers spilled their contents, and grotesque phantoms walked the halls. A neighbor told them the nefarious pirate Lafitte had painted the house blood red and sold slaves by the pound from it. All varieties of wickedness had occurred in that ghastly seaside cottage, which remained haunted despite the coats of paint and white curtains Amelia had applied to purify it. Now the entire family caught yellow fever. Robert, Calvin, Alexander, and Andrew, who was born on December 5, after the epidemic had passed, died in the pirate's den that had been turned into a family home.

After recovering, Amelia and her daughters ran a boardinghouse and sold ladies notions, but their efforts failed. Then, with $5.18 in her pocket, she took Mary, Alice, and Lilly to New York, where friends helped them start a school. For a while, they lived in rooms that once had been rented by Edgar Allan Poe. Later, the Reverend Henry Ward Beecher started Amelia on her literary career by introducing her to the editorial staff of the *Christian Union*.

Amelia's personal life was as exciting as any plot she devised. Most of her stories reveal her sympathy for feminism. Perhaps her own experiences as a wife and a mother convinced her the suffragists deserved to prevail. She noted that men valued children more than they did their wives because they could replace their spouses while their children were parts of themselves that could not be duplicated. The author of women's romances recast her memories in the Cinderella formula, but she, like the Gilded Age itself, embodied several contradictions. For example, she repeatedly professed her love for and absolute faith in her husband, yet she emphasized his myopic judgment. Despite her business acumen, Amelia believed herself to be psychic and looked to her dreams for clues about the future as well as explanations of the past. Her success as an author enabled her to retire to Cherry Croft, a cottage on Storm King Mountain in Cornwall-on-Hudson, New York.

Amelia Barr's story illustrates how one author, among many others, either inadvertently lived the same story she wrote or else subconsciously edited both texts and experiences until they repeated the archetypes preserved in the collective unconscious. "[Barr's] career has been an admirable illustration of the capacity of woman under stress of sorrow to conquer the world and win success."[41] That same description captured many romances and domestic novels.

Many women—similar in background, temperament, and ultimate triumph over crushing hardship—claimed as their own personal experience this variation on the Cinderella scenario as the prince's death prompted them to excel as writers to pay the bills. In this fractured Victorian version of the cherished Alger tale, the heroine often proved herself more resourceful and more worthy of reward than her foolish deceased husband.

Such life stories and the resulting fiction filled readers' need to believe in something greater than themselves. The predictable real-life stories encouraged the multitude to relish the magic of the written word. The world might deny closure, but narratives ended happily. In fact, authors of harmless mirth served as public benefactors, argued P. T. Barnum, who never entirely convinced his critics that wholesome entertainment revived the soul. The autobiographies reassured readers that, in life as in books, lucky coincidences introduced daring youths to benefactors, who, like fairy godparents, would transform them into middle-class citizens. Moreover, these testimonials demonstrated that, in the real world as in fiction, diligence earned public esteem; even those faced with massive disappointments and formidable obstacles balanced materialism and spirituality.

Chapter 7

The Repulsive Fascination of Fires

Natural laws explain why fires burn. But most people in the Gilded Age were more interested in the majesty of the flames than in their physical properties. The deadly beauty of fire and the power of ancient narrative patterns, such as the Judgment Day archetype, fascinated popular bards. Science gave nineteenth-century readers a tidy system for categorizing their experiences, a set of pigeonholes that made the irrational forces of nature conform to a logical scheme. Even storms fit into precise explanations of natural phenomena. However, despite the accuracy of meteorological equipment or the brilliance of scientists, no one could explain why lightning struck certain individuals but skipped over their companions or why tornadoes flattened some homes but not others. Therefore, a key mystery of the universe—why some suffered while others escaped—remained inscrutable. The tension between tidy facts and chaotic reality made people thirst for affective explanations that filled the gaps left by science.

Narrative formulas invoked the magic of ancient amulets. Encountering proven solutions repeatedly in plots gave readers the courage to face destruction and the hope to rebuild their tattered lives. Icarus rode once more through the clouds via elevators, and Ajax found the golden fleece where it belonged—in the slaughter yards of Chicago or on Wall Street in New York. Reporters as well as popular bards relied upon the success archetype to interpret disasters.

The typewriting bards supplied fanciful explanations for phenomena written off as chance by scientists. Experts explained how the droughts and atmospheric conditions of autumn of 1871 turned expanses of the Midwest into a tinderbox. However, the factual details of the great fires in Chicago and Peshtigo, Wisconsin, did not satisfy the human need to place such events in perspective by connecting present tragedies to past narratives concerning calamities. The authors of popular fiction recast the facts in terms of the myths that had sustained the community for generations. The Reverend E. P. Roe retold the legend of Noah's Flood. In his version, God spared a handful of worthy individuals rather than just one pure family. Instead of washing away humanity's sins, the Almighty purified Chicago, the modern Sodom and Gomorrah, with flames. Like Roe, the Reverend E. J. Goodspeed declared in his *History of the Great Fires*, "[The] mercy of the fire spared men of might in trade, art and journalism. . . . Many such true hearts were strengthened in their attachment to God . . . there was no such thing as despondency or gloom, for [their] treasures were laid up above the reach of the flames, [their] hope did not consist in earthly prosperity but in the mercy of Jesus Christ."[1]

Certainly this quotation illustrates how writers applied traditional biblical teachings to the present. This chapter examines three devastating fires in terms of their narrative potential. Why did Americans filter such calamities through the success paradigm's imperative to reconcile materialism with spirituality? Why did martyrdom haunt the corridors of public discourse? These disasters were not anomalies; carelessness and fatalism increased the danger of conflagrations, regardless of where citizens lived. Indeed, blazes generated speculation about Judgment Day as well as a need to justify the suffering of the innocent and the escape of the guilty. The Chicago Fire simultaneously repelled and intrigued readers.

To Goodspeed, Roe, and their fellow idealists, the conflagration proved God loved everyone equally since the rich and the poor alike emerged penniless from the smoldering ruins. Only a few had insured their property. The ordeal forced survivors to rebuild their lives and, thus, to make the "Young Giant," as Goodspeed called Chicago, "more splendid than before." He and Roe believed "faith supplemented nature."[2] Many interpreted the tragedies at Chicago and Peshtigo in terms of the biblical book of Revelation. In *Fire at Peshtigo*, Robert W. Wells explains:

> Others, believing that the day of judgment was surely come, fell upon the ground and abandoned themselves to its terrors. Indeed, this apprehension that the last day was at hand pervaded even the strongest and most mature minds. All the conditions of the prophecies seemed to be fulfilled. The hot atmosphere filled with smoke supplied the "signs in the sun and in the moon and in the stars." The sound of the whirlwind was as "the sea and the waves roaring," and everywhere there were "men's hearts failing them for fear and for looking after those things, which were coming on the earth: for the powers of heaven shall be shaken."[3]

Hell on Earth?

The Chicago Fire blazed in the public's imagination, while the conflagration that decimated Peshtigo, Wisconsin, and northern Michigan received cursory attention. Three hundred may have perished in Chicago. At least twelve hundred died during the same night up north. The city fire satisfied expectations better than the forest fire because many equated the word *urban* with *perdition*. A gaudy, art-infested metropolis full of temptations deserved to burn up. A vast stand of timber, broken only by wild meadows and pure farm settlements, should be spared. Nevertheless, storms of embers made 8 October 1871 Judgment Day for citizens of both Chicago and Peshtigo.

People across the nation had read news items about Chicago's self-made go-getters and self-crowned royalty. Many admired the railroad hub's ballrooms, theaters, museums, and billiard halls, as well as its factories, stockyards, and financial offices. Most aspired to visit "The Pearl of the Midwest," but only a few knew of Peshtigo before the disaster. On the morning of October 9, mostly ashes remained in Peshtigo; a third of Chicago had burned up. Although the fires occurred almost simultaneously, they differed logistically and in story potential.

Many plots portrayed the Irish stereotypically. The tendency to treat them as scapegoats fueled popular mistrust of cities, luring ministers and journalists to speculate on the cosmic meaning of the Chicago conflagration, despite the forest fire's greater toll in death and destruction. The Chicago Fire had a culprit—Mrs. O'Leary, whose cow had kicked over a kerosene lamp; this assigned agency to the horror. In Roe's account of the Chicago Fire, the hero gets his first job when a drunken Irish snow shoveler collapses despite his wife's tears and the priest's threats.[4]

Although many in Peshtigo pleaded with Providence for mercy, no one took the blame for starting the blaze. The flaming tornado was driven by wind, not triggered by bovine peevishness. Atmospheric conditions and drought, rather than the carelessness of a foreigner, caused the Peshtigo Fire. Nevertheless, survivors told tales reflecting ethnic stereotypes. For example, some recounted the adventures of obnoxiously pious Scandinavians like "Praying Peter" Bernson, who lived outside Sturgeon Bay and constructed a "pipeline to heaven." Each day he prayed, and God told him exactly what to do to save his house, clothes, and cows. "Peter and all that was his were saved to the utmost."[5]

The anecdotes passed through the sieve of history stress perseverance and quick thinking. The ones who died were those who panicked, gave up, or unwittingly stepped into the path of the fiery cyclone. Many who lived refused to recall their ordeal. The stories about the fires represent the extroverts' experiences and story-making abilities. While entire families were incinerated, some of their names endure as footnotes to the chronicle of the calamity. Sometimes neighbors kept their memories alive by describing how they had died. Wells's study, *Fire and Ice,* places the conflagration in a cultural context. Despite their accuracy, the vignettes provide more insight into the North Country's values than factual evidence. The anecdotes bring the victims back to life, if only for as long as it takes to read a paragraph.

Consider Joseph Lasure. He watched his wife and four sons perish as the family fled across the Sugar Bush clearing. His favorite child, Floy, could have escaped, but she kept stopping to encourage him. Suddenly, sparks ignited the dry, knee-deep grass. "Then her dress caught. For a moment, she stood there, this bright and beautiful child, her clothing a torch in the light of the blazing pines."[6] Her father mourned the loss of his hope for the future, his nine-year-old daughter. The story of that doomed family with the French name still evokes pain, partly because it fits into the narrative formula of self-sacrifice. Floy loved her father enough to risk her own life to save his; and, had it been possible, he would have taken her place on the pyre. Long after Peshtigo had risen from the ashes and was, like the forest around it, thriving with new growth spawned by the fire, Lasure still grieved for his daughter. Floy belongs to the ranks of martyrs who die so that others may live.

Those who sacrificed themselves for others deserved salvation. The success paradigm promised them the ultimate reward, a place in heaven. Although protagonists do not die in the bardic tales, often somebody makes that supreme sacrifice for loved ones. Train accidents as well as forest fires inspired stories about selfless heroes who died so that others might live. For example, "Heroes of the Railway Service," in the March 1899 issue of the *Century Magazine,* points out that working on the railroad proved fatal for many: "The washouts of spring, the blinding dust of summer, the treacherous fogs of autumn and the icy car-tops of winter, all teach [the engineer] to be careful of his hold in this world, lest he slip suddenly into the next."[7]

Indeed, many railroad engineers risked their lives to protect strangers. In accounts of real disasters, engineers followed the same code of honor as the heroes of dime thrillers. Catastrophes plunged the true-hearted into an abyss of suffering where their altruism inspired hope and selflessness in ordinary folks. Consider the conflagration of 1 September 1894, in which 418 souls perished and 2,000 lost their homes while eight villages collapsed into smoldering rubble. The flames cut a swath of 350 square miles in northern Minnesota and Wisconsin, destroying property valued at more than a million dollars. Nellie Bly met the hardware-store tycoon she later married while traveling on the train to cover this sensational blaze for the *New York World.* Her love story provides a poignant counterpoint to the harrowing legend of "The Limited's Last Run."

Fact and mythic license blended even in the news reports, until the brave and felicitously named engineer, James M. Root, satisfied his generation's hunger for a sacrificial lamb. Long after flames had entered his cab, Root stayed at his post. As the blaze engulfed the tracks ahead of the station in Hinckley, Minnesota, the engineer pushed the throttle to reverse, hoping to back up six miles to Skunk Lake, a mud-hole. Many of his twenty-five paying passengers risked their own lives to help the throng facing cremation jam onto the cars. "On through this weird scene the *Limited* sped, the situation growing more alarming at every mile. . . . On rushed the train through the fiery, hot breath of the pursuing flames, for a stop would have been fatal to all on board," reported the *New York Times.*[8]

One chronicler of the disaster claimed that Root had "backed his train through a wall of flames and over the burning Grindstone Creek bridge all the way to Duluth . . . saved 350 lives, but his hands were burned fast to the throttle."[9] The reporters quoted three witnesses who described their express ride through hell, which, in news parlance, became "one of the most thrilling events" of the calamity. This news report resembles an adventure story:

> The baggage car was soon a mass of flames, which streamed back over the tender and engine, setting fire to the engineer's clothes and scorching his face and hands. On either side of the engine there was a stream of flames, but never for an instant did Engineer Root flinch. To remain was apparently certain death for him, but could he hold out for four miles the passengers might possibly escape. To have deserted his post would have been certain death for all on board. Back of him stood his trusty fireman.[10]

Playing a modern Sancho Panza or Man Friday, Root's loyal fireman dumped water from the holding tank onto his clothing as Root backed the speeding train through the fiery corridor of trees toward the refuge of the mud flats. Windows cracked. Woodwork peeled. Seats hissed and crackled. "The smoke from the forest fires was so dense lamps were lighted in the cars."[11] Men stationed themselves at the doors to prevent panicking riders from flinging themselves from the platform onto the tracks. Some tourists leaped through the windows in their frenzy to evade the fire, which was devouring the *Limited.*

Just two minutes ahead of the conflagration, Root reached Skunk Lake. The passengers stumbled to the water, pulling unconscious traveling companions to safety. Some travelers on the *Limited* later remembered that terror, rather than exhaustion, had prevailed. For example, C. A. Vandever of Davenport, Iowa, told the *New York Times,* "Men and women were driven perfectly frantic by the heat, together with the fear of an impending horrible death."[12] Mrs. Lawrence agreed with him: "People screamed and men jumped through the car windows. There was no humanity in it. Every fear-crazed person was for himself, and they did not care how they got out of the swirling, rushing avalanche of flame."[13] Nevertheless, both journalists and Vandever said that two men carried the courageous engineer, whose burns and cuts from the broken glass made his recovery seem unlikely, to Skunk Lake. Together, the wounded railroad crew and two hundred passengers huddled submerged in the mud, ducking their heads repeatedly to prevent their hair from bursting into flames.[14] The ground smoldered for four hours.

Praising the crew for remaining calm, the writer for *Century Magazine* said that, when the survivors crawled out of the water, engineer Root, "as if guided by instinct," staggered to his cab and passed out on the charred driver's seat.[15] Vandever noted that the conductor "lost his head entirely and seemed to be raging in a perfect fever of insanity." The *New York Times* lamented that the man "had gone crazy from the intense heat, and it was doubtful whether he [would] ever recover."[16] The curator of the Hinckley Fire Museum explained that Root had stayed on the floor of the engine all night and lived because it was the sole car not consumed in the flames. She said that, through the years, with every retelling of his harrowing experiences, Root had embellished the story.[17] Since most of the train had burned to the ground and he had sustained severe injuries, Root became the hero of the legend of "The *Limited's* Last Run."

The name of the train ironically echoed the spiritual reality that was of concern to most individuals. Humans remain "limited" even when their technology permits them to challenge nature. The Reverend William Wilkinson collected anecdotes from the survivors and crew of the *Limited.*[18] True to the doctrine of predestination, the brave engineer could not save everyone. For those fleeing the fire, the train embodied the eye of the needle—at least in terms of immediate salvation. A flurry of embers pelted them as they attempted to gain passage on the *Limited.*

Some who boarded the train died anyway. Two Chinese brothers smothered in the day coach. Dozens fell or leapt onto the blazing tracks. A few suffocated as they stepped into Skunk Lake. Moreover, although Root stopped the train once, he had to retreat before everyone who was trying to escape the fiery cyclone could board because the train itself had ignited. He could hear the roar of destruction thundering toward the *Limited* at an estimated clip of eighty miles an hour.

The engineer's quandary captured public attention. He wrote a play about his dance with the Grim Reaper. It closed in New York after only one performance, probably because he did not know how to turn the raw drama of his ordeal into compelling theater. The incident contained symbolic kernels that fit popular assumptions about heroic sacrifice and death. In fact, the epidemic of train wrecks during the Gilded Age generated a continuous stream of news items about brave martyrs who were reminiscent of those heroes in formula tales who died so that others might live, according to Katie Letcher Lyle. In *Scalded to Death by the Steam,* Lyle compared the stories about railroad disasters with the ballads that converted those tragedies into enduring testimonies of human courage and frailty.[19]

Like the heroes in ballads and paperbacks, Root disregarded his own pain. Only his quick thinking saved 250 riders on that unlucky St. Paul and Duluth Railroad carrier. *Century Magazine's* account ended on this mythic note: "It was a long time before Engineer Root recovered from his wounds and burns."[20] The reminder of the hero's sacrifice satisfied the need for narrative closure. Similarly, Root's *New York Times* obituary in 1911 assured readers that the engineer had retired from the railroad with a pension three years before his demise. True to the luck-and-pluck code, he had worked hard and, ultimately, had earned official recognition. The *Times* saluted Root as the "Saver of Many Lives," declaring that "Root was in charge . . . of the best train on the road crowded with passengers . . . [and] showed great heroism in one of the most disastrous forest fires in the Northwest."[21] In the horse operas, the star cowboy always rode the finest mount; therefore, despite budgets and the tacky confines of reality, the reporter put the hero in the conveyance his bravery merited—the best train on the road.

Like Root, potboiler heroes risked their lives rescuing others. Factual and fictional accounts of tragedies retold the drama of sacrifice and occasional martyrdom. Newspapers ran anecdotes concerning survivors. The cultural emphasis upon the useful and the practical influenced writers. Progress promised improvement, not death. The protagonist who tempted fate but lived to tell about it heartened readers. On the other hand, in formula stories, outcasts earned salvation by dying so that others might live. For example, a recovered alcoholic sustains fatal head injuries to shield the heroine of *In His Steps* (1897) from a beer bottle flung by a rioter.

Fires as Evidence of Predestination

In Eleanor Porter's novel, *The Turn of the Tide* (1908), the heroine realizes that she loves her rich benefactor only after assuming he has died saving others in a factory explosion. Of course, he lives. In the world of romantic formulas, good deeds and hard work—even amid destruction—guaranteed the survival of the fittest. Such plots offered hope to those who daily were reminded of the ubiquity of death. Indeed, in 1892, Henry C. Adams told *The Forum's* readers that, every year, 1 out of every 135 railroad employees died, while 1 in 12 sustained injuries. "In no other occupation, not even in mining, which is a most dangerous occupation, can such results be shown."[22] The examples of heroism on the rails in the *Century Magazine* were culled from hundreds of incidents.

No account of fatal altruism exceeded several paragraphs, but the anecdotes concerning engineers who lived received longer treatment. In fact, the Hinckley disaster took up nearly half the space devoted to describing accidents. Disaster accounts illustrated the limits of earthly power, money, or prestige when confronted with the wrath of storms or accidents. Despite reality's nasty tendency to obliterate the innocent along with the guilty, narratives enforced the success archetype and bestowed the gift of life upon those who deserved it.

This need to salute life in the face of death might explain why some stories are repeated more frequently than others and why some writers chose the living rather than the dead as the focus of their reports of the Peshtigo Fire. An interviewer designated twenty-year-old Lovell Reed as the "pluckiest hero of the fire," rather than Floy Lasure, who, like pure children in stories from the American colonial period, reminded adults of God's love for those who suffer to spare others. The child's death and her father's grief touched the deepest chords of empathy.

Moreover, while Floy had no power over the sparks that ignited her dress, Lovell took the situation into his own hands, displaying Yankee gumption—a trait the public always applauded. Story makers thwarted mortal efforts to evade fate. Lovell's experience fit this pattern. To avoid cremation, Lovell stabbed himself twice in the chest. His suicide went awry when he dropped the knife. Just as Lovell bent over to retrieve it, the flames skipped over him. Those standing beside him died, but he fled to the river. The adult's resignation and his act of desperation, not the child's bravery and self-sacrifice, won laurels. To many respecters of progress, Lovell's self-preservation and strength commanded attention. On the other hand, few could ignore the dear daughter's love for her father. Probably both stories appealed to readers because both encapsulated part of the affective truth. Nevertheless, to some individuals, embracing fate without hesitation epitomized heroic behavior because many still respected predestination.

Another Peshtigo tale featured a roughneck "of huge frame and generous impulses," who risked losing his sawmill rather than endanger his two brothers and neighbors. Personal sacrifice crept into this plot via ruinous property loss. First, that curmudgeon cursed the Lord. According to the minister, who interviewed survivors for his chronicle of the fire, when the roaring flames pierced the dark smoky sky like an avenging sword, the blasphemous mill owner knew the Almighty had the upper hand. "'Go home. Nothing more can be done for us,' he shouted, 'God can do as He pleases.'"[23]

Then, a drop of rain bounced off his forehead. The tired firefighters redoubled their efforts, and, with the help of that faint spray of rain, they turned the fire into steam, just as it was converging upon the sinner and his mill. Of course, no one knew who the elect were. That God let innocent children die but saved a gnarled blasphemer fit the narrative pattern. Moreover, the old man prospered only after he had recognized the majesty of God and repented. "The rough man dropped upon his knees; great tears rolled down his face. His hands were clasped, head bowed, and he agonized to express his thanks. Suddenly, he sprang to his feet, vigorously swinging his hat, and with the most earnest intensity shouted, 'Hurrah for God! Hurrah for God!'"[24]

"Hurrah for God!" reflected a theme in many anecdotes about the Peshtigo Fire. Perhaps the legend of the rowdy sawmill owner who found God amid the ashes conformed to emotional rather than historical authenticity. Did any such person really escape the blaze that closely? Since the rain did not fall until the afternoon after the fire had leveled Peshtigo, he would have had to be living up north in the wilds not yet connected by railroads, and, of course, the miracle would have had to happen during the day.

Historian Robert Wells concludes that the story would have made a better sermon had lightning struck the blasphemer. The wicked as well as the saintly fit into the grand scheme of the universe, according to the tenets of predestination, which remained fixed in many people's minds. But, by 1871, the social climate had changed enough so that stories about a merciful God and the redemption of the least worthy were fashionable.

The constant threat of fire throughout the nineteenth century made hell on earth a daily possibility. History's trail of ashes began with immense prairie and forest fires before white settlements arose in the New World. Of course, the first immigrants fought fires to preserve their colonies. For example, Jamestown burned to the ground in 1676. Residents of New Orleans fled, as 856 buildings collapsed in a wave of flames that swept over the city in 1788. New York City lost thirteen acres—and 654 structures—to the infamous blaze of 1835. By 1871, regardless of where they lived, most had witnessed as well as read about deadly blazes.

Moreover, even after the Great Fire of 1871, Chicago planners did not eliminate the congestion and shoddy construction that had fueled the conflagration. Fifty fires a year plagued the hundred blocks between Harrison Street and the Chicago River, which extended north and west to Lake Michigan. "The most striking general aspect of the record is the paradoxical conjunction of a high rate of burning with the highest type of business ability in the occupants of the burned premises." The author of that statement, writing in an architectural journal, urged city inspectors to enforce laws requiring buildings to install sprinklers in "so-called conflagration-breeders."[25]

In fact, during the nineteenth century, fire was omnipresent. Conflagrations wiped out entire towns as well as neighborhoods and villages. Goodspeed listed the Chicago blazes of 1857, 1859, 1866, and 1868 as well as the New York fires of 1835 and 1845 in his "Histories of the Great Fires of the Past."[26]

The success archetype embedded in the bardic tales may have contributed to people's fatalistic attitude toward conflagrations. The paradigm promised material rewards to the deserving. Moreover, spiritual rather than material riches endured. Death delivered the virtuous to heaven. The assurance of salvation or the hope of an afterlife may have made fires seem part of the natural order that ultimately separated good from evil. Blazes eluded control and struck the rich as well as the poor. Theater and reality blended as crowds applauded the firefighters. The beauty and excitement of conflagrations generated free entertainment more dramatic than any tragedy presented on the stage.

In New York City, people bought booklets containing lists of the number of bells rung for fire alarms. A throng of curious observers chased fires engines. Harold S. Walker, who years later served as a fire protection engineer in Marblehead, Massachusetts, remembered going to the Chelsea conflagration on Palm Sunday afternoon in 1908: "I got home about midnight. In the course of events, I ruined an almost new coat that I had been given for Easter. If I recall correctly, my mother said very little about it. Maybe she didn't like the coat any more than I did. I never had to wear it again."[27] Although John A. Cregier's father tried to "whip it out" of him, at age seven John ran after Engine Number Thirty-Four. Later, John joined the New York City Fire Department.

One of the most sensational of New York City's numerous memorable fires flattened P. T. Barnum's American Museum on 13 July 1865. In a few hours, the attractions Barnum had spent over two decades collecting crumbled into mounds of ashes studded with embers. Barnum had taken most of the wild animals on tour, but the firefighters had to kill some whales, crocodiles, and snakes that could not be led from the building. The seals padded after their rescuers to safety, providing one of the few moments of levity during the tragic afternoon in which the hoaxes, marvels, and oddities that had delighted children of all ages vanished in the flames. Ironically, the blaze entertained the very individuals who had patronized the museum. Although Barnum's customers regretted losing the place where many of their conversations and dreams had been born, they could not resist the crimson and gold charm of the deadly leveler.

The public imagination refused to permit Barnum's amusement palace to fall in flames caused by carelessness like any normal building. Gossip created more dramatic, more significant causes than the faulty flue in an adjoining restaurant that actually had started the blaze. One rumor declared that southern sympathizers had torched the emporium of wonders to preserve Jefferson Davis's honor. A diorama depicting the deposed Confederate president, sneaking away from captors disguised in his wife's petticoats, had enraged the disgruntled Rebels.[28]

This was the final conflagration the New York City volunteer fire department extinguished. "It was their last hurrah, a spectacular ending to a spectacular era in New York."[29]

Gruesome "Slices of Life"

When her older siblings left her at home, Mabel Osgood Wright howled as Aunt Kinnie Haven's Sunday coach careened down Broadway to get as near as possible to the blaze that consumed Barnum's American Museum in 1865. Indeed, as Michael Schudson pointed out in *Discovering the News,* "the interest in fire was not just child's play."[30] As noted above, New York vendors sold alarm manuals to citizens. Mabel carried her tattered, pink-jacketed "Bell Guide" in her pocket. "For some years after the fire engines were drawn by horses, instead of, as in the early 1860s, by the volunteers running a foot, this bell was sounded from the watch tower, and it was by counting strokes we might locate it," she noted.[31] As a wee lass, Mabel ate five raw oysters and slid the sixth down the front of her dress to retain her reputation as a "tommy" when a pushcart operator took her to the harbor to watch a ship sink in a swirl of embers after igniting buildings on the wharves.

Mabel recalled missing the Barnum fire: "The other great fire I went to, to use an Irish bull, was one, which I didn't see until after it was out, and then I smelt it." She cried disconsolately as her siblings raved about the astounding museum blaze. Mary Daly, the family's cook, comforted Mabel: "We'll have a grand time, I'll warrant thee, seeing what isn't there any more." Mary took the disappointed little girl to see the ruins the next morning. Mabel remembered this outing in her autobiography, *My New York* (1926): "There was enough confusion and smoke left to satisfy any one, and my curiosity was soon gratified for I not only saw what was not there, but the smell of the smolder is yet a vivid memory." Even when reduced to a gutted hulk, Barnum's Home of Humbugs stirred the child's imagination. He understood the tyranny of fire better than some of his contemporaries because his museum burned three times, as well as two of his mansions and the winter quarters of "The Greatest Show on Earth."[32]

Fire smoldered in the public imagination because it incinerated rural hamlets, prairies, forests, and cities. Both popular bards and newspaper writers described the losses, along with the heroism of those who suffered or died trying to save loved ones. The success archetype amplified many of these stories. Unlike most modern fires, which tend to consume one or two buildings, the blazes of a hundred years ago, given faulty construction, wooden buildings, and inadequate firefighting equipment, often consumed vast areas. Sometimes only a few died. For example, the fire of 1838 that reduced Charleston, South Carolina, to charred rubble claimed four lives. Everyone escaped in the St. Louis blaze of 1849 that engulfed fifteen blocks and twenty-five steamboats.

In *The Darkest Hours: A Narrative Encyclopedia of Worldwide Disasters from Ancient Time to the Present,* Jay Robert Nash indicates that many more buildings were destroyed in what is now the United States between 1667 and 1920 than between 1911 and 1976. In fact, from the Colonial Era to just before World War I, thirty-six conflagrations leveled fourteen cities or towns and gutted more than one thousand buildings in four cities, between one hundred and five hundred buildings in eight other places, and more than fifty but fewer than one hundred buildings in four different neighborhoods. On the

other hand, during the years after 1911, only six major blazes occurred. Two wiped out towns, one consumed fifty blocks in Cleveland, one left five thousand homeless in Pittsburgh, and two others
flattened between fifty and one hundred buildings.[33]

As the comparison is based on only the largest fires, a tally of all
fires in the nation probably would add up to much larger sums. Statistics never "include the very large number of fires that go unre-
ported and of which no note is made."[34] The data suggest that the
nature of fires changed as progress led to innovation in prevention
and firefighting techniques. The respect for religion often associated
with the nineteenth century, as well as a recurrent interest in the millennium, may have arisen partly from the presence of conflagrations.
Writers probably felt compelled to devise fiery plot twists because
readers understood that, but for the grace of God, they would be cre-
mated at home, in railroad cars, in theaters, on steamboats, or in commercial buildings. No one was safer than anyone else. Indeed, viewing fires fascinated people as long as the danger did not creep too
close to home.

Ironically, often the tragedies that struck individuals hardest were
those that interested the public and the press least. Impersonal fires
broke the monotony. Spectacular catastrophes dominated conversations and front-page headlines. Some accidents neither inspired ban-
ner headlines nor made the roster of *The Darkest Hours,* an encyclopedia of disasters, but shattered families. The death of a loved one
personalized calamity. For example, on 23 March 1883, the *Alexandria (Louisiana) Town Talk* told its readers about a woman whose piety led to her demise: "On Friday last at Bridgeport, Conn., while
Mrs. Ann Roland was kneeling in front of a stove, saying her prayers,
a live coal fell on her clothing, setting her on fire. She was shockingly
burned and died from her injuries. Her three daughters were badly
burned in trying to extinguish the flames."[35]

Such notices reminded readers of their vulnerability, even within
their homes. Lightning, which long had been associated with divine
wrath, also struck without mercy or reason. *Town Talk* reported the
tragic end of a child's game: "This afternoon the three little daughters
of Jacob Morrowitz were playing in the street, under an umbrella,
when they were struck by lightning. The two older girls, aged nine
and eleven, died instantly, and the third, aged 6, was paralyzed on the
right side, but will recover." An item on the front page recounted the
sad fate of the steamer *Graphles,* which burst into flames near Victoria,
British Columbia, on 6 May 1883, cremating 750 passengers.[36]

Of course, trains contributed to the grim chronicle of events. The

New York Daily Tribune reported in gruesome detail a horrible train wreck in Alton, Illinois. Reporters, like novelists, may have described the injuries minutely to attain realism and so to present "slices of life" exactly as they had witnessed them. The accounts reported physical evidence of what had happened to victims: "The oil, wherever it had touched the skin, had burned deep into the flesh, while such portions of the flesh as escaped entire destruction were blistered, and in many cases were blackened, by the intense heat. The lips were terribly swollen and discolored, and the eyes of all five were burned out entirely. Every vestige of hair was burned off the face and head, and in many places the skull and cheek bones were exposed."[37]

To modern critics, the gory descriptions suggest an unhealthy preoccupation with morbidity. Commenting on the success of *Science,* a new weekly magazine, and on the increased attention to scientific aspects of news by reporters, the editor of the *Muncie (Indiana) Daily News* predicted in 1885 that metropolitan readers soon would demand a daily devoted entirely to science.[38] A century ago, inclusion of dire details in accounts of disasters perhaps corresponded to printing verbatim reports of meetings and acts of Congress. Shocking items may have accomplished then what the television camera achieves today. If a picture can substitute for a thousand words, then, in the era when news photos had not become economically feasible, reporters may have tried to convey the terror of random calamities, such as train wrecks, through the use of verbal images that depicted the suffering precisely as it occurred, no matter how cruel the reality was. Some slices of life, in fact, were slabs of hell.

Despite the daily danger of fire and the news reports of tragedies elsewhere, people living along the northern frontier accepted the seasonal threat of immolation. Their religious convictions may have helped them cope with the possibility of destruction posed by the annual autumn forest fires. Smoke had hung over Peshtigo for several weeks before the conflagration in 1871. The associate editors of the *Chicago Daily Tribune,* James W. Sheahan and George P. Upton, explained, "The fires were about them in every direction, but they had fought them off with the appliances so familiar to frontier men and dreamed of no danger."[39]

People ignored the grit. Despite the drought, farmers set their pasture-making fires as usual. Lumberjacks relied upon the sparks kindled by lightning to clear out underbrush. Railroad builders let piles of tailings and trash smolder. Peat bogs glowed where spontaneous combustion, swamp gas, or an unknown agent had ignited them. Every fall, the night sky occasionally was lit with flares from a distant fire, and ashes blew in from the north. "The threat of fire, the main topic of conversation in the region that fall, seemed like someone else's problem to the families who lived in the Sugar Bushes."[40]

To many in Chicago in 1871, too, the threat seemed impersonal. Despite the calls the night before, the fire department expected the problem to ease up, not worsen. While the drought had been partly responsible for precipitating the crisis in both Chicago and Peshtigo, the carelessness of the victims, and their inability to sense the danger until it was too late, sealed their doom. Too many citizens enjoyed watching fires to take them seriously, until the whirlwind of flames had swept away their homes, neighborhoods, world.

Perhaps such people intuitively cast themselves as protagonists in the romance called life. Certainly the divine author would reward pluck with luck. Chasing fire engines brought individuals vicarious thrills, much like watching sports events or going to the theater. Reality heightened the interest, but life had a nasty way of imposing unhappy endings on delightful displays of courage and pyrotechnics. Thrill seekers still chase fire engines. However, most depend upon television docudramas, "Unsolved Mysteries," or action reports taped by "Rescue 911" and "Forty-Eight Hours" for armchair adventure. Of course, television news broadcasts, including Cable News Network (CNN), provide disaster junkies with constant video gratification since, every minute, someone somewhere bumbles fatally.

A nineteenth-century journalist declared that "the greater proportion of the conflagrations . . . of any of our large cities . . . are the direct result of carelessness and malice."[41] This waste occurred because "Americans are a notoriously reckless people, and a spirit of speculation prevails among them. Fortunes are quickly made as quickly spent, and it is indubitably this spirit of speculation that makes them careless to an extraordinary degree."[42] The number of fires reported steadily rose between 1876 and 1885, from 9,301 to 14,114. The eerie common denominator of large and small fires often was carelessness. Just two months after the Hinckley (Minnesota) Conflagration of 1894, John Gifford warned that, while lightning caused some blazes, human agents—incendiaries, shiftless individuals, and locomotives—started most forest fires. Gunners, tramps, and boys left embers from campfires or flicked their lit cigarettes, cigars, or matches into the brush. In homes as well as in the woods, carelessness took its toll. Defective flues caused most household fires. The failure to line wall partitions or the spaces between ceilings and floors with nonflammable substances caused commercial blazes. Indeed, in construction as well as in everyday life, "the perils of fire [seemed] to be ignored entirely."[43]

Perhaps the spate of disaster stories in newspapers encouraged readers to hope that misfortune would strike only strangers. G. W. De Succa, editor of the *Austin (Nev.) Reese River Reveille*, observed on 29 June 1875: "But as disasters never come single, we have, in today's dispatches, accounts of an immense conflagration in Spain and destructive tornadoes in Wyoming and Michigan, involving loss of life as well as of property."[44] The nearly daily occurrence of fires and mayhem made tragedy commonplace on the western frontier, as well as along the East Coast. No matter where one lived, either going to work or staying home frequently amounted to playing Russian roulette.

Amid such uncertainty, the success archetype embedded in the bardic tales gave readers a refuge from the grim possibilities of modern life. In the realm of the imagination, justice always prevailed. Through diligence and loyalty, virtuous souls earned the respect of a fairy-godparent benefactor who enabled them to advance to the middle class. The story always ended happily. If one's home burned down, that tragedy opened marvelous opportunities. If one's parents died, that loss spurred orphans to develop their potential. If crisis struck, a lucky break soon followed. Nobody honest, good, or faithful died young without going to heaven in a blaze of glory. And nobody in love (appropriately, of course!) ever died. The rags-to-riches paradigm kept the promises that life broke routinely.

Chapter 8

Fantastic Reality and Realistic Fantasy

> For now we see in a mirror dimly, but then face to face. Now I know in part; then I shall understand fully, even as I have been fully understood.
>
> —Corinthians I

Business leaders Elias Colbert and Everett Chamberlin agreed with novelist Roe, author of *The Great Conflagration,* that the Chicago Fire would bring "good out of evil" by "scorching out the Aristocracy."[1] The journalistic as well as public reaction to fires and disasters during the Gilded Age amounted to looking through a glass dimly, hoping to see clearly. Reporters peered into that dark mirror while covering events, especially those involving the rich. This chapter compares how journalists and the popular bards commented on the wealthy.

The rich simultaneously embodied and contradicted clichés about success. Some, including Carnegie and Barnum, had earned their fortunes through diligence and luck, much like Alger heroes. Other millionaires, including the Vanderbilts and the Astors, had inherited their money. The prevalent belief in prosperity as a reward for gumption often distorted journalists' perceptions. Merle Curti concluded, "In the post–Civil War decades, the idea of success through self-effort as a possibility for everyone became vastly more popular and widespread than ever before."[2]

Historian Lee Soltow's analysis of census records indicates that in 1850 about a quarter of the white men in the United States owned 92 percent of the real estate in the country. However, he concludes that from 1850 on and probably earlier a gulf separated the rich cadre from the poor multitude. Nevertheless, the number of wealthy families increased dramatically during the Gilded Age. By January 1891, "half of the national wealth [was owned] by 40,000 families and . . . three-fourths of it [was] in the possession of 250,000 families," or less than 10 percent of the population. Reporters, sociologists, and popular bards speculated about the impact of wealth upon individuals and about the consequences of tolerating an elite of millionaires capable of controlling the political and social arenas. The success paradigm illustrated how money corrupted people, just as it eroded democracy by generating a working class in the European sense of the term.[3]

A Social Gospel advocate, the Reverend Washington Gladden, warned that financial inequity spawned slums and would cause a revolution unless the chasm between the rich and poor disappeared.[4] Predicting that "the billionaire will bring an army of paupers in his train," one thinker called for tax laws to balance the distribution of resources skewed by "the evolution of such enormous fortunes, absolutely inconceivable 40 years ago as an American possibility."[5] However, many poor families enjoyed improvements in their standard of living and modest occupational advancements. They considered themselves members of the middle class and hoped that their children would rise socially and economically.

The aristocracy in the United States experienced an uncomfortable expansion as the newly wealthy demanded social recognition. Suddenly, the old bastions of propriety found themselves forced to socialize with vulgar upstarts, who, in Alger fashion, had turned wheat, pulp, barbed wire, or some other common thing into gold. Newspapers described in detail the parties, weddings, and escapades of both groups and boosted circulation by covering squabbles among them.

In addition to columns listing the names of those who had risen to the top, dailies around the country published articles about the richest available women, according to George Juergens, the author of *Joseph Pulitzer and the New York World.*[6] The interest in high society permeated the papers, regardless of their size or location. Even the *Alexandria (Louisiana) Town Talk* ran items about wealthy women in nearly every issue. On 1 July 1883, its editor noted that the queens of society at the Grand Prix had "pleased the eye immensely" in their reversible silk dresses adorned with fruit and flowers. One English lady in blue satin stole the show: "On the front of the dress is embroidered in rainbow jets an enormous cat, and a cat in smaller proportions adorns the parasol."[7] The sumptuous clothes bespoke a make-believe world where, in contrast to events in reality, stories ended happily.

Some news as well as fiction gave even those believers just barely earning subsistence wages in tenement industries, in sweatshops, in factories, or on farms the most potent weapon imaginable against hard times—magic. Of course, this sword worked only in spiritual territory. But that was enough. Formulas persist because they provide reassurance in a risky world. Juergens and other scholars miss the point when they complain that Alger repeats the same plot over and over.

Alger believed in the archetype and realized that the formula had to be repeated exactly; otherwise, the myth lost its potency. Cawelti suggests that readers enjoyed predicting what would happen next. Repetition enabled people to recognize literary conventions. Even William Dean Howells and Jack London invoked traditional motifs and symbols. Joseph Campbell explains why the myths embedded in those Gilded Age serials are crucial to all generations, including our own: "People say that we're all seeking meaning for life; I don't think that's what we're really seeking. I think that what we're seeking is an experience of being alive, so that our life experiences on the purely physical plane will resonate within our own innermost being and reality, so that we actually feel the rapture of being alive. That's what it's all finally about, and that's what these clues help us to find within ourselves."[8]

Reporters and fiction writers searched for clues to determine what particular life experiences meant. News items, as well as the serials and poems published in many newspapers, frequently retold the sacred success story. For example, on 2 April 1875, the *Austin (Nev.) Reese River Reveille* saluted the Hoffman Brothers, proprietors of a dry goods store, who had "started on a small scale" and sold their goods for reasonable prices, thereby earning fair profits. The editor noted: "They are not hoggish and don't care to get rich suddenly. They prefer to expand their business gradually, so as to rest on a sure foundation; but they will not object to owning a three-story brick house chock full of goods, in a year or two."[9]

Fiction was expected to lionize this myth, which might be titled "The Hare and the Tortoise Do Wall Street." Journalists, especially by the end of the era, strove to make the news—including items about society figures—factual. Particularly in the early decades of the Gilded Age, editors devoted many columns to real incidents that demonstrated the power of the rags-to-riches archetype. These examples suggest the broad line of thought but do not constitute a random sample. The selected items reflect general patterns observed by other scholars also.

In fact, in *Sensational Designs,* Jane Tompkins notes that diaries, letters, success tracts, advice books, and other imaginative works resembled fiction: "These forms of non-fictional discourse, when set side by side with contemporary fiction, can be seen to construct the real world in the image of a set of ideals and beliefs in exactly the same way that novels and stories do. So much so that in certain instances, unless one already knows which is fiction and which is fact, it is impossible to tell the difference."[10] Tompkins expands the literary canon to encompass these non-fiction creations as well as popular pieces and domestic novels by women. All these forums for public conversation, plus newspapers and magazines, questioned the sudden emergence of an aristocracy determined by wealth.

Juergens explains that public opinion about the extremely wealthy ran the gamut from admiration to castigation. This divergence cut across classes so greatly that Carnegie wrote *The Gospel of Wealth* to instruct millionaires in how to serve the poor without denying the latter the bracing stimulus of poverty. Carnegie's triumph over adversity reinforced the public's belief that all things were possible in the land full of self-made men and women. Pulitzer was a self-made publisher, but he questioned Carnegie's assumption that the wealthy would act wisely on behalf of the destitute. "The newspaper, like the people who read it, did not know whether to admire those newly emerged eminences or to oppose and condemn them."[11]

The cult of success might be traced to *Poor Richard's Almanac* or *McGuffey's Readers*, but it gained its greatest strength between 1870 and 1910. During that period, William Makepiece Thayer, Orison Swett Marden, and other inspirational authors wrote self-help tracts and biographies of cultural heroes worth emulating.[12] The titles of their publications reflect the optimistic expectations of those who codified the success archetype and those who willed that sacred prototype into actuality. In two works, *Pushing to the Front, or Success Under Difficulties, a Book of Inspiration and Encouragement to All Who Are Struggling for Self-Elevation Along Paths of Knowledge and Duty,* and *The Secret of Achievement: A Book Designed to Teach the Highest Achievement Is That Which Results in Noble Manhood and Womanhood,* Marden predicted prosperity for those who persevered while fulfilling their responsibilities. In texts and biographies for young people, he focused on exemplars like Abraham Lincoln and Florence Nightingale, who had transformed hardship into hard cash. His upbeat advice circulated across the nation for nearly half a century in *Aim High: Hints and Help for Young Men; Women Who Win, or Making Things Happen; Onward to Fame and Fortune, or Climbing Life's Ladder;* and numerous collections of accolades to successful citizens.

By 1900, besides *Success,* a monthly magazine, readers were buying *Successful American, Success: An Illustrated Magazine for the People,* and *Eternal Progress.* Small-town newspapers espoused the doctrine of success. For instance, on 16 January 1896, John M. Vrooman, editor of the *Lewiston (Montana) Fergus County Argus* urged his readers to "Keep Everlastingly at It": "The line between success and failure is so fine that we scarcely know when we pass it—so fine that we are often on the line and do not know it. . . . A little more persistence, a little more effort, and what seemed hopeless failure may turn to glorious success. There is no failure except in no longer trying. There is no defeat except from within, no really insurmountable barrier save our own inherent weakness of purpose."[13] Of course, those lucky enough to be born penniless automatically had incentives for "keeping everlastingly at it."

One striking example of a hero too good to rise to financial glory appeared in the *Wenatchee (Washington) Advance* on 19 January 1895, in the form of a tribute to the editor, who was retiring after spending his life boosting newspapers in the West. L. E. Kellogg "stuck to the printers trade and lost opportunities," not because he lacked drive or intelligence, but because he was "lacking in business qualifications—that is, the knack of trading and bartering and scheming and circumventing and gouging."[14] Kellogg did not advance in the commercial world. However, in true Alger fashion, he attained middle-class respectability. His successor at the paper concluded: "Our acquaintance with Mr. Kellogg has continued since '83. We have always found him an industrious, conscientious, well-meaning newspaper man, laboring faithfully for the communities in which he lived, aiding individuals and making a good local paper. Personally, we found him a generous, self-sacrificing, warm-hearted gentleman, a good citizen and a true friend."[15] Kellogg had earned the respect of his neighbors, a feat that eluded many millionaires.

Scoffing at the pretensions of the wealthy, tiny items illuminated the love-hate relationship between the rich and the poor. For example, on 27 June 1895, the *Fergus County Argus* recycled a quip from the *Chicago Tribune* about a careless young man who went to bed without removing his gloves after returning from his dinner club. At about 3 A.M., he woke his wife, screaming, "Lobelia, Lobelia! I believe on my soul I am paralyzed! There isn't a bit of feeling in my hands!"[16] The editor of the *Town Talk* reminded his readers just how common even the mightiest ultimately become: "Instances have been observed of nails growing on the stumps of amputated fingers, and when the coffin containing the corpse of the great Napoleon was opened long after his death at St. Helena, his toenails had grown clear through his boots, and his hair stuck through the chinks of the coffin."[17]

In some stories about the wayward rich, poor judgment proved deadly. On 13 April 1893, the *New York Daily Tribune* reported that a rich man had died in a quarrel with a hack driver in Hickman, Kentucky, over a quarter. The one-paragraph, front-page story explained that the white hack driver was "possessed of a considerable fortune and an ungovernable temper."[18]

On 3 January 1896, the *Argus* depicted fatal foolishness.[19] In this tale of shipwrecked love, a Parisian, who had been rejected by "the object of his affection" because illness had caused him to go bald, bought an elaborate, curly wig. The cruel maiden ridiculed him at a restaurant. She tossed his toupee to a companion and slapped him when he tried to retrieve it. She and her high-society friends laughed until he stabbed her in the throat, ending the jolly dinner party. The bald paramour went to jail, and the druggist who treated the cold-hearted siren predicted she would die.

Such newspaper stories probably were based on real incidents. However, the retelling of the story always emphasized the details most pertinent to the cultural contexts of the readers. The names often dropped out entirely. What mattered was what happened to the fool who wasted money and time trying to please a haughty belle. The French incident proved the wisdom of the advice N. P. Willis had passed on to the lovelorn on 10 October 1895: "The plainest features become handsome unawares when associated only with kind feelings, and the loveliest face disagreeable when linked with ill humor or caprice. People should remember this when they are selecting a face which they are to see every morning across the breakfast table for the remainder of their lives."[20]

Numerous news stories resembled potboiler plots. Many popular bards as well as reporters pointed out that, while physical beauty faded, integrity endured. Although authors equated beauty with goodness, some, including E. D. E. N. Southworth in *A Beautiful Fiend* (1873), reminded readers that peachy looks did not guarantee angelic behavior. On the other hand, the "fiend's" foil was beautiful and virtuous. General Lew Wallace also created an evil temptress in *Ben-Hur* (1880). Naturally, corrupt fictional beauties lusted after money and prestige.

The paradox of the decadent yet successful wealthy fascinated the writers of cliff-hangers and created conflicts for the *New York World,* according to Juergens. Pulitzer's liberal, pro-labor, pro-reform policies clashed with the paper's minute coverage of the splendid excesses of the aristocracy. However, rather than serving as the battleground for inconsistencies, as Juergens suggests, Pulitzer's editorial page actually grafted the success paradigm onto the news and, in the process, justified old ideals by filtering them through factual reportage.

The *World* foreshadowed the points which Carnegie delineated in *The Gospel of Wealth* and which Edward Eggleston, General Lew Wallace, George Cable, and other popular writers proclaimed. As a result, readers knew that not even the richest person could buy redemption. The emergence of a wealthy upper class prompted the popular bards to experiment with scenarios about individuals who accrue goods and still remain spiritual. Thus, by the end of the nineteenth century, the success archetype gradually had expanded to encompass guidelines for making the philanthropic expenditure of capital an acceptable route to salvation. Greed, shiftlessness, and debauchery, not prosperity, condemned irresponsible millionaires.

The perfidy of sons whose rich, parasitic parents lavished luxuries upon them and, in so doing, extinguished any flame of ambition that hard work might have sparked, was a common theme in the formula stories. Many rich sons became "dudes," men excessively concerned about their clothes and appearance. Preachers and editors criticized the vanity and wastefulness of the wealthy who indulged their children. Sudden inheritance ruined heirs. On 31 December 1885, a front-page story in *The Muncie (Indiana) Daily News* was titled "Unable to Stand Good Fortune": "Herrick Williams, a young man moving in respectable circles here [Auburn, New York], was arrested for wife beating. A short time ago by the death of his father, he fell heir to $50,000. This sudden acquisition seemed to turn his brain, and he began to drink heavily. Lately he has been more intoxicated than usual, and in a quarrel with his wife he pummeled her in a brutal fashion. Her face is much disfigured. Williams's friends refused to bail him out."[21]

"Exaggerated unselfishness of their parents" spoiled the character of children by denying them the satisfaction of ministering to others.[22] Pulitzer never tired of lambasting Commodore Cornelius Vanderbilt and his "boorish" son, William Henry. One editorial, especially, emphasized how the sins of the father had been visited upon the son: "What respect is due to a man who counts his wealth by the hundred million and spends it wholly for the gratification of his own whims and pleasures? . . . Who in the coarse and vulgar language of a horse jockey extols his son, not for his culture, not for his virtues, not for his industry, not for his patriotism or public spirit, but for his sharpness in Wall Street gambling and because 'he never squeals.'"[23]

This editorial sounds like a passage from *In His Steps* (1897) or *Looking Backward* (1888). Fiction writers contrasted wicked, selfish, rich parents, whose cupidity ruins their children with wholesome, struggling families, whose sons and daughters rise above poverty mostly because suffering has taught them how to live. A variation on this theme of the heartless father appeared on 9 February 1895, in the *Wenatchee (Washington) Advance's* account of Daisy Gardner's $10,000 breach-of-promise suit against George Stone. His father imprisoned him in a walk-in vault in Chicago to prevent him from marrying the virtuous but penniless telegraph operator.[24] The solitude convinced the young man not to marry Daisy.

In popular plots, the pampered, thoughtless rich always sneer at the destitute. The younger Vanderbilt was no exception. When asked to defend railroad policies in Michigan City in 1882, he retorted, "Let the public be damned!"[25] Pulitzer pounced on the remark, noting that "the words are as appropriate to him as the bristles on a hog. All the dollars in the world cannot remove innate vulgarity. They can only make it more offensive by coating it over with insolence and swagger."[26]

The elder Vanderbilt had not been referring to pigs when he said his son did not squeal. He meant that, like a pedigreed hunting dog, his son could take punishment without yelping. Neither reference was very flattering. However, the comparison of the rich boy to a dog might have amused some who had read Margaret Deland's *John Ward, Preacher*. The indolent, rude millionaire, whose father had made his fortune in buttons, behaved like a cur toward a pure maiden and was soundly cuffed about the ears by a masterful young attorney who worked and, therefore, led a saintly life.

Not all lazy fathers were millionaires. In books, diligent fathers died young. In the real world, newspapers ran anecdotes about gold-bricking papas. The *Town Talk* quoted "old Mrs. Jones," who recalled that her first husband was so lazy he refused to shovel a path to the front gate. Instead, "he . . . [lay] on the lounge and [pinched] the baby's ears with nippers until the neighbors came rushing in to see what was the matter, and thus tread down the snow."[27] Such editorial hyperbole contrasted with the child abuse Alger and Eleanor Hodgson Porter documented in plots featuring street children who worked eighteen hours a day to avoid being beaten.

Frequently, fictional rich fathers, who broke their children's spirits instead of their bodies, lost their souls along with their fortunes speculating. The Reverend Washington Gladden said that honest buying and selling provided a vital service. Fearing that the gambling mania might destroy the nation, the preacher denounced speculation: "The poor man's loaf grows small as the gambler's gains increase. Every cent made by this class of men is taken from the industrial classes with no compensation."[28]

These "parasites of commerce" were just as guilty as if they had gone "about picking [their] neighbors' pockets or setting their harvest fields on fire."[29] The *Town Talk* agreed, joking that, while "Jay Gould is worth $600,000,000, we are worth, let's see—five, ten, fifteen—we are worth only $000,000,015."[30] Gladden lamented the lack of public concern and the tendency of newspapers to "deal gingerly" with speculators, the enemies of society. The *New York World* did not "deal gingerly" with speculators. In fact, Pulitzer's editorials about gambling on Wall Street decried the system of piracy that allowed an elite to amass tremendous wealth. He warned: "Do not dream of becoming a Money King as soon as you secure a gilt gingerbread crown and brass scepter."[31] It is no wonder many writers of formula stories made their villains speculators.

Besides denouncing speculators, the plots focused on the aristocratic pretensions of the wealthy. For example, in *Barriers Burned Away* (1872), Christine fills her room with naked statues and other European masterpieces reflecting her paganism. She fancies herself a German princess and expects to retire to a castle on the Rhine with her father once they sell enough art in America to finance the move. Pulitzer rebuked as unpatriotic the rich who bought European treasures but did not support American artists. He ridiculed them for putting coats-of-arms on their coaches and dressing like the English or French.

On 17 March 1883, the editor of the *Town Talk* declared that foreign standards had eroded national values. He condemned the "dude," a variety of masher. Unlike mashers, however, dudes exuded phoniness, were fascinated by Continental tomfoolery, and connived to join high society: "The dude is from 19 to 28 years of age, wears trousers of extreme tightness, is hollow-chested, effeminate in his ways, apes the English and distinguishes himself among his fellow men as a lover of actresses. The badge of his office is the paper cigarette, and his bell-crown English opera hat is his chiefest joy."[32]

Kasson makes the same observations about "dandies," who delighted in embarrassing innocent maidens by leering at them at the opera. Indeed, the dandies formed packs and trained their lorgnettes on their prey. "To stare at a woman in such a way was to violate her modesty and assault her honor, even to group her with the prostitutes and painted women of the city."[33] The dandies and dudes were exaggerated manifestations of Americans imitating Europeans.

Many plots mentioned the evil influence of the Old World upon the new Republic. The Angel in Gene Stratton-Porter's romance *Freckles* (1904) fretted that the relatives of the man she loved would be flawed spiritually because they were Irish nobles. Most authors included a scene or an aside suggesting that true nobility arose from character, not birth. The marriages most likely to succeed united Americans, who had worked their way up the social ladder, unencumbered by aristocratic ties or pretentious claims. *The Muncie (Indiana) Daily News* quoted a minister who was "preaching without gloves on: God won't keep a young girl pious long who has her waist encircled seven times a week by the arms of a spider-legged dude."[34]

Nevertheless, the editor of the *Fergus County Argus* reminded readers in Lewiston, Montana, of the "American Fondness for Titles," which made "Military Designations as Plent[iful] as Blackberries: Why, hang it, we dote on titles. Just see how many of the rich girls go gunning for titles abroad and are willing to accept broken down specimens of humanity for husbands simply because they call themselves dukes or marquises or counts or what not."[35] Pulitzer renounced those *nouveau riches* individuals who bought prestige for their children by arranging marriages with bluebloods who could offer prestige but no cash. Just as writers of formula stories suggested that marrying for gold instead of love led to disaster, Pulitzer predicted: "A girl who sells herself or allows herself to be sold for a title without love or affection sacrifices the best attributes of womanhood. What has she a right to expect except a cold, calculating life, full of frivolity or of abuse?"[36] Pulitzer praised Vanderbilt for not putting on aristocratic airs. Vanderbilt kept his coat-of-arms small, his wife did not carry a poodle, and his children all married "plain Americans."[37] The publisher preached from the editorial columns the sanctity of love based on character rather than on bank balances.

In fact, one very lengthy feature about Caroline Astor's marriage to Orme Wilson, a regular guy who had nothing to give her but love, resembled a Cinderfella story. Many readers devoured variations of this plot in romances. Would money corrupt him? Would he become a whiskey-guzzling billiard addict with a red nose and gout in his toes? In the formula tales, Wilson would have been lucky had no worse fate awaited him!

In addition to commenting on the evils of ill-gotten money and vanity, newspaper stories and popular fiction also considered changes in lifestyle women experienced during the Gilded Age. Many took jobs in the city. The bicycle freed them from cumbersome garments, and the typewriter created new employment options. Pulitzer's lists of wealthy women in his feature pages proved everyone could be royal; obviously, the Alger archetype fascinated readers. Of course, headlines told the familiar story of those who had pulled themselves up by their own bootstraps: "The Legal Fraternity of New York—Men Who Have Worked Up from the Ranks," "Go-a-Headative Men," "Men of Mark and Push," "Men Who Grasp at Fortune as She Flies."[38]

A decade before Edward Bok, the editor of the *Ladies Home Journal,* discovered the popularity of photographic spreads featuring the mansions of the wealthy, the *New York World* took its readers inside the homes of the famous. While few could afford to emulate the rich, many enjoyed dreaming about living in a palace. These articles appealed to people in the same way that fairy tales opened the portals of the imagination. "The very inaccessibility of their style made them more than ever like figures out of a familiar and well-loved fairy tale."[39]

The homes and their rich owners, the enterprising go-getters who had scrambled to the top, embodied success. Technology offered opportunities, but each invention increased the risks of daily living. Money could not buy immunity from disease or disaster. People as well as nature caused calamities. Acts of God smote everyone, rich and poor alike. Religion supplied the narrative closure that machines could not provide. The success paradigm bridged the gap between material facts and spiritual satisfaction. Roe, Sheldon, and kindred bards felt called to bring the Kingdom of God to earth via fantasy. Sheldon urged writers to push humanity "along the track of millennial progress" by keeping fiction "freed from the stain of mercenary motives."[40]

Facts could not replace narration because, while science explained *how* lightning and other phenomena occurred, it could not explain *why*. Why did one survivor of a steamboat explosion float to safety on a log while hundreds of passengers around her drowned? Why did fires skip over sinners but immolate the pious? Why did lightning strike one child rather than another?

Perhaps the most essential queries science could not answer were: What is success? Is money without public esteem enough? Can anyone live on respect without remuneration? What, indeed, determined who succeeded and who failed? Did Providence or blind luck decide who prospered? What made one bobbin boy stand out from the rest?

Since science could not answer such inquiries with logic, the public bards sought solutions in the heart and in the imagination. The formula stories and news reports arose within a cultural context in which the Alger archetype rendered reality intelligible and made bearable losses caused by human carelessness or natural disasters. The success archetype proposed spiritual solutions for impenetrable mysteries. The formula perpetuated the paradigm and changed when war shattered the world in the second decade of the twentieth century. Until that international crisis, luck-and-pluck myths attached meaning to earthly experiences and provided insights into spiritual obligations. This inquiry still demands attention. Can the material success offered by the secular world provide the inner peace formerly attained through religion? Does hell still crackle just in the afterlife, or have thing-worshipers created it here on earth?

The Inevitability of Sinking

Success in the Nineties

"People have come here not for wealth but for a better 'way of life.' America blurred the boundary between the material and the spiritual." So Daniel J. Boorstin, a Pulitzer Prize winning historian, teacher, and best-selling author of books about the American experience asserted in *Parade Magazine* in 1994.[1] His essay, echoing the success archetype that popular bards have woven into formula tales for centuries, views religion, language, law, and wealth as the bricks of consensus. Just as the rags-to-riches paradigm specifies, luck (or, as Boorstin puts it, "the happy accidents of history") made this country unique. Moreover, Boorstin credits the passion for improving everybody's standard of living with thwarting avarice.

In the "Land of the Unexpected," citizens simultaneously developed their ideals and exploited geographical opportunities.[2] Boorstin praises the immigrants and pioneers for evolving a boisterous way of life and a buoyant outlook that, to this day, shape American values. The search for meaning in life always has entailed balancing spiritual and material needs. Yet, in that same issue of *Parade*, Erica Jong, author of the novel, *Fear of Flying*, points out that turning fifty upsets many Americans, especially women, because of the social equation of happiness with youth and physical beauty. The merry-go-round of exercise, diet, and appearance belies the discontent seething below the wrinkle-free surface. "As human beings, we long for some ritual that tells us we are part of a tribe, part of a species, part of a generation. . . . What about our need—women and men—to prepare for death in a culture that often mocks spirituality?"[3]

Jong's concerns reflect a cardinal difference between the Gilded Age (1870–1910) and the 1990s. A century ago, the artisans of popular culture respected the spiritual dimensions of existence. Today, movies like *Pretty Woman* pervert the Cinderella archetype to make prostitution a route to respectability. On the other hand, *Curly Sue, Forrest Gump,* and similar films tell stories about poor individuals who, through diligence, overcome obstacles and, thus, merit the assistance of a benefactor before rising into the middle class. These characters serve something larger than self.

Indeed, John-Boy, a character on *The Waltons*, shows cable viewers that serving family, God, and community can lead to felicity.[4] The television series traces a lad's rise from barefooted schoolboy to newspaper owner and editor and then to middle-class respectability as an evening news anchor in New York City. Each episode illustrates the key to "Getting the Most Out of Life"—remembering that "tough-minded optimists approach problems with a can-do philosophy and emerge stronger from tragedies."[5] On Walton's Mountain the values preserved in the success archetype—diligence, perseverance, thrift, abstemiousness, honesty, loyalty, and, of course, family love—prevail as the epitome of earthly treasure.

In fact, today the success archetype lives even in the Mario Brothers video games, in which players strive to overcome incredible odds and vanquish forces of evil; they rise slowly, level by level, until winning the ultimate title. Some sequences repeat the princess-in-trouble motif while others recast the action in exotic locales. The game reduces to bleeps and splashes of color the Alger archetype that distinguishes the United States from all other nations.

The proliferation of media has created new channels for the traditional paradigm, but romance novels still repeat the essential sequence of events through details chosen to mirror present exigencies. For example, in the early 1990s, Yarrow Press reissued several novels written by Dawn Powell during the 1940s. In *A Time To Be Born*, the heroine, Amanda Keeler, who grew up on the wrong side of the tracks, flees to the city, where she entices a married man away from his wife and convinces him to promote her writing career. Her machinations succeed so completely that she attains international fame. Another character in the story, Vicky Haven, rises like Cinderella with Amanda as her fairy godmother.

Danielle Steel's novel, *Star*, like its long-forgotten cliff-hanger predecessors, appeared in several popular culture channels. *Good Housekeeping* magazine praised the writer for "always being on the best-seller list" and featured her new "winner" in thirteen pages with eight illustrations as the "Novel of the Month."[6] In autumn of 1993, NBC presented the "fatuous modern fairy tale." The reviewer for *People* magazine gave "this perfectly bland, egregiously predictable fable of virtue rewarded" a grade of D+.[7] However, many viewers relished escaping into the fantasy kingdom of stock characters and absolute consequences preserved in romances like *Star*. In *Sensational Designs*, Jane Tompkins explains that yesterday's readers of sentimental tales sought remedies for maladies of the soul that manifested themselves in ugly physical realities—wife abuse, slum epidemics, vices.[8]

The heroine of *Star*, Crystal Wyatt, flees when her neighbors falsely and viciously blame her for her brother's death. The naïve maiden's passionate affair with Spencer Hill, a man twice her age, nearly destroys them both. She dazzles Hollywood with her beauty and captivates audiences with her singing. Alas, Spencer has married out of concern for the security of his career, rather than for true love (the worst sin a character can commit in the tear-stained realm of romance). As a result, the heartbroken Crystal falls under the spell of an evil man. After being charged with murdering the cad, she calls Spencer, an attorney, to defend her. He proves her innocent but cannot save her career. She returns to her hometown pregnant and in disgrace. Ultimately, Crystal and righteousness prevail: she wins an Academy Award, and Spencer—relieved to be free of the corrosive career that has brought him only pain and estrangement from Crystal—divorces his indifferent wife. "Time, however, heals all wounds, and justice will triumph," says a book review.[9] This observation sounds like the asides popular bards inserted in their plots a century ago.

As romances like *Star* and *A Time To Be Born* continue to sell briskly, so do success tracts. Indeed, in 1993 Bianca Leonardo edited a paperback edition of the Reverend Russell Conwell's *Acres of Diamonds*. Advertisements claimed the minister had delivered the lecture six thousand times, earning more than $4 million, the equivalent of $145 million today. Moreover, "Conwell lived a SELFLESS LIFE and died 'in harness' at age 82. He lived many lives in one because he literally worked 16 hours a day, seven days a week. HE BELIEVED THAT EACH OF US IS PLACED HERE ON EARTH FOR ONE MAIN PURPOSE—TO HELP OTHERS. . . . The truths and principles in this book are as valid today as when the great humanitarian lived. . . . *Acres of Diamonds* is a spiritual book."[10]

Books in Print (1993–94) lists 1,006 self-help volumes. All of them promise to reveal the secrets of success. Many urge novices to balance financial and spiritual goals. For instance, in *Going Nowhere Fast: Step off Life's Treadmills and Find Peace of Mind*, Melvyn Kinder decries "the treadmill mentality . . . that occurs when people seek happiness through outward success and achievements instead of within themselves."[11] Kinder's insight echoes the moral of scores of nineteenth-century mysteries, dime novels, romances, idea novels, horse operas, and children's serials built around the success prototype.

Steamy romances of the 1990s, nostalgic motion pictures, family-oriented reruns, video games, and similar popular culture forums often convey the age-old success archetype. That seminal model remains implanted in our subconscious, despite efforts to deny the efficacy of faith in unquantifiable things. Although skeptics may dismiss "Cinderella" as trivial, even the most jaded, secularly-oriented individual still enjoys magic. Science and technology often supply miracles acceptable to those who must see blueprints to believe in the power of the mind and the soul. Despite an official view that the empirical world is the only form of reality, however, the longing for marvels finds expression in the safe havens of whimsy, including formula tales, advertising, cartoons, and movies. Sometimes nicknames and slogans remind people of the ancient mysteries.

In fact, until recently, "Magic" wore tennis shoes and held court in soft drink commercials. Then Magic retired. His name and face, amid the tattooing of basketballs, had become commonplaces of the society. Nevertheless, once Magic stopped playing ball, he dropped out of circulation, and the corporations hired new athletic *wunderkinder* to sell their wares. The styrofoam heroes of the late twentieth century no longer command respect for intellectual contributions, political leadership, raw courage, or moral fiber. Instead, public relations firms and advertising agencies package the heroes of the nineties much as they market macaroni or bug spray. Athletes whose skills merit praise fall victim to this cash-and-carry system of adulation. Through product endorsements and clever management, a few players rise to Olympian heights as exemplars, illogically expected to be perfect.

Although athletes provide positive role models for youths, the excessive focus on them as the culture's vanguard reflects a false equation of money and image with heroism. A fixation on power and prestige has led to the debunking of historical heroes, under the mistaken assumption that the discrepancy between details about the private lives of public figures and the exaggerated legends concerning them exposes intellectual dishonesty. However, legends—as a form of folklore—disregard historical accuracy to magnify some vital characteristic. Legends embroider an incident or develop a plot around a single noble trait and, simultaneously, remind listeners that the Great Ones lived common lives made extraordinary by their uncommon virtue.

In the name of historical fact-finding, debunking the legends of such figures as George Washington, Thomas Jefferson, Abraham Lincoln, Martin Luther King, Jr., Harriet Tubman, Eleanor Roosevelt, and Helen Keller has robbed several generations of Americans of their ethical ties to past generations. Legends exist to arrest attention. Thus they are to be remembered not as historical fact, but rather as engaging examples of admirable behavior. Heroes embody a community's highest aspirations spiritually and morally. Over time, legends elevate the hero from the mundane earthly plane to the lofty sphere of dreams and possibilities.

In contrast, role models, including athletes and celebrities, demonstrate how to achieve goals in the here-and-now. Some biographies become classics, but many, especially when published as short magazine or newspaper articles, appeal mostly to contemporary readers. Discovering heroes helps to ground an individual in a specific heritage and stimulates a narrative sense of self. Retelling heroic adventures keeps the American Dream of rising through pluck and luck alive. As greed spreads like a deadly virus through the body politic, the mandate to pursue the spiritual dimensions of success lapses, leaving behind rampant self-interest. Heroes lose prestige. Moreover, the hallmark Yankee expectation that one will do better than one's predecessors becomes unrealistic.

De Tocqueville observed in 1830 that even citizens carving homes out of the wilderness were obsessed by the fear of sinking—of failing to earn enough money to buy the trappings associated with rising in the world.[12] This materialism contrasted with the emphasis upon honor in the early national era—a time when public service and dedication to community well-being were the measure of personal character. The rise of individualism and the triumph of Jacksonian democracy exacerbated the tension between private goals and public responsibilities. The Civil War and the technological implosion of the Gilded Age made people feel that the self was pitted against a world dominated by strangers rather than existing in harmony with neighbors or kin. The popular bards defanged strangers, creating a sanctuary within which timeless values prevailed, despite the inequities created in the wake of progress. In *The American Myth of Success*, social historian Richard Weiss concludes that Christians, including Gene Stratton-Porter, the author of *Freckles*, ambivalently resolved the conflict between the expectation that mobility would stimulate prosperity and the need for stability within families as well as communities.[13] To retain altruism while praising fair profit, writers adapted the sacred success archetype to contemporary conditions, thus keeping it relevant.

By 1900, with generous, wealthy social leaders highly visible, it had become hard for many American still to believe in the dream of attaining middle-class respectability and hence becoming superior to the scandalous rich. Andrew Carnegie espoused his "gospel of wealth" to justify the presence of a cadre who comprised less than 10 percent of the population but controlled nearly 90 percent of the nation's resources.[14] Conwell and a legion of highly esteemed personages embraced the steel mogul's scheme. Conwell's question—"Who would want to be poor, anyhow?"—powerfully captured the belief that, in America, only the lazy and the shiftless were indigent.[15]

Gospel of Wealth instructed the rich to fund ventures designed to teach the downtrodden to help themselves. Muckrakers pointed out the cruelty and the hypocrisy of some of these so-called benefactors, who had prospered through shady business practices. Modern authors continue to protest hollow gifts. In "About Ed Ricketts," John Steinbeck denounces philanthropy as "a kind of frightened restitution . . . a shoddy virtue" that massaged the consciences of the perpetrators of economic injustice. "One only has to remember some of our wolfish financiers who spend two-thirds of their lives clawing fortunes out of the guts of society and the latter third pushing it back."[16]

In the 1990s, financial sharks who served prison sentences became heroes to a public committed to making money at any cost. Indeed, according to the *New York Times*, flocks of adoring students surrounded Michael Milken in the halls at the University of California at Los Angeles when he lectured there after being imprisoned twenty-two months for securities fraud. Some students resented his presence, but many considered Milken a great man, a visionary who—like Galileo—was persecuted for his revolutionary ideas. He hired a public relations firm to "package" him as a misunderstood genius and not a creative thief.[17] Although he paid more than a billion dollars in fines, the deposed Junk Bond King is still rich and recently established an educational television network to broadcast his lectures directly to universities.

Milken did not repent. Instead, he blamed "the system" for being too stodgy to appreciate his particular talents. Moreover, he rose from convict to guru by mixing charisma with the promises of profit that always appeal to the ambitious. His popularity in the classroom as a role model underscores the inevitability, for those who follow in his footsteps, of sinking. Ann Landers periodically publishes a list of would-be greenback tigers who discovered, too late, that "money and power [do not] open a magic door to happiness."[18] Three of the eight Landers mentions committed suicide, two died destitute, two went to jail, and one died in a sanitarium.

Like the go-getters Landers describes, some executives work hard and cut corners to reap profits, at tremendous cost to their personal lives. "Including his own case among those cited, psychologist [Melvyn]

Kinder . . . demonstrated how outwardly enviable lives are achieved through enormous effort and often at the expense of personal relationships and other kinds of growth and fulfillment."[19] The success paradigm promises rewards for diligence but recommends aiming for middle-class respectability; acquiring too much capital blunts the spirit and diminishes sensitivity toward others.

Corporate insensitivity assumes many forms. For example, the goal of making as much money as possible has replaced the old-fashioned principle of striving to build a dedicated workforce that produces high-quality products. Thousands of employees, including white-collar workers, are displaced when factories are closed to balance ledgers.[20] The need for corporations to survive as Wall Street entities has led to the demise of many of their local branches. Workers left unemployed by a sudden romping of bears and bulls must retrain for jobs that usually will not allow them to maintain their prior standard of living. Middle-aged employees who have advanced through the factory from unskilled laborer to expert suffer most. They must accept the inevitability of sinking. According to *Business Week*, when a plant making pain killers closed in Elkhart, eight hundred workers endured "A Living Hell in Indiana."[21] Some sent out a hundred resumes but still did not secure employment. Others lived on credit cards. The closing of General Motors plants also put thousands of hard-working Americans in unemployment lines. Unfortunately, when making money replaces striving to earn a fair profit by providing quality services that generate jobs, those who do not play high-finance Russian roulette feel the consequences.

The inevitability of sinking frees people from the rut of materialism only so long as enough opportunity exists for workers to support themselves. The obsession with getting rich quickly prods the schemers of the 1990s into investing in mail-order scams, dialing 900 numbers, asking psychics for advice, buying lottery tickets, gambling heavily at casinos, or competing on television game shows. Buying things to affirm success saps resources and generates stress: "Americans apparently feel poorer now than they did thirty years ago when real incomes were substantially lower than their present levels."[22]

For the Rominger family, whose members reside in the hills along the coastal range eighty miles north of San Francisco, success means doing their chores each morning. Four generations of Romingers have tilled the soil. Like his father and his grandfather before him, Rick Rominger has never wanted anything beyond the chance to grow crops. "In the context of lives so integrated, the words *family* and *home* recover some of the meaning lost in the hypermobile twentieth century. . . . Success of the family is itself the Romingers' ambition. 'Our goal in life is not to go out and make a lot of money, to see how big a house or fancy a car we can have,' says Rick. 'It's just to be farmers, to work and to be with our family.'"[23]

The Romingers feel a sense of purpose and a shared fate. Money cannot buy the satisfaction they feel. The inevitability of sinking may free some Americans from the fear of losing face because in the 1990s many—if not most—Americans will fall instead of rise financially before reaching retirement age. The bitter loss of opportunity experienced by thousands during the recent recession has created doubt about the meaning of success. The formula for success promises rewards for pluck and luck as long as the individual takes advantage of chances and earns the respect of a benefactor. Rising to the middle class requires perseverance and integrity.

Today, many start out in the middle class and then keep pushing to rise in the system. The stress of evaluating self-worth in terms of vocation or annual salary leads to despair and to a sense of sinking rather than rising because no amount of money or power is enough. "So the culture of mass consumption develops around a core of unfulfilled longing, in which advertising promises that the goods we can buy carry with them the states of consciousness we desire and in which the broken promises of each purchase lead to new yearnings."[24] When life degenerates into a race for power and possessions, the winner is always doomed, eventually, to lose to a younger, a stronger, a wealthier contender.

Popular bards always have celebrated the wisdom and serenity that are inherent in aging when people invest their energies in life-giving activities at work, at home, and in the public arena. Perhaps Americans still love Cinderella because she represents the triumph of the soul over earthly burdens. In the 1990s, abuses of the success prototype are forcing citizens to abandon unhealthy goals that are focused on the acquisition of things and the exercise of power. Instead, Americans are cultivating their sense of wonder, implementing their belief in positive thinking, and seeking satisfaction in everything they do—especially in communing with others.

Works Analyzed

Note: A work fitting into more than one category was categorized according to its dominant traits, and none is listed twice.

Children's Serials

L. Frank Baum, *The Wizard of Oz*, 1900
James Otis (James Otis Kaler), *Toby Tyler; Or, Ten Weeks with a Circus*, 1881
James Otis (James Otis Kaler), *Josiah in New York; Or, A Coupon from the Fresh Air Fund*, 1893
Eleanor Hodgman Porter, *Cross Currents: Margaret's Story*, 1907
Eleanor Hodgman Porter, *The Turn of the Tide: The Story of How Margaret Solved Her Problem*, 1908
Alice Caldwell Hegan Rice *Captain June*, 1907
Laura Richards, *Captain January*, 1893

Dime Novels

Horatio Alger, *Phil the Fiddler; Or, The Story of a Street Musician*, 1872
Horatio Alger, *Luke Walton*, 1889
Edward S. Ellis, *Wyoming*, 1888
Burt L. Standish (Gilbert Patten), *Frank Merriwell's School Days*, 1900

Domestic Fantasies

George W. Cable, *John March, Southerner*, 1894
Edward Eggleston, *The Hoosier School-Master*, 1871
Opie Read, *The Jucklins*, 1894

Idea Portraits

Edward Bellamy, *Looking Backward*, 1888
Charles M. Sheldon, *In His Steps*, 1897
Mark Twain and Charles Dudley Warner, *The Gilded Age* (2 vols.), 1873
Elizabeth Stuart Phelps Ward, *Beyond the Gates*, 1883
Elizabeth Stuart Phelps Ward, *The Gates Ajar*, 1868
Elizabeth Stuart Phelps Ward, *The Gates Between*, 1887
Kate Douglas Wiggin, *The Birds' Christmas Carol*, 1887

Mysteries

Nick Carter (John Russell Coryell), *Nick Carter's Mysterious Case; Or, the Road House Tragedy,* 1896

Anna Katharine Green, *The Leavenworth Case,* 1878

Anna Katharine Green, *The Circular Study,* 1900

Harlan Page ("Old Sleuth") Halsey, *Fly-Away Ned,* 1895

Mary Roberts Rinehart, *The Circular Staircase,* 1900

Regional Tales

Alice Caldwell Hegan Rice, *Mrs. Wiggs of the Cabbage Patch,* 1901

Ann Stephens, *Phemie Frost's Experiences,* 1874

Religious Books

Margaret Deland, *John Ward, Preacher,* 1888

E. P. Roe, *Barriers Burned Away,* 1872

Gen. Lew Wallace, *Ben-Hur: A Tale of the Christ,* 1880

Romances, Girls'

Frances Hodgson Burnett, *A Little Princess,* 1888

Eleanor Porter, *Pollyanna,* 1913

Margaret Sidney, *Five Little Peppers and How They Grew,* 1880

Gene Stratton-Porter, *Freckles,* 1904

Kate Douglas Wiggin, *Rebecca of Sunnybrook Farm,* 1903

Kate Douglas Wiggin, *Polly Oliver's Problem,* 1893

Romances, Women's

Amelia Barr, *Jan Vedder's Wife,* 1885

Mary Jane Holmes, *Edith Lyle's Secret,* Late 1870, early 1880

E. D. E. N. Southworth, *The Beautiful Fiend,* 1873

E. D. E. N. Southworth, *Victor's Triumph,* 1875

Success Tracts

P. T. Barnum, *The Art of Money-Getting,* in *Struggles and Triumphs,* 1884

Andrew Carnegie, *Gospel of Wealth,* 1900

Russell Conwell, *Acres of Diamonds,* 1887

Westerns

E. L. Wheeler, *Deadwood Dick on Deck; Or, Calamity Jane, the Heroine of Whoop Up—A Story of Dakota,* 1885

Owen Wister, The Virginian: A Horseman of the Plains, 1902

Notes
Abbreviations

AWW   Linda Mainiero, ed., *American Women Writers: A Critical Reference Guide, from Colonial Times to the Present.* New York: Ungar, 1979.

DAB   *Dictionary of American Biography.* New York: Scribners, 1946–58.

DLB   *Dictionary of Literary Biography.* Detroit: Gale Research, 1978–.

NAW   Edward T. James III, ed., *Notable American Women: A Biographical Dictionary, 1607–1950.* Cambridge, Mass.: Harvard Univ. Press, Belknap Press, 1971.

NCAB   *National Cyclopedia of American Biography.* New York: J. T. White, 1893–.

Introduction

1. Joseph Campbell, *An Open Life: Joseph Campbell in Conversation with Michael Toms* (New York: Larson, 1988), 21.
2. Walter A. Shelburne, *Mythos and Logos in the Thought of Carl Jung: The Theory of the Collective Unconscious in Scientific Perspective* (Albany: State Univ. of New York Press, 1988), 49.
3. Paul Boyer, *When Time Shall Be No More: Prophecy Belief in American Culture* (Cambridge, Mass.: Belknap Press, Harvard Univ., 1992).
3. Carol S. Pearson, Awakening the Heroes Within: Twelve Archetypes to Help Us Find Ourselves and Transform Our World (San Francisco: Harper, 1991), 1.
4. Stewart H. Holbrook, *The Age of the Moguls* (Garden City, N.Y.: Doubleday, 1953), 7.
5. James W. Carey to Paulette Kilmer, 21 Dec. 1991, in Marquette, Mich.
6. Shelburne, *Mythos and Logos,* 51.
7. Ibid., 33.
8. "The Gospel According to St. Matthew and the Gospel According to St. Mark," *The Interpreter's Bible: New Testament Articles* (New York: Abingdon, 1951), 7, 483–84.

9. Charles M. Laymon, ed., *The Interpreter's One-Volume Commentary on the Bible: Introduction and Commentary for Each Book of the Bible, Including the Apocrypha* (New York: Abingdon, 1971), 634.
10. Northrop Frye, *The Great Code: The Bible and Literature* (New York: Harcourt Brace Jovanovich, 1982).
11. Shelburne, *Mythos and Logos,* 45.
12. Frye, *Great Code,* 140.

Chapter 1. News and Fiction

1. *Alexandria (La.) Town Talk,* 3 Oct. 1883, 2:3. The notice carries no headline.
2. Henry Nash Smith, *The Virgin Land: The American West as Symbol and Myth* (Cambridge, Mass.: Harvard Univ. Press, 1950), xi.
3. Michael Denning, *Mechanic Accents: Dime Novels and the Working Class Culture in America* (New York: Verso, 1987).
4. Christine Bold, "The Voice of the Fiction Factory in Dime and Pulp Westerns," *Journal of American Studies* 17 (Apr. 1983): 29–46.
5. Lewis Atherton, in *Main Street on the Middle Border* (Chicago: Quadrangle, 1954), describes the late 19th century as the age of the useful and practical.
6. Richard Weiss, *The American Myth of Success: From Horatio Alger to Norman Vincent Peale* (New York: Basic Books, 1969), 11.
7. John G. Cawelti, *Adventure, Mystery and Romance: Formula Stories as Art and Popular Culture* (Chicago: Univ. of Chicago Press, 1976); James D. Hart, *The Popular Book: A History of America's Literary Taste* (New York: Oxford Univ. Press, 1950); Frank Luther Mott, *Golden Multitudes: The Story of Best Sellers in the United States* (New York: Macmillan, 1947).
8. Jane Tompkins, *Sensational Designs: The Cultural Work of American Fiction, 1790–1860* (New York: Oxford Univ. Press, 1985), esp. chap. 7, "Is It Any Good? The Institutionalization of Literary Value," 186–201; and Mary Kelley, *Private Woman, Public Stage: Literary Domesticity in 19th-Century America* (New York: Oxford, 1984).

Chapter 2. The Magic Formulas
of the People's Press

1. Peter Conn, *Literature in America: An Illustrated History* (London: Cambridge Univ. Press, 1989), 209.
2. "Fashion in Fiction," *Blackwood's Edinburgh Magazine* 166, no. 1008 (Oct. 1899): 532.
3. Mott, *Golden Multitudes,* 122. Also see Mary Noel, *Villains Galore: The Heyday of the Popular Story Weekly* (New York: Macmillan, 1954), 303. *Letters of Hawthorne to William D. Ticknor, 1851–1864* (New York: Houghton, 1910), 1, 75. Also see Caroline Ticknor, *Hawthorne and His Publisher* (1913; 1969).
4. Charles M. Sheldon, *In His Steps: What Would Christ Do?* (New York: Burt, 1897; rpt. as *In His Steps,* Chicago: Ulrich, 1899). See Stanley Kunitz and Howard Haycraft, *Twentieth-Century Authors: A Bibliographic Dictionary of Modern Literature* (New York: Wilson, 1942), 1273–74; Stanley Kunitz and

Howard Haycraft, *First Supplement to Twentieth-Century Authors* (New York: Wilson, 1955), 902; and Paul S. Boyer, "In His Steps: A Reappraisal," *American Quarterly* 1, no. 1 (Spring 1971): 60–78.

5. "Fashion in Fiction," *Blackwood's Edinburgh Magazine* 166, no. 1008 (Oct. 1899): 536.

6. Jess Stein, ed., *The Random House Dictionary*, rev. ed. (New York: Random, 1988), 1312.

7. Max Weber, *The Protestant Work Ethic and the Spirit of Capitalism*, trans. Talcott Parsons (New York: Scribners, 1958); qtd. in Weiss, *American Myth of Success*, 20.

8. Elliott Oring, *Folk Groups and Folklore Genres: An Introduction* (Logan: Utah State Univ. Press, 1986).

9. Kelley, *Private Woman, Public Stage*, 323.

10. For insight into the literary giants of the Gilded Age (1870–1910) who wrote about business and success, see Irvin G. Wyllie, *The Self-Made Man in America: The Myth of Rags to Riches* (New Brunswick, N.J.: Rutgers Univ. Press, 1954); and Robert Falk, "The Writer's Search for Reality," in *The Gilded Age*, ed. H. Wayne Morgan (Syracuse, N.Y.: Syracuse Univ. Press, 1970). Paul F. Boller, Jr., reconstructs the historical context of the Victorian era in his *American Thought in Transition: The Impact of Evolutionary Naturalism, 1865–1900* (Lanham, Md.: Univ. Press of America, 1981).

11. Henry Nash Smith, *Virgin Land*, 95.

12. James D. Hart, *The Oxford Companion to American Literature*, 4th ed. (New York: Oxford Univ. Press, 1965), 390.

13. Conn, *Literature in America*, 248.

14. Lewis Mumford, *The Brown Decades: A Study of the Arts in America, 1865–1895* (New York: Harcourt Brace, 1931; rpt. New York: Dover, 1971).

15. Conn, *Literature in America*, 209.

16. Weiss, *American Myth of Success*, 15.

17. Walter T. K. Nugent, *Money and American Society, 1865–1880* (New York: Free Press, 1968), 34–36.

18. Vernon L. Parrington, *The Beginnings of Critical Realism* (New York: Harcourt Brace, 1930).

19. George Santayana, *The Genteel Tradition: Nine Essays*, ed. Douglas L. Wilson (Cambridge, Mass.: Harvard Univ. Press, 1967). Several authors find Santayana's criticism insightful: Henry F. May, *The End of American Innocence: A Study of the First Years of Our Time, 1912–1917* (New York: Knopf, 1957); Van Wyck Brooks, "America's Coming-of-Age," in his *Three Essays on America* (New York: Dutton, 1934), 13–112; Malcolm Cowley, "The Revolt Against Gentility," in his *After the Genteel Tradition* (Carbondale: Southern Illinois Univ. Press, 1964), 9–26; and Parrington, *Beginnings of Critical Realism*, n. 11. Also see Falk, "Writer's Search for Reality," 224.

20. Herbert G. Gutman, *Work, Culture and Society: Working-Class and Social History* (New York: Vintage Books, 1976), chap. 4: "The Reality of the Rags-to-Riches Myth," 209–33.

21. Lawrence W. Levine, *Highbrow/Lowbrow: The Emergence of Cultural Hierarchy in America* (Cambridge, Mass.: Harvard Univ. Press, 1988).

22. David Paul Nord, "Working-Class Readers: Family, Community, and Reading in Late-19th-Century America," *Communication Research* 13, no. 2 (1986): 156–81.

23. Walter R. Fisher, *Human Communication as Narration: Toward a Philosophy of Reason, Value and Action* (Columbia: Univ. of South Carolina Press, 1987). See Fisher, "Narration as a Human Communication Paradigm: The Case of Public Moral Argument," *Communication Monographs* 51, no. 1 (Mar. 1984): 1–22.

24. Paul A. Carter, *The Spiritual Crisis of the Gilded Age* (DeKalb: Northern Illinois Univ. Press, 1971).

25. Nord, "Working-Class Readers," 161–62. All statistics in this paragraph were drawn from this excellent essay.

26. Hart, *Popular Book*; and Mott, *Golden Multitudes*.

27. Cawelti, *Adventure, Mystery and Romance,* esp. chap. 2, "Notes Toward a Typology of Literary Formulas," 38.

28. Stephen Crane, *Maggie, A Girl of the Streets: A Story of New York (1893): An Authoritative Text; Backgrounds and Sources; The Author and the Novel; Reviews and Criticism,* ed. Thomas A. Gullason (New York: Norton, 1979).

29. David S. Reynolds, *Faith in Fiction: The Emergence of Religious Literature in America* (Cambridge, Mass.: Harvard Univ. Press, 1981), 211.

30. Hart, *Popular Book*; Mott, *Golden Multitudes;* Edmund Pearson, *Dime Novels; Or, Following an Old Trail in Popular Literature* (Boston: Little, Brown, 1929); and Quentin Reynolds, *The Fiction Factory; Or, From Pulp Row to Quality Street* (New York: Random, 1955).

31. Henry Nash Smith, "The Scribbling Women and the Cosmic Success Story," *Critical Inquiry* 1 (Sept. 1974): 51.

32. Mark Twain, *Contributions to* The Galaxy, *1868–1871,* ed. Bruce R. McElderry, Jr. (Gainesville, Fla.: Scholars' Facsimiles and Reprints, 1961), 128.

33. James D. Hart, "Platitudes of Piety: Religion and the Popular Modern Novel," *American Quarterly* 6, no. 4 (Winter 1954): 320.

34. Reynolds, *Faith in Fiction,* 205.

35. E. P. Roe, *Barriers Burned Away* (New York: Dodd, Mead, 1872); Lew Wallace, *Ben-Hur: A Tale of the Christ* (New York: Harper, 1880); and Margaret Deland, *John Ward, Preacher* (London: Warne, 1887; rpt. Boston: Houghton Mifflin, 1888).

36. Mott, *Golden Multitudes,* 172.

37. Sheldon, *In His Steps*; and Edward Bellamy, *Looking Backward: 2000–1887* (Boston: Ticknor, 1888; rpt. as *Looking Backward,* Cleveland: World, 1945).

38. Kate Douglas Wiggin (Mrs. G. C. Riggs), *The Birds' Christmas Carol* (San Francisco: C. A. Murdock, 1887; rpt. New York: Apple Classics, 1972).

39. Elizabeth Stuart Phelps (Ward), *The Gates Ajar* (Boston: Fields Osgood, 1868; rpt. ed. Helen Sootin Smith, Cambridge, Mass.: Harvard Univ. Press, Belknap Press, 1964); Phelps, *Beyond the Gates* (Boston: Houghton Mifflin, 1883); and Phelps, *The Gates Between* (Boston: Houghton Mifflin, 1887).

40. Mark Twain and Charles Dudley Warner, *The Gilded Age: A Tale of Today* (Hartford, Conn.: American, 1873).

41. Cawelti, *Adventure, Mystery and Romance,* 261, and chap. 9, "The Best-Selling Social Melodrama," 263–95.

42. George Cable, *John March, Southerner* (New York: Scribner's, 1894; rpt. New York: Garrett, 1970).

43. Janice A. Radway, *Reading the Romance: Women, Patriarchy and Popular Literature* (Chapel Hill: Univ. of North Carolina Press, 1984), on "the reading process," 11–17.

44. Russell Conwell, *Acres of Diamonds* (Old Tappan, N.J.: Revell, 1983); Andrew Carnegie, *The Gospel of Wealth* (New York: Century, 1901); P. T. Barnum, *Struggles and Triumphs* (Buffalo, N.Y.: Courier, 1884); P. T. Barnum, *Humbugs of the World: An Account of Humbugs, Delusions, Impositions, Quackeries, Deceits and Deceivers Generally, in All Ages* (New York: Carleton, 1866).

45. For insight into the relationship between thinking and language, see Marshall Blonsky, *On Signs* (Baltimore, Md.: Johns Hopkins Univ. Press, 1985); Umberto Eco, *A Theory of Semiotics* (Bloomington: Indiana Univ. Press, 1979); Roland Barthes, *Elements of Semiology,* 11th ed. Trans. Annette Lavers and Colin Smith (New York: Hill and Wang, 1986); and Noam Chomsky, *Language and Mind* (New York: Harcourt Brace, 1968). For insight into the relationship between story making and attaching meaning to experience, see Walter J. Ong, *Orality and Literacy: The Technologizing of the Word* (New York: Methuen, 1982); Ronald C. Arnett, *Communication and Community: Implications of Martin Buber's Dialogue* (Carbondale: Southern Illinois Univ. Press, 1968); Paulo Freire and Donaldo Macedo, *Literacy: Reading the Word and World* (South Hadley, Mass.: Bergin and Garvey, 1987); and Paul Ricoeur, "Narrative Time," *Critical Inquiry* 7, no. 1 (Autumn 1980): 176.

46. James W. Carey, "Editor's Introduction: Taking Culture Seriously," *Sage Annual Review of Communication Research* 15 (1988): 15.

47. Ibid.

48. Ibid.; David Thorburn, "Television as an Aesthetic Medium," *Sage Annual Review of Communication Research* 15 (1988): 48–66.

49. Joseph Campbell, *Myths To Live By: How We Re-Create Ancient Legends in Our Daily Lives to Release Human Potential* (New York: Bantam, 1972).

50. Thorburn, "Television as an Aesthetic Medium," 56. See John Fiske and John Hartley, "'Reading' Television," in their *Reading Television* (New York: Rutledge, 1990), 85–100; and H. Newcomb and R. S. Alley, *The Producer's Medium* (New York: Oxford Univ. Press, 1983).

Chapter 3. "Book Soap"

1. John Tebbel, *A History of Book Publishing in the United States: The Expansion of an Industry, 1865–1919,* 2 vols. (New York: Bowker, 1975), 2:487.

2. "The Literature of Our Sunday Schools," pt. 2, *Hours at Home: A Popular Monthly of Instruction and Recreation* 10, no. 5 (Mar. 1870): 455.

3. Weiss, *American Myth of Success,* 35.

4. For insight into religion in the U.S. during the 19th century, see Atherton, *Main Street on the Middle Border*; and Stephen E. Berk, *Calvinism Versus Democracy: Timothy Dwight and the Origins of American Evangelical Orthodoxy* (Hamden, Conn.: Archon, 1974).

5. Anthony Comstock, "Half-Dime Novels and Story Papers," in his *Traps for the Young* (New York: Funk and Wagnalls, 1883), 20–24. Quotations in this paragraph come from Anthony Comstock, "Vampire Literature," *North American Review* 153, no. 417 (July 1891): 159–71. See Morton Keller, *Affairs of State: Public Life in Late-Nineteenth-Century America* (Cambridge, Mass.: Harvard Univ. Press, Belknap Press, 1977), 515.

6. Bradford K. Pierce, D.D., "The Probable Intellectual and Moral Outcome of the Rapid Increase in Libraries," *Library Journal* 10, nos. 9–10 (Sept.–Oct. 1885): 235. Also see George Putnam, "Influence of Fiction for Good or Evil in Relation to Public Libraries," *Catholic World* 67 (July 1898): 570–72.

7. William Wallace Cook, *The Fiction Factory* (Ridgewood, N.J.: Editor Company, 1912), 41.

8. For biographical information, see *DAB* 1:10–12; Stanley J. Kunitz and Howard Haycraft, *American Authors, 1600–1900: A Biographical Dictionary of American Literature* (New York: Wilson, 1938); John H. Barrows, *Henry Ward Beecher: The Shakespeare of the Pulpit* (New York: Funk and Wagnalls, 1893); Lyman Beecher Stowe, *Saints, Sinners and Beechers* (New York: Blue Ribbon Books, 1934); Harriet Beecher Stowe, "Henry Ward Beecher," in Harriet Beecher Stowe, *The Lives and Deeds of Our Self-Made Men*, rev. and ed. Rev. Charles E. Stowe, chap. 18, pp. 509–71 (Boston: Estes and Lauriat, 1889); and the negative appraisal, which was a standard reference for much of the 20th century: Paxton Hibben, *Henry Ward Beecher: An American Portrait,* introd. Sinclair Lewis, American Newspapermen Series, 1790–1933 (1927; New York: Press of the Reader's Club, 1942). Rev. Beecher's sermons contain autobiographical material. See the *Plymouth Pulpit* (the weekly that suspended publication between 18 Sept. 1875 and 4 Oct. 1882), vols. 1–10 (1868–73), and the new series, vols. 1–7 (1873–84); and *Sermons by Henry Ward Beecher from Verbatim Reports by T. J. Ellinwood,* 2 vols. (New York: Ford, 1868). Beecher's essays include *Star Papers; Or, Experiences of Art and Nature* (New York: Derby, 1855), and *New Star Papers; Or, Views and Experiences of Religious Subjects* (New York: Derby, 1859); both contain articles from the *Independent*. Henry Ward Beecher, *Eyes and Ears* (Boston: Ticknor and Fields, 1862), contains pieces also printed in the following: the *New York Ledger*; Henry Ward Beecher, *Freedom and War: Discourses on Topics Suggested by the Times* (Boston: Ticknor and Fields, 1863); and Henry Ward Beecher, *Lectures and Orations by Henry Ward Beecher,* ed. Newell D. Hillis (New York: AMS Press, 1970).

9. Robert Wiebe, *The Search for Order, 1877–1920* (New York: Hill and Wang, 1967).

10. Wolfgang Schivelbusch, *The Railway Journey: The Industrialization of Time and Space in the 19th Century* (Berkeley: Univ. of California Press, 1977), 41.

11. James W. Carey, "Technology and Ideology: The Case of the Telegraph," in

Prospects: An Annual of American Cultural Studies, ed. Jack Salzman (Cambridge Univ. Press, 1983), 303–25.

12. Daniel J. Boorstin, "Consumption Communities," in *The Americans: The Democratic Experience,* by Daniel J. Boorstin, 89–157 (New York: Vintage, 1974).

13. Ira V. Brown, review of Clifford E. Clark, Jr., *Henry Ward Beecher: Spokesman for a Middle-Class America* (Urbana: Univ. of Illinois Press, 1978), in *American Historical Review* 84, no. 4 (Oct. 1979): 1153. Constance M. Rouke, *Trumpets of Jubilee: Henry Ward Beecher, Harriet Beecher Stowe, Lyman Beecher, Horace Greeley, and P. T. Barnum* (New York: Harcourt Brace, 1922), assesses the roots of Beecher's popularity and success. The most recent biography of Beecher is Halford Ryan, *Peripatetic Preacher* (Westport, Conn.: Greenwood, 1990).

14. This account of the suicide hoax appeared in the *Austin (Nev.) Reese River Reveille,* 2 Apr. 1876, 2:2. The editorial admitting the hoax appeared on 3 Apr. 1876, 2:1.

15. *Austin (Nev.) Reese River Reveille,* 2:1, contains a list of Beecher's accomplishments. The paragraph about the reaction to his suicide appeared 3 Apr. 1876, on 3:3; the item about the trial appeared the same day, on 2:2.

16. For insights into the scandal, see Altina L. Waller, *Rev. Beecher and Mrs. Tilton: Sex and Class in Victorian America* (Amherst: Univ. of Massachusetts Press, 1982); Paul A. Carter, *Spiritual Crisis of the Gilded Age*; and William G. McLoughlin, *The Meaning of Henry Ward Beecher: An Essay on the Shifting Values of Mid-Victorian America, 1840–70* (New York: Knopf, 1970). For the case transcript, see *Theodore Tilton v. Henry Ward Beecher, Action for Crim. Con . . . Verbatim Report by the Official Stenographer* (New York: McDivitt, Campbell, 1875), 3 vols.; and Austin Abbot, *Official Report of the Trial of Henry Ward Beecher* (New York: G. W. Smith and Co.,1875), 2 vols.

17. *Daily Alexandria (La.) Town Talk,* 14 Oct. 1883, 3:1.

18. Paul A. Carter, *Spiritual Crisis of the Gilded Age,* 115.

19. Ibid.

20. Hart, *Oxford Companion to American Literature,* 67.

21. Paul A. Carter, *Spiritual Crisis of the Gilded Age,* 125.

22. Ibid.

23. In the late 1850s, separately but simultaneously, Sir Henry Bessemer in England and William Kelly in America, pioneered what is known as "the Bessemer process" for forcing air into molten pig iron. The development of the open-hearth method and the Thomas-Gilchrist process for removing impurities enabled manufacturers to use ores that, using the Bessemer process alone, were unsuitable for steel production. The first steel mills primarily made rails for railroad builders, because steel rails had proved ten times more durable than iron rails. However, by the 1880s, the construction of the forerunners of skyscrapers, with steel skeletons, made Bessemer steel obsolete, because of "its unpredictable tendency to break under strain." See John A. Garraty, *The New Commonwealth, 1877–1890* (New York: Harper and Row, 1968), 90–91.

24. John F. Kasson, *Civilizing the Machine: Technology and Republican Values in America, 1776–1900* (New York: Penguin, 1986).

25. Charles Monroe Sheldon, "What Is a Sermon?" *Outlook* 49, no. 7 (24 Feb. 1894): 363.

26. "Samuel F. Dunham Dead: He Was the Inventor of the 'Hokey Pokey' or Ice Cream Brick," *New York Times*, 8 Oct. 1907, 11:5.

27. Kate Douglas Wiggin, "Children's Rights," *Scribner's Magazine* 12, no. 2 (12 Aug. 1892): 242–48.

28. Ibid., 243.

29. "Laughs at Auto Havoc, Chauffeur Leaves His Victim Dying—Defies and Eludes Police," *New York Times*, 8 Oct. 1907, 11:4.

30. Alan Trachtenberg, *Brooklyn Bridge: Fact and Symbol* (New York: Oxford Univ. Press, 1965). Also see Helen Campbell, *Darkness and Daylight; Or, Lights and Shadows of New York Life—A Woman's Story of Gospel, Temperance, Mission, and Rescue Work, with Hundreds of Thrilling Anecdotes and Incidents, Personal Experiences, Sketches of Life and Character, Humorous Stories, Touching Home Scenes, and Tales of Tender Pathos, Drawn from the Bright and Shady Sides of City Life* (Hartford, Conn.: Worthington, 1891).

31. Kasson, *Civilizing the Machine*, 163.

32. Ibid., 152–53. Also see Atherton, *Main Street on the Middle Border.*

33. Comstock, "Vampire Literature," 159–71.

34. "A Lesson from the Revolution," *Publishers Weekly* 18, no. 7:186–87, qtd. in Tebbel, *History of Book Publishing*, 2:171.

35. Ibid.

36. Tebbel, *History of Book Publishing*, 2:5–6.

37. Cawelti, *Adventure, Mystery and Romance*, 260–95. Roe, *Barriers Burned Away.*

38. Mott, *Golden Multitudes*, 5.

39. George Du Maurier, *Trilby* (New York: Harper, 1894). Also see Hart, *Popular Book*, 194–97; and Mott, *Golden Multitudes*, 249.

40. William H. Harvey, *Coin's Financial School* (Chicago: Coin, 1894). Also see Mott, *Golden Multitudes*, 170–71; and Hart, *Popular Book*, 194–97.

41. Anthony Hope, *The Prisoner of Zenda* (New York: Holt, 1894). Also see Mott, *Golden Multitudes*, 208; and Hart, *Popular Book*, 192–93.

42. Ian Maclaren (Rev. John Watson), *Beside the Bonnie, Bonnie Briar Bush* (New York: Dodd, Mead, 1894). Also see Hart, *Popular Book*, 197.

43. Margaret Marshall Saunders, *Beautiful Joe* (Philadelphia: Judson, 1894). Also see Mott, *Golden Multitudes*, 165.

44. Edward Weeks, *This Trade of Writing* (Boston: Little, Brown, 1935). See Mott, *Golden Multitudes*, 7.

45. Mark Twain, *Tom Sawyer* (Hartford, Conn.: American, 1876). W. Somerset Maugham, *Of Human Bondage* (New York: Modern Library, 1915).

46. Alice Caldwell Hegan Rice, *Mrs. Wiggs of the Cabbage Patch* (New York: Century, 1901); Edward Eggleston, *The Hoosier School-Master* (New York: Orange and Judd, 1871).

47. Frances Hodgson Burnett, *The Little Princess: Being the Whole Story of What Happened to Sara Crewe, Now Told for the First Time* (New York: Scribners,

1905). Gene Stratton-Porter, *Freckles* (New York: Doubleday and Page, 1904). Lew Wallace, *Ben-Hur.*

48. Burt L. Standish (Gilbert Patten), Frank Merriwell Series No. 1; the paperback set includes these titles: *Frank Merriwell's School Days, Frank Merriwell's Chums, Frank Merriwell's Foes, Frank Merriwell's Trip West, Frank Merriwell Down South, Frank Merriwell's Bravery, Frank Merriwell's Hunting Tour, Frank Merriwell at Yale,* and *Frank Merriwell's Sports Afield* (all, rpt. New York: Smith Street, 1971). The last page of *Frank Merriwell's School Days,* 252, promises "All Titles Always in Print."

49. Lew Wallace, *The Prince of India* (New York: Harper, 1896).

50. Owen Wister, *The Virginian: A Horseman of the Plains* (New York: Macmillan, 1902). Also see Mott, *Golden Multitudes,* 207; and Hart, *Popular Book, passim.*

51. Irving Bacheller, *Eben Holden* (Boston: Lothrop, 1900). See Mott, *Golden Multitudes,* 203–5; Hart, *Popular Book,* 206–7.

52. Stratton-Porter, *Freckles.*

53. Frances Hodgson Burnett, *Little Lord Fauntleroy* (New York: Scribners, 1886).

54. John Habberton, *Helen's Babies: With Some Account of Their Ways, Innocent, Crafty, Angelic, Impish, Witching and Repulsive. Also a Painful Record of Their Actions During Ten Days of Their Existence, by Their Latest Victim* (Boston: Loring, 1876). See Mott, *Golden Multitudes,* 159–60.

55. Hall Caine, *The Deemster* (New York: Appleton, 1888). See Mott, *Golden Multitudes,* 182.

56. Ralph Connor, *Black Rock* (New York: Revell, 1898). See Mott, *Golden Multitudes,* 197–98; and Hart, *Popular Book, passim.*

57. Mme. Sarah Grand (Mrs. Frances Elizabeth [Clarke] McFall), *The Heavenly Twins* (New York: Cassell, 1893). See Mott, *Golden Multitudes,* 181–82, 249; Hart, *Popular Book,* 173.

58. Lucy M. Montgomery, *Anne of Green Gables* (Boston: Page, 1908). See Mott, *Golden Multitudes,* 217–18; and Hart, *Popular Book,* 213.

59. Raymond Howard Shove, *Cheap Books Produced in the United States: 1870–1891* (Urbana: Univ. of Illinois Library, 1937), ix–x, *passim.* Also Tebbel, "Cheap Books and Paperbacks," in *A History of Book Publishing in the United States: The Expansion of an Industry, 1865–1919,* by John Tebbel (New York: Bowker, 1975), 1:481–511.

60. Shove, *Cheap Books,* ix.

61. Charles Dudley Warner, "Editor's Drawer," *Harper's Magazine* 73, no. 487 (1886): 807.

62. "The American Book Market," *Publishers Weekly* 35, no. 896 (Mar. 1889): 191–92. The quotation is from the *Boston Herald.*

63. Shove, *Cheap Books,* 36. Also see Tebbel, *History of Book Publishing,* 1:132–33; and Andrew Lang, "Literary," *Public Opinion* 6, no. 17 (1889): 356

64. Alexis de Tocqueville, *Democracy in America* (New York: Knopf, 1945), vol. 1:424.

65. T. B. Peterson, "Catalogue of Books," published at back of E. D. E. N. Southworth, *Victor's Triumph* (Philadelphia: T. B. Peterson, 1875); 2d quota-

tion is from p. 12. Shove, *Cheap Books*, has two parts of interest here. For descriptions of the Petersons and their competitors, see "Representative Publishers of Cheap Books," pt. 1, 53–105.And "Publishers [Like Harper or Holt] Whose Cheap Books Were Not the Most Important Part of Their Publishing Activities" are described in pt. 2, 106–28. In Madeleine B. Stern, ed., *Publishers for Mass Entertainment in 19th-Century America* (Boston: Hall, 1980). See Tebbel, "Cheap Books and Paperbacks," 1:481–511.

66. "Obituary: Theophilus B. Peterson," *Publishers' Weekly* 37 (10 Jan. 1891): 27–28; Stern, *Publishers for Mass Entertainment*, 229–35; Noel, *Villains Galore*, *passim*; "The Bookmakers: Reminiscences and Contemporary Sketches of American Publishers, T. B. Peterson and Brothers," *New York Evening Post*, 24 Feb. 1875, 19; Tebbel, *History of Book Publishing* 2:488; and Helen Waite Papashvily, *All the Happy Endings: A Study of the Domestic Novel in America, the Women Who Wrote It, the Women Who Read It, in the 19th Century* (Port Washington, N.Y.: Kennikat, 1972), 98, *passim*.

67. Shove, *Cheap Books*, 2.

68. Stern, *Publishers for Mass Entertainment*, 234.

69. For the "List of the Best Cook Books Published," see Southworth, *Victor's Triumph*, catalog at end, p. 2.

70. *Frank Forester's Sporting Scenes . . . And Characters*, catalog, 3, in Southworth, *Victor's Triumph*, catalog at end, p. 3.

71. *Q. K. Philander Doestick's Funny Books*, catalog at end, p. 3. "Harry Cockton's Eight Laughable Novels," 10; and "American Humorous Books," catalog at end, p. 11.

72. "Humorous Illustrated Books," catalog at end, p. 8.

73. *Beautiful Snow! New & Enlarged Edition* and "other poems never before published" were advertised in catalog at end, p. 10.

74. "New and Good Books by the Best Authors," catalog at end, p. 10.

75. *Green's Works on Gambling*, catalog at end, p. 4; "T. S. Arthur's Great Temperance Books," catalog at end, p. 7; and *Dow's Patent Sermons*, catalog at end, p. 4.

76. "Model Speakers and Readers," catalog at end, p. 7.

77. Albert Johannsen, *The House of Beadle and Adams and Its Dime and Nickel Novels: The Story of a Vanishing Literature*, 2 vols., with foreword by John T. McIntyre (Norman: Univ. of Oklahoma Press, 1950) 1:361.

78. Ibid.

79. See Henry Nash Smith, *Virgin Land*, 227–29.For biographical information about Mrs. Metta Victor, see: Kunitz and Haycraft, *Nineteenth-Century American Authors*, 774; William Taylor, "Metta Victor," in *NAW* 3:519–20; (Sarah Josepha Hale,) *A Woman's Record; Or, Sketches of All Distinguished Women, from The Creation to A.D. 1868. Arranged in Four Eras with Selections from Authoresses of Each Era. Illustrated by 230 Portraits Engraved on Wood by Lossing and Barritt*, 3d rev. ed. (New York: Harper, 1870), 734–35; Kathleen L. Maio, "Metta Victor," *AWW* 3:31–33; and "Death of Mrs. Victor: An Authoress Well Known a Quarter of a Century Ago," *New York Times*, 27 June 1885, 8:5.

80. Charles E. Rosenberg, *The Care of Strangers: The Rise of America's Hospital System* (New York: Basic, 1987).

81. Johannsen, *House of Beadle and Adams,* 1:376–77.

82. Ibid., 1:364–72.

83. Atherton, *Main Street on the Middle Border,* 67.

84. Johannsen, *House of Beadle and Adams,* 1:405–6, 395–403.

85. Ibid., 384–95.

86. Katie Letcher Lyle, *Scalded to Death by the Steam: Authentic Stories about Railroad Disasters and the Ballads That Were Written about Them* (Chapel Hill, N.C.: Algonquin, 1988).

87. See preface and catalog in back of Southworth, *Victor's Triumph.*

88. "Chronicle and Comment: Four of a Kind," *Bookman* 7 (Dec. 1907): 340. Besides Mrs. Holmes, the critic mentions Susan Warner (*The Wide, Wide World* [New York: Putnam, 1885]), Susanna Cummins (*The Lamplighter; Or, a Girl's Struggle* [New York: Grossett, n.d.; rpt. Boston: Hewett, 1854]), and Laura Jean Libbey (*A Fatal Wooing* [New York: Munro, 1883]). See Tompkins, *Sensational Designs*; and Kelley, *Private Woman, Public Stage.*

89. Papashvily, *All the Happy Endings,* 203–4; and Sue G. Walcutt, "Laura Jean Libbey," in *NAW* 2:402–3.

90. Cook, *Fiction Factory,* 53.

91. Ibid.

92. "Laura Jean Libbey Hoped to Achieve Immortality: Story Writer Had Her Tombstone Erected in Her Lifetime and Lingered Near It to Hear People Discuss Her Fame," *New York Times,* 2 Nov. 1924, sec. 7, 11:1. This article appeared between the obituary, "Laura Jean Libbey, Novelist, Dies at 62: Author of More than 50 Ardent Love Stories Succumbs in Her Brooklyn Home; Worked Almost to End; *Lovers Once but Strangers Now* and *When His Love Grew Cold* Among Her Popular Works," 26 Oct. 1942, sec. 2, 7:1; and the notice of the disposition of her will, "Laura Jean Libbey Leaves $5 to Husband; Her Total Estate Is Estimated at More Than $11,000—Gives Burial Directions," on 7 Nov. 1924, 21:3. This article contains valuable insights concerning Libbey's cultural significance. For criticism of her work, see Noel, *Villains Galore, passim*; Papashvily, "Common Sense in the Household," in Papashvily, *All the Happy Endings,* 199–200; Hart, *Popular Book,* 213; and Mott, *Golden Multitudes,* 10. For biographical information, see Walcutt, "Laura J. Libbey," *NAW* 2:402–3, and Cathy N. Davidson, "Laura Jean Libbey," *AWW* 3:3–5. Albert Payson Terhune, *To the Best of My Memory* (New York: Harper, 1930), 208–12 and n. 87.

93. Washington Gladden, "Christianity and Popular Amusements," *Century Magazine* 29, no. 3 (Jan. 1885): 384.

94. C. Hugh C. Holman and William Harmon, *A Handbook of American Literature,* 5th ed. (New York: Macmillan, 1986), 391.

95. Carlin T. Kindilien, "Adeline Whitney," *NAW* 3:599.

96. Justin Kaplan, *Mr. Clemens and Mark Twain: A Biography* (New York: Simon and Schuster, 1966), 201.

97. "Old Sleuth Passes Away: H. P. Halsey Author of the Famous Detective Stories, Dies Suddenly; Wrote Nearly 700 Books," *New York Times,* 18 Dec. 1898, 7:2.

Chapter 4. The Fear of Sinking

1. Fiske and Hartley, *Reading Television,* esp. "Reading Television" and "The Modes of Television," 109–27.
2. Ricoeur, "Narrative Time," 176.
3. Denning, *Mechanic Accents,* 152–53.
4. Garraty, *New Commonwealth.*
5. Herbert G. Gutman, "The Reality of the Rags-to-Riches Myth," in Gutman, *Work, Culture and Society,* chap. 4, 209–33 (New York: Vintage, 1967).
6. Advertisement, *Boca Raton (Florida) Sun* 6, no. 17 (26 Apr. 1988): 3.
7. Ibid.
8. Atherton, *Main Street on the Middle Border,* 68–76.
9. Orvin Larson, *American Infidel: Robert G. Ingersoll, A Biography* (New York: Citadel, 1962), 160.
10. Tocqueville, *Democracy in America,* 2:164.
11. George J. Edward, "Bellamy: Utopia, American Plan," *Antioch Review* 14, no. 2 (Summer 1954): 184.
12. Conwell, *Acres of Diamonds,* 1 and 10.
13. Ibid., 10.
14. Ibid., 16.
15. Ibid.
16. John Gilmer Speed, "The Great American Showman," *Harper's Weekly* 35, no. 1791 (7 Apr. 1891): 289.
17. Barnum, *Struggles and Triumphs,* 38.
18. A. H. Saxon, "P. T. Barnum: Universalism's Surprising 'Prince of Humbugs,'" *The World* 2, no. 3 (May–June 1988): 5–7, 50. Saxon, a theater historian, edited *The Autobiography of Mrs. Tom Thumb: Some of My Life Experiences, by Mrs. Countess M. Lavinia Magri, formerly Mrs. General Tom Thumb, with Assistance of Sylvester Bleeker* (Hamden, Conn.: Archon, 1979) and *Selected Letters of P. T. Barnum* (New York: Columbia Univ. Press, 1983), and authored *P. T. Barnum: The Legend and the Man* (New York: Columbia Univ. Press, 1989).
19. Saxon found this quotation in Barnum's tract, "Why I Am a Universalist" (Boston: Universalist Publishing Co., 1895).
20. Saxon, "P. T. Barnum" 5.
21. Barnum, *Struggles and Triumphs,* 37.
22. Ibid.
23. Saxon, "P. T. Barnum" 5.
24. Ibid.
25. M. R. Werner describes P. T.'s faith in Werner, *Barnum* (New York: Harcourt Brace, 1923), 284; see 282–87.
26. Phelps, *The Gates Between.*
27. E. L. Wheeler (Edward Lytton), *Deadwood Dick on Deck; Or, Calamity Jane, the*

Heroine of Whoop-Up: A Story of Dakota (New York: Beadle and Adams, 1885), 27. See Henry Nash Smith, *Virgin Land,* 99–102, 116–19.

28. Ihab H. Hassan, "The Idea of Adolescence in American Fiction," *American Quarterly* 10, no. 3 (Fall 1958): 312.

29. "Mrs. Daniel Lothrop," *Publishers Weekly* 6 (9 Aug. 1944): 501.

30. Elizabeth Johnson, "Margaret Sidney vs. Harriet Lothrop," *Horn Book* 47, no. 3 (June 1971): 313. She makes the statement in Margaret M. Lothrop, *The Wayside House: Home of Authors* (New York: American, 1940), 171–72.

31. *The Random House College Dictionary,* 1st rev. ed. (New York: Random House, 1984), 938.

32. "Old Sleuth" (Harlan Page Halsey), *Fly-Away Ned* (New York: Parlor Car, 1895; rpt. New York: Arno, 1974), for Popular Culture in America: 1800–1925 series.

33. Tom H. Towers, "The Insomnia of Julian West," *American Literature* 47, no. 1 (Mar. 1975): 53.

34. Tocqueville, *Democracy in America,* 2:165.

35. David B. Davis, "Ten-Gallon Hero," *American Quarterly* 6, no. 2 (Summer 1954): 117.

36. Ibid.

37. Wister, *The Virginian,* 201.

38. Weiss, *American Myth of Success,* 78.

39. Phelps, *Gates Ajar,* xxix.

40. Ann Stephens, *Phemie Frost's Experiences* (New York: Carlton, 1874), 58.

41. Ibid., 57.

42. Tocqueville, *Democracy in America,* 2:140.

43. Atherton, *Main Street on the Middle Border,* 111.

44. Halsey, *Fly-Away Ned,* 18.

45. Roe, *Barriers Burned Away,* 415.

46. Wister, *The Virginian,* 366.

47. Andrew Carnegie, "The Advantages of Poverty," *Nineteenth Century* 29 (Mar. 1891): 379.

48. Barnum, "The Art of Money-Getting," in *Struggles and Triumphs: Life of P. T. Barnum, Written by Himself, Including His Golden Rules for Money-Making, Brought Up to 1888,* by P. T. Barnum (Buffalo, N.Y.: Courier, 1888), 177, 178.

49. Wister, *The Virginian,* 310.

50. Henry M. Littlefield, "The Wizard of Oz: Parable on Populism," *American Quarterly* 16, no. 1 (1964): 55. R. Hal Williams comments on Baum's work and the Populist movement in his *Years of Decision: American Politics in the 1890s* (New York: Wiley, 1978), 105.

51. Littlefield, "Wizard of Oz," 57.

52. Ibid.

53. Nick Carter (John Russell Coryell), "Nick Carter's Mysterious Case; Or, The Road-House Tragedy," in Robert Clurman's collection of original stories, *Nick Carter, Detective: Fiction's Most Celebrated Detective (Six Astonishing Adventures),* introd. Robert Clurman (New York: Macmillan, 1963), 6.

54. Carnegie, *Gospel of Wealth,* 16–17.

55. Ibid.

56. Conwell, *Acres of Diamonds*, 23.

57. Rice, *Mrs. Wiggs of the Cabbage Patch*, 4.

58. Wiggin, *Birds' Christmas Carol*, 17.

59. Tocqueville, *Democracy in America*, 1:308.

60. Carnegie, *Gospel of Wealth*, 9.

61. Conwell, *Acres of Diamonds*, 33.

62. Sheldon, *In His Steps*, 281.

63. Ibid., 280.

64. Ibid., 371.

65. Horatio Alger, *Luke Walton* (Philadelphia: Porter and Coates, 1889), 344.

66. Carnegie, *Gospel of Wealth*, 43.

67. Mary Roberts Rinehart, *The Circular Staircase* (New York: Grosset and Dunlap, 1908), 215.

68. Conwell, *Acres of Diamonds*, 37.

69. Ibid.

70. Ibid., 21.

71. Anna Katharine (Rohlfs) Green, *The Circular Study* (Garden City, N.Y.: Doubleday Page, 1900), 207.

72. Wheeler, *Deadwood Dick on Deck*, 3.

73. Anna Katharine Green, *The Leavenworth Case* (1878; rpt. New York: Putnam, 1901), 408.

74. Conwell, *Acres of Diamonds*, 23.

75. Garraty, *New Commonwealth*, 318–19.

76. Ibid., 319.

77. Mumford, *Brown Decades*, 22.

78. Ibid.

79. Bellamy, *Looking Backward*, 156.

Chapter 5. Why Children Read Success Tales

1. Weiss, *American Myth of Success*, 35.

2. "How the World's Wealth Has Grown," *Literary Digest* 48, no. 26 (27 June 1914): 1568.

3. Harriet Beecher Stowe, *Uncle Tom's Cabin; Or, Life Among the Lowly* (Boston: Jewett, 1852).

4. Hart, *Oxford Companion to American Literature*, 871. C. B. Tillinghast, *Forum* 16 (Sept. 1893): 62. See Frank Luther Mott, *A History of American Magazines, 1865–1885* (3 vols., Cambridge, Mass.: Harvard Univ. Press, 1938), 1:142–44, on the impact of the novel; Hart, *Oxford Companion to American Literature*, 871.

5. For criticism of Stowe's writing, see Noel, *Villains Galore*, 302–3; Jean W. Ashton, *Harriet Beecher Stowe: A Reference Guide* (Boston, Mass.: Hall, 1977); Charles Foster, *The Rungless Ladder: Harriet Beecher Stowe and New England Puritanism* (Durham, N.C.: Duke Univ. Press, 1954); Alice C. Crozier, *The Novels of Harriet Beecher Stowe* (New York: Oxford Univ. Press,

1969); G. Kimball, "The Religious Ideas of Harriet Beecher Stowe: Her Gospel of Womanhood," Ph.D. diss., Univ. of California at Santa Barbara, 1976); Florentine T. McCray, *The Life Work of the Author of* Uncle Tom's Cabin (New York: Funk and Wagnalls, 1889); Mott, *Golden Multitudes*, 114–22; Hart, *Popular Book*, 110–12; R. Gordon Kelly, ed., *Children's Periodicals of the United States* (Westport, Conn.: Greenwood, 1984); Tompkins, *Sensational Designs*; Kelley, *Private Woman, Public Stage*; and Papashvily, *All the Happy Endings*. Harriet Beecher Stowe collaborated with her son, Charles Edward Stowe, on the *Life of Harriet Beecher Stowe* (Boston: Houghton Mifflin, 1889; rpt. Detroit: Gale, 1976). That account "conveys her self-image and her own interpretations of her life," says Barbara M. Cross, "Harriet Beecher Stowe," *NAW* 3:393–401. Also see Gayle Kimball, "Harriet Beecher Stowe," *AWW* 4:172–78.

6. For biographical information on Stowe, see Kunitz and Haycraft, *American Authors, 1600–1900*; John Adams, *Harriet Beecher Stowe* (New Haven, Conn.: College and Univ. Press, 1963); Catherine Gilbertson, *Harriet Beecher Stowe* (New York: Appleton-Century, 1937); Johanna Johnston, *Runaway to Heaven* (Garden City, N.Y.: Doubleday, 1963); C. M. Rourke, *Trumpets of Jubilee*; and Lyman Beecher Stowe, *Saints, Sinners and Beechers*. The best biography, Forrest Wilson's *Crusader in Crinoline* (Philadelphia: Lippincott, 1941), explores Stowe's experiences as inspirations for her fiction. For contemporary accounts, see "The Success of Harriet Beecher Stowe," *Putnam's Magazine* 1 (Jan. 1853): 97; and Annie Adams Fields, *Life and Letters of Harriet Beecher Stowe* (Boston: Houghton Mifflin, 1898).

7. May Hill Arbuthnot, *Children and Books*, 3d ed. (Glenview, Ill.: Scott-Foresman, 1964), 35–36.

8. Hart, *Oxford Companion to American Literature*, 689, defines Puritanism as "an attitude of a party within the Established Church of England, which under Elizabeth and the Stuarts desired a more thoroughgoing reformation of the Church in the direction of Continental Protestantism. At first the Puritans wished only to eliminate certain ceremonial vestments and rituals, and, having no doctrinal quarrel, they were not Separatists (q.v.), but definitely believed in a state church. As the conflict grew that led to the Revolution of 1640–60, there arose many political Puritans whose main interest was in the establishment of parliamentary authority as opposed to the regal theory of divine right. The Puritan movement was at its height when it found an outlet in American colonization, and, though the Pilgrims (q.v.) were Separatists, the later colonists were primarily Puritans who came from the English middle class. The Puritans' doctrine, as expressed in the Cambridge Platform (1646), was Calvinistic (q.v.) in theology and Congregational (q.v.) in church polity. The word *Puritan* is used to refer either to this theology or to this polity. Later the word has been used to denote a strictness in morality that verges on intolerance, and refers to a supposed parallel with the moral severity of the early New England settlers."

9. Hart, *Oxford Companion to American Literature*, 34–38. Donna E. Norton, *Through the Eyes of a Child: An Introduction to Children's Literature*, 2d ed. (Columbus, Ohio: Merrill, 1987), 48–49.

10. Edna Kenton, "The Pap We Have Been Fed On: The Old-Time Books for Children," *Bookman* 44, no. 4 (June 1916): 374.

11. Ibid. Quotations also ibid.

12. Kunitz and Haycraft, *American Authors, 1600–1900,* 273. Amy H. Dowe, "Elsie Finds a Modern Champion: G. B. Stern, English Novelist, Is More of an Authority on Elsie Dinsmore Than Most Americans," *Publishers Weekly* 122, no. 27 (31 Dec. 1932): 2384. Also see Janet Elder Brown, "The Saga of Elsie Dinsmore," *University of Buffalo Studies* 17 (July 1945): 75–129.

13. Stanley Kunitz and Howard Haycraft, eds., *British Authors of the 19th Century* (New York: Wilson, 1936), 559. Also see S. Kelly, *The Life of Mrs.* [Mary Martha Butt] *Sherwood* (London: Darton, 1854); "Life of Mrs. Sherwood," review of S. Kelly, *The Life of Mrs. Sherwood,* from the *Christian Remembrancer,* rpt. in *Littell's Living Age* 43, no. 528 (25 Nov. 1854): 339–62; "Life of Mrs. Sherwood," review of S. Kelly, *The Life of Mrs. Sherwood,* from the *Spectator,* rpt. in *Littell's Living Age* 41, no. 526 (17 June 1854): 602–5; Sir Paul Harvey, ed., *The Oxford Companion to English Literature,* 4th ed., (New York: Oxford Univ. Press, 1985), 751; and Clarence L. Barnhart, ed., *The New Century Handbook of English Literature* (New York: Appleton-Century-Crofts, 1956), 996.

14. Kunitz and Haycraft, *British Authors,* 559.

15. "The Literature of Our Sunday-Schools," pt. 3, *Hours at Home* 10, no. 6 (Apr. 1870): 454–55.

16. Florence Wilson, "Faces We Seldom See: The Author of the 'Elsie' Books," *Ladies Home Journal* 20, no. 5 (Apr. 1893): 3.

17. Kindilien, "Martha Farquharson Finley," 620. See Anne Eaton, chap. 6, "The American Family," in *A Critical History of Children's Literature: A Survey of Children's Books in English from Earliest Times to the Present, Prepared in Four Parts,* ed. Cornelia Meigs (New York: Macmillan, 1953), 226–31. See Mott, *Golden Multitudes,* 10; and Papashvily, *All the Happy Endings,* 170.

18. M. Sarah Smedman, "Martha Finley (Martha Farquharson)," *DLB* 42:182. *American Writers for Children,* ed. Glenn E. Estes (1985).

19. Kunitz and Haycraft, *American Authors, 1600–1900,* 272.

20. Agnes Repplier, "Little Pharisees in Fiction," *Scribner's Magazine* 5, no. 20 (Nov. 1896):718–24.

21. Wilson, "Faces We Seldom See," 3. For biographical information on Martha Farquharson (Martha Finley), see Kindilien, "Martha Farquharson Finley," 1:619–20; Kunitz and Haycraft, *American Authors, 1600–1900,* 272; William Coyle, ed., *Ohio Authors and Their Books* (Wethersfield, Conn.: World Action, 1962), 207–10; Frances E. Willard and Mary A. Livermore, *American Women: A Revised Edition of* Women of the Century: *1500 Biographies with over 1,400 Portraits: A Comprehensive Encyclopedia of the Lives and Achievements of American Women during the 19th Century* (New York: Mast, Crowell, and Kirkpatrick, 1897), 226, 290; and *Baltimore Sun,* 31 Jan. 1909.

22. Dowe, "Elsie Finds a Modern Champion," 2384. Two articles that debunk the Elsie myth are G. B. Stern, "Onward and Upward with the Arts: Elsie Reread,"

New Yorker 12, no. 4 (14 Mar. 1936): 53–55; and Ruth Suckow, "Elsie Dinsmore: A Study in Perfection; Or, How Fundamentalism Came to Dixie," *Bookman* 66 (Oct. 1927): 126–33.

23. Papashvily, *All the Happy Endings,* 173–74.

24. Smedman, "Martha Finley (Martha Farquharson)," 182. See Jacqueline Jackson and Phillip Kendall, "What Makes a Bad Book Good: Elsie Dinsmore," *Children's Literature* 7 (1978): 45–67; and Honore Morrow, "My Favorite Character," *Bookman* 62 (Jan. 1926): 546–47.

25. Papashvily, *All the Happy Endings,* 170.

26. Eaton, "American Family," 620.

27. Dowe, "Elsie Finds a Modern Champion," 2384.

28. Papashvily, *All the Happy Endings,* 170. She evaluates domestic novels in terms of sex roles and rebellion against the constraints of Victorian social mores; see "The Death of the Master," 63–74, and "The Mutilation of the Male," 75–94.

29. Wilson, "Faces We Seldom See," 3.

30. Dowe, "Elsie Finds a Modern Champion," 2385–86.

31. Ibid., 2385.

32. R. Gordon Kelly, *Children's Periodicals,* 455. Louisa May Alcott, *Little Women* (Boston: Roberts, 1867).

33. "Common Salt," *Chautauquan: A Monthly Magazine Devoted to the Promotion of True Culture* 8, no. 32 (Nov. 1887): 82. The magazine was the organ of the Chautauqua Literary and Scientific Circle.

34. "New Books," *Dial* 3, no. 32 (Dec. 1882): 174.

35. "The Gayworthys," *Littell's Living Age* 88, no. 1129 (20 Jan. 1866): 256. Adeline Dutton Train Whitney, *The Gayworthys: A Story of Threads and Thrums, by the author of* Faith Gartney's Girlhood, 2 vols. (London: Sampson, Low and Marston, 1866).

36. Elinor Whitney Field, "The Neighborhood Stories of Mrs. A. D. T. Whitney," *Horn Book* 29, no. 6 (June 1953): 185.

37. For biographical information on Mrs. Adeline Dutton Train Whitney, see Florine Thayer McCray, *Ladies Home Journal* (Oct. 1888); *Critic* 40, no. 2 (Feb. 1902): 109; the *Boston Evening Transcript,* 21 Mar. 1906; Kindilien, "Adeline Dutton Train," 3:599–600; Kunitz and Haycraft, *American Authors, 1600–1900,* 722–24; and Harriet Beecher Stowe, *Our Famous Women: Comprising the Lives and Deeds of American Women Who Have Distinguished Themselves in Literature, Science, Art, Music and the Drama, or Are Famous as Heroines, Patriots, Orators, Educators, Physicians, Philanthropists, etc., with Numerous Anecdotes, Incidents and Personal Experiences* (Hartford, Conn.: Worthington, 1884).

38. Field, "Neighborhood Stories," 184.

39. "*Golden Hours: A Magazine for Boys and Girls,*" in *Children's Periodicals of the United States,* ed. R. Gordon Kelly (Westport, Conn: Greenwood, 1984), 182–83. See Hart, *Popular Book,* 97; Mott, *Golden Multitudes,* 20, 102; and Hart, *Oxford Companion to American Literature.* For biographical information, see David E. Smith, "Louisa May Alcott," in *NAW* 1:27–31; Alma Payne, "Louisa May Alcott," in *AWW* 1:28–31; C. L. Meigs, *The Story of the Author of Little*

Women: Invincible Louisa (Boston: Little, Brown, 1933); Belle Moses, *Louisa May Alcott: Dreamer and Worker—A Story of Achievement* (New York: Appleton, 1909); M. S. Porter, "The Recollections of Louisa May Alcott," *Atlantic Monthly* 65 (Mar. 1890): 420–21; Josephine Lazarus, "Louisa May Alcott," *Century Magazine* 42, no. 1 (May 1891): 59–67; and Maria S. Porter, "Recollections of Louisa May Alcott," *New England Magazine* 6 (Mar. 1892): 2–19.

40. "The Literature of Our Sunday Schools," pt. 1, *Hours at Home* 10, no. 4 (Feb. 1870): 295. Also see S. S. Green, "Sensational Fiction in Public Libraries," *Library Journal* 4, no. 9 (Sept. 1879): 347–48.

41. Gary Scharnhorst with Jack Bales, *The Lost Life of Horatio Alger, Jr.* (Bloomington: Indiana Univ. Press, 1985), 118.

42. "Literature of Our Sunday Schools," pt. 1, 295.

43. S. S. Green, "Sensational Fiction," 348.

44. Robert Falk, "Notes on the Higher Criticism of Horatio Alger, Jr.," *Arizona Quarterly* 19 (Summer 1963): 151–67; John Seelye, "Who Was Horatio? The Alger Myth and American Scholarship," *American Quarterly* 17, no. 4 (Winter 1965): 751.

45. Dee Garrison, "Cultural Custodians of the Gilded Age: The Public Librarian and Horatio Alger," *Journal of Library History* 6 (Oct. 1971): 327–36.

46. Ibid.

47. Herbert R. Mayes, *Alger: A Biography Without a Hero* (New York: Macy-Masius, 1928); Jack Bales, "Herbert R. Mayes and Horatio Alger, Jr.; Or, The Story of a Unique Literary Hoax," *Journal of Popular Culture* 8, no. 2 (Fall 1974): 317–19; and Scharnhorst with Bales, *Lost Life of Horatio Alger*.

48. See Seelye, "Who Was Horatio?," 749.

49. Garrison, "Cultural Custodians of the Gilded Age"; Scharnhorst with Bales, *Lost Life of Horatio Alger*; Malcolm Cowley, "Books in Review: The Alger Story," *New Republic* 113, no. 11 (10 Sept. 1945): 319–20; and John G. Cawelti, "Portrait of the Newsboy as a Young Man: Some Remarks on the Alger Stories," *Wisconsin Magazine of History* 45 (Winter 1961–62): 79–83.

50. See Seelye, "Who Was Horatio?" 755.

51. Garrison, "Cultural Custodians of the Gilded Age," 335, n. 16: "This judgment of the attitude of most public librarians is primarily based upon a complete and detailed reading of the *Library Journal, 1876–1904.*" See Mary Salome Cutler, "Sunday Opening of the Libraries," *Library Journal* 14 (May–June 1889): 176–90; C. C. Soule, "The Boston Public Library," *Library Journal* 17 (Mar. 1892): 88–91; F. M. Crundan, "What of the Future?" *Library Journal* 22 (Oct. 1897): 5–11; and Lindsay Swift, "Paternalism in Public Libraries," *Library Journal* 24 (Nov. 1899): 608–18.

52. Cutler, "Sunday Opening of Libraries," 178–79.

53. Frank K. Walter, "A Poor but Respectable Relation—The Sunday School Library," *Library Quarterly* 12 (1942): 371. See R. Gordon Kelly, *Children's Periodicals,* 92–98; Gillian Avery, "The Evangelical Child, 1818–1880," in her *Childhood's Pattern: A Study of the Heroes and Heroines of Children's Fiction, 1770–1950* (London: Hodder and Stoughton, 1975): 92–120; and Noel, *Villains Galore,* 164–65.

54. Herbert Putnam, "The Relation of Free Public Libraries to the Community," *North American Review* 498, no. 166 (June 1898): 660. All quotations in this paragraph came from this source.

55. Wiebe, *Search for Order,* 14.

56. "The Literature of Our Sunday-Schools," pt. 3, *Hours at Home* 10, no. 6 (Apr. 1870): 560.

57. Kate Douglas Wiggin, *Rebecca of Sunnybrook Farm* (Boston: Houghton Mifflin, 1903; rpt. New York: Scholastic, 1988).

58. Walter, "A Poor but Respectable Relation," 372.

59. "Isabella M. Alden, Noted Author Dies: Wrote Under the Name, Pansy, More Than 120 Books for World-Wide Public," *New York Times,* 6 Aug. 1930, 21:5. This article claimed that "Pansy" had published her first piece in the local newspaper at age 8, but the *NCAB* and Paul R. Messbarger, "Isabella M. Alden," in *NAW* 1:31–32, reports that "Pansy" was 10 years old. See Sarah K. Bolton, *Successful Women* (Buffalo, N.Y.: Moulton, 1893); Willard and Livermore, *American Women,* 13–14; the foreword by Grace Livingston Hill in Isabella M. Alden, *An Interrupted Night* (Boston: Lippincott, 1884; rpt. Lathrop, 1929), 5–22; and *Woman's Who's Who of America, 1914–15.*

60. "Isabella Macdonald Alden," *NCAB* 10:405.

61. "Understanded [*sic*] of the People," *New York Times,* 6 Aug. 1930, 20:4.

62. "J. T. Trowbridge: Friend of Boys," *Outlook* 112 (23 Feb. 1916): 412.

63. Ibid.

64. Samuel Scoville, Jr., "Rescue, Robbery and Escapes," *Forum* 74, no. 1 (July 1925): 85.

65. Martha H. Brooks, "Sunday School Libraries," *Library Journal* 4, no. 9 (Sept. 1879): 338.

66. Eaton, "The American Family," in Meigs, *Critical History of Children's Literature,* 169.

67. R. Gordon Kelly, *Children's Periodicals,* 381. Catherine Morris Wright, "Mary Mapes Dodge," *AWW* 1:518–19. For biographical information, see Marilyn H. Karrenbrock, "Mary Mapes Dodge," *DLB* 42:146–60; Kunitz and Haycraft, *American Authors, 1600–1900,* 221; *New York Times,* 22 Aug. 1905, 7:6; Henry Steele Commager, "Dodge, Mary Elizabeth Mapes," in *NAW* 1:495–96; William Fayal Clarke, "St. Nicholas: In Memory of Mary Mapes Dodge, Died Aug. 21, 1905," *St. Nicholas* 32, no. 12 (Oct. 1905): 1059–71; Alice B. Howard, *Mary Mapes Dodge of St. Nicholas* (New York: Messner, 1943); Sarah S. McEnery, "Mary Mapes Dodge: An Intimate Tribute," *Critic* 47 (Oct. 1905): 310–12; Lucia Gilbert Runkle, "Mary Mapes Dodge," in *Our Famous Women: An Authorized Record of the Lives and Deeds of Distinguished American Women of Our Times*, ed. Elizabeth Stuart Phelps, et al. (Hartford, Conn.: Worthington, 1886), 276–94; and Catherine Morris Wright, *Lady of the Silver Skates: The Life and Correspondence of Mary Mapes Dodge* (Jamestown, R.I.: Clingstone, 1979).

68. Clarke, "St. Nicholas: In Memory," 1066.

69. Marilyn Karrenbrock, "Mary Dodge Mapes," *DLB* 150.

70. Clarke, "St. Nicholas: In Memory," 1066.

71. "Mary Mapes Dodge Dead: The Poet, Author, and Editor of St. Nicholas Magazine," *New York Times,* 22 Aug. 1905, 7:6.
72. Eaton, *Critical History of Children's Literature,* 285.
73. Earnest Elmo Calkins, "St. Nicholas," *Saturday Review of Literature* 22, no. 2 (4 May 1940): 7. Also see Clarke, "St. Nicholas: In Memory," 1059–71; and Alice Jordan, "Good Old St. Nicholas," *Horn Book* 19 (Jan.–Feb. 1943): 56–62. For information about *Wide Awake,* see Mott, *History of American Magazines,* 508–9; and R. Gordon Kelly, *Children's Periodicals,* 454–60.
74. R. Gordon Kelly, *Children's Periodicals,* 507–14; and Mott, *History of American Magazines,* 6–8.
75. Hart, *Oxford Companion to American Literature,* 230.
76. Jordan, "Good Old St. Nicholas," 61.
77. Ibid., 57.
78. Mary Mapes Dodge, "Children's Magazines," *Scribner's Monthly* 6 (July 1873): 352.
79. Ibid., 352–53.
80. Clarke, "St. Nicholas: In Memory," 1064.
81. Jordan, "Good Old St. Nicholas," 61.
82. For standard biographical information about "Oliver Optic" (William Taylor Adams), see Johannsen, *House of Beadle and Adams,* 2, 7–8; Kunitz and Haycraft, *American Authors: 1600–1900;* "William Taylor Adams," Carol Gay, *DAB* 42; "William Taylor Adams," *NCAB* 6:102–3; and "Death of Oliver Optic, *New York Times,* 28 Mar. 1897. For information on "Oliver Optic's" magazines, see Mott, *History of American Magazines,* 174–78, 210; and R. Gordon Kelly, *Children's Periodicals,* 311–17. Kelly describes Mayne Reid in chap. 7, "Education and Arts," esp. 175, 176, 179, and 219; and gives information on Reid's publishing ventures, 317–21.
83. For assessments of Adams's writing, see Jane Bingham and Grayce Scholot, *Fifteen Centuries of Children's Literature: An Annotated Chronology of British and American Novels in Historical Context* (Westport, Conn.: Greenwood, 1980), 186–88, 205; R. L. Darling, "Authors vs. Critics: Children's Books in the 1870s," *Publishers Weekly* 192 (16 Oct. 1967): 25–27; Gene Gleason, "Whatever Happened to Oliver Optic?" *Wilson Library Bulletin* 49 (May 1975): 647–50; "A New Oliver Optic Series," no. 258, 3, no. 258: 286; *Critic* (3 Apr. 1897); *Munsey's Magazine* (Oct. 1886); R. Gordon Kelly, *Children's Periodicals,* 311–16, 325–26, 428–35; *American Bookseller* 23 (1888): 289–90; and *American Bookseller* 24 (1889): 8–11; Alban Eric, "William Taylor Adams," *Midland Monthly* (Dec. 1897): 560–62; *Critic* 30:242–43; "The Author of One Hundred Successful Books," *Literary Digest* 14 (10 Apr. 1897): 700; and Hart, *Oxford Companion to American Literature,* 9–10.
84. Gay, "William Taylor Adams," *DAB* 42:16.
85. Quentin Reynolds, *Fiction Factory,* 5. Both quotations are from this source.
86. Hart, *Oxford Companion to American Literature,* 9.
87. R. Gordon Kelly, *Children's Periodicals,* 314.
88. Tebbel, *History of Book Publishing,* 2:271.

89. *Burlesque* was a "popular stage entertainment that originated in mid-19th century New York, deriving from the minstrel show, variety theater, and travesties. Often considered somewhat illicit, it became very popular, and from New York companies grew the Columbia and mutual circuits ("wheels") throughout the country and the Weber and Fields Music Hall and Minsky's. It featured dialect and slapstick comedians who specialized in *double entendre*; travesties of popular drama and current events; scantily dressed chorus girls; and song-and-dance acts. Today [1965] only a few theaters feature burlesque." Burlesque did not promise striptease; that feature was added in the twentieth century. Hart, *Oxford Companion to American Literature,* 119.

90. Johannsen, *House of Beadle and Adams* 2:7.

91. Louisa May Alcott's condemnation of "optical delusions" can be found in her "Eight Cousins," *St. Nicholas* 2 (1875): 616–17. His reply, "Sensational Books for Boys," ran in *Oliver Optic's Magazine* 17, no. 266 (1875):717–18.

92. Roberts Brothers in Boston published Alcott's novels. See *DAB* 16.

93. Kunitz and Haycraft, *American Authors, 1600–1900,* 19.

94. R. Gordon Kelly, *Children's Periodicals,* 94.

95. "Books for Children of All Ages," *Nation* 5 (26 Dec. 1867): 524.

96. "Gay, William Taylor Adams," *DAB* 42:16. See John Rowe Townsend, *A Sense of Story* (Philadelphia: Lippincott, 1971).

97. Kunitz and Haycraft, *American Authors, 1600–1900,* 13.

98. Scoville, "Rescue, Robbery and Escapes," 88.

99. William Holmes McGuffey, *McGuffey's First Eclectic Reader,* rev. ed. (New York: Van Nostrand Reinhold, 1879), 37–41. For biographical information on William Holmes McGuffey, see Rebecca Lukens, "William Holmes McGuffey," *DLB* 42:271–75; Stanley W. Lindberg's introduction in Lindberg, *The Annotated McGuffey: Selections from the McGuffey Eclectic Readers, 1836–1920* (New York: Van Nostrand Reinhold, 1976); and Harvey C. Minnich, *William Holmes McGuffey and His Readers* (New York: American, 1936). For assessments of the cultural impact of the readers, see Atherton, *Main Street on the Middle Border;* Alice McGuffey Ruggles, *The Story of the McGuffeys* (New York: American, 1950); John H. Westeroff, III, *McGuffey and His Readers* (New York: Abingdon, 1978); and Carol Kammen, "The McGuffey Readers," in *Children's Literature: Annual of the Modern Language Association Group on Children's Literature and the Children's Literature Association* 5 (1973): 58–63.

100. *McGuffey's First Eclectic Reader,* 93–94.

101. Ibid., "Preface," iii.

102. Weiss, *American Myth of Success,* 33–35.

Chapter 6. Biography—Truth or Legend?

1. Ernest G. Bormann, "Symbolic Convergence: Organizational Communication and Culture," *Communication and Organizations: An Interpretive Approach,* ed. Linda L. Putnam and Michael E. Pacanowsky (Beverly Hills, Calif.: Sage, 1983), 99–122.

2. Ronald C. Arnett, *Communication and Community: Implications of Martin Buber's Dialogue* (Carbondale: Southern Illinois Univ. Press, 1986), 171.

3. The three examples of press treatment of the Carnegie legend are quoted from "In Praise of Mr. Carnegie," *Review of Reviews* 13, no. 6 (June 1896): 741. Homer David Bates, "The Turning Point of Mr. Carnegie's Career," *Century Magazine* 76, no. 3 (July 1908): 333; and "Andrew Carnegie Dies of Pneumonia . . . Started Out as a Poor Boy," *New York Times,* 12 Aug. 1919, 1:1.

4. Hamilton Holt, "The Carnegie That I Knew," *Independent* 99 (23 Aug. 1919): 253.

5. "Owen Wister Dies; Wrote 'Virginian' Novel That Resulted from the Advice of Physician Sold 1,500,000 Copies; Also Active in Politics; Was Biographer of Theodore Roosevelt—Author of Other Historical Works," *New York Times,* 22 July 1938, 17:2.

6. E. P. Roe, "The Elements of Life in Fiction," *Forum* 5 (Apr. 1888): 236.

7. Margaret Bloom, "George W. Cable: A New Englander in the South," *Bookman* 73, no. 4 (June 1931): 403.

8. Edward Eggleston, "Formative Influences," *Forum* 10 (Nov. 1890): 286. See Henry Nash Smith, *Virgin Land,* 233–42.

9. Eggleston, "Formative Influences," 286.

10. Ibid.

11. Ibid.

12. Carol Farley Kessler, "Elizabeth Stuart Phelps Ward," *AWW* 327.

13. "Elizabeth Stuart Phelps Ward," *Outlook* 97, no. 6 (11 Feb. 1911): 299.

14. "Elizabeth Stuart (Phelps) Ward," *NCAB* 9:369, and Kunitz and Haycraft, *American Authors, 1600–1900,* 779–80.

15. Mrs. Emma (E. D. E. N.) Southworth, *The Haunted Homestead and Other Novelettes, With an Autobiography of the Author* (Philadelphia: Peterson, 1860).

16. Geoffrey T. Hellman, "Mary Roberts Rinehart: For 53 Years She Has Been America's Best-Selling Lady Author," *Life* 20, no. 7 (18 Feb. 1946): 61.

17. Kate Douglas Wiggin, "When I Was a Little Girl," *Ladies Home Journal* 32, no. 4 (Apr. 1915): 10. The honorary title, "The Lady of the Twinkle and the Tear," appeared in the *New York Times,* 13 Sept. 1923: "Kate D. Wiggin Dies in London. American Novelist Fails to Rally from the Effects of an Operation Last June. Her Stories of Childhood. Author of *Rebecca of Sunnybrook Farm* Began Her Career as a Kindergarten Teacher."

18. Stanley A. Pachon, "Mary Roberts Rinehart and the Nickel Novels," *Dime Novel Roundup* 31, no. 6 (June 1963): 55.

19. Barbara Welter, "Mary Roberts Rinehart," *NAW* 4:577.

20. Mary H. Krout, "Personal Reminiscences of Lew Wallace," *Harper's Weekly* 49, no. 2518 (25 Mar. 1905): 409.

21. "The Gospel of Wealth," *Outlook* 67, no. 10 (9 Mar. 1901): 571.

22. Eggleston, "Formative Influences," 285.

23. Amelia Barr, *All the Days of My Life: An Autobiography—The Red Leaves of a Human Heart* (New York: Appleton, 1913), 52.

24. "Mary Roberts Rinehart," *NCAB* 100:486.

25. Eggleston, "Formative Influences," 285.

26. All quotations in this paragraph are from Bruce Barton, "Conversation Between a Young Man and an Old Man: Bruce Barton at 34, Russell H. Conwell at 78," *American Magazine* 92, no. 1 (July 1921): 15, 108. Barton's bestseller, *The Man Nobody Knows: A Discovery of the Real Jesus* (New York: Grossett and Dunlap, 1925), depicts Christ as a salesman.

27. Lucy Ward Stebbins, "Kate Douglas Wiggin as a Child Knew Her," *Horn Book* 26, no. 6 (Nov.–Dec. 1950): 447.

28. Mary R. P. Hatch, "The Author of the Leavenworth Case," *Writer* 2, no. 7 (July 1888): 159.

29. "Dey Released in Denver. Reprimand Only for Nick Carter Author, Who Impersonated Officer," *New York Times,* pt. 2, 24 Aug. 1913, 1.

30. Dennis R. Rogers, "The Pseudonyms of Edward Ellis," *Dime Novel Round-Up* 26, no. 12 (15 Dec. 1958): 148.

31. Elizabeth Johnson, "Margaret Sidney vs. Harriet Lothrop," 144.

32. Anne Commire, "Harriet Mulford Stone Lothrop," *Something about the Author,* 20:112. This series of books, which features children's authors, resembles the *DLB*.

33. Commire, "Harriet Mulford Stone Lothrop," 114.

34. Southworth, *Haunted Homestead,* 30.

35. Hatch, "Author of the Leavenworth Case," 159.

36. Barr, *All the Days of My Life,* 21–22.

37. Ibid., 241.

38. Ibid., 100.

39. Ibid., 107.

40. Ibid., 146.

41. Willard and Livermore, *American Women,* 57.

Chapter 7. The Repulsive Fascination of Fires

1. E. J. Goodspeed, *History of the Great Fires: Chicago and the West—A Proud Career Arrested by Sudden and Awful Calamity; Towns and Counties Laid Waste by the Devastating Element. Scenes and Incidents, Losses and Sufferings, Benevolence of the Nations, Etc., with a History of the Rise and Fall of Chicago, the "Young Giant," to Which Is Appended a History of the Great Fires in the Past, Illustrated and Sold Only by Subscription* (New York: Goodspeed, 1871), 218.

2. Ibid., table of contents, viii.

3. Robert W. Wells, *Fire and Ice: Two Deadly Disasters, Fire at Peshtigo* (Ashland, Wis.: Northword, 1983), 86.

4. The Chicago Fire was treated by contemporaries in: James W. Sheahan and George P. Upton, *History of the Great Conflagration. Chicago: Its Past, Present and Future. Embracing a Detailed Narrative of the Great Conflagration in the North, South and West Divisions. Origin, Progress and Results of the Fire. Prominent Buildings Burned, Character of Buildings, Losses and Insurance. Graphic Description of the Flames, Scenes and Incidents, Loss of Life, the Flight of the People. Also, a Condensed History of Chicago, Its Population, Growth and Great Public*

Works. And a Statement of All the Great Fires of the World (Chicago: Union, 1871). Also see Elias Colbert and Everett Chamberlin, *Chicago and the Great Conflagration: With Numerous Illustrations by Chapin and Gulick from Photographic Views Taken on the Spot* (Cincinnati, Ohio: Vent, 1871); and Howard G. Earl, "Peshtigo's Night of Horror: The Fire That Killed 1200 Souls in a Forest So Remote, On a Day So Infamous, That Its Story Was Hidden from History," *Esquire* 225, no. 2 (Aug. 1952): 34.

5. Sheahan and Upton, "History of the Great Conflagration," 56.

6. Wells, *Fire and Ice*, 84.

7. Charles De Lano Hine, "Heroes of the Railway Service: Notes from Experience," *Century Magazine* 35, no. 5 (Mar. 1899): 653.

8. The fire itself, including the train rescue, was described in "Hundreds Perish in Forest Fires. Western Towns Destroyed and Citizens Burned to Death in Their Crumbling Houses. Terrible Scenes of Suffering at Hinckley. The Minnesota Town Completely Wiped Out by the Flames, and Many of Its Inhabitants Perish—One Hundred-Forty-Three Bodies Already Recovered and More in the Ruins—Other Towns Swept Up by the Fire—The List of Dead Will Probably Reach Four Hundred," *New York Times,* 3 Sept. 1894, 1:1–6. See "Race for Life with Flames: How Engineer Root Brought the Limited to a Place of Safety," *New York Times,* 3 Sept. 1894, 1:6.

9. William Watts Folwell, *Minnesota: The North Star State* (New York: Houghton Mifflin, 1908), 349–50. *The WPA Guide to Minnesota: Compiled and Written by the Federal Writers' Project of the Works Progress Administration* (St. Paul: Minnesota Historical Society Press, 1985), 295.

10. "Race for Life with Flames," 1:6.

11. Ibid.

12. Ibid.

13. Ibid.

14. Estimates of the number on the train varied from Hine's figure, 200, to passengers' guesses of about 100. The exact figure cannot be calculated.

15. Hine, "Heroes of the Railway Service," 653.

16. "Race for Life with Flames," 2:2.

17. Telephone conversation with Jeanne Coffey, curator of the Hinckley Fire Museum, 6 Feb. 1990. Coffey explained that news accounts exaggerated Root's heroism. She also noted that Root wrote, produced and starred in a play about the Hinckley nightmare. It closed after the first performance in New York. His attempt to bring his experiences to the stage suggests the close relationship between life and fiction.

18. William Wilkinson, *Memorials of the Minnesota Forest Fires in the Year of 1894* (Minneapolis: Norman E. Wilkinson, 1895); and Grace Swenson, *From the Ashes: The Story of the Hinckley Fire of 1894* (St. Cloud, Minn.: North Star, 1979).

19. Lyle, *Scalded to Death by the Steam.*

20. Hine, "Heroes of the Railway Service," 654.

21. "Saver of Many Lives Dead: Engineer J. M. Root Displayed Great Heroism in Minnesota Forest Fire," *New York Times,* 15 Dec. 1911, 13:5.

22. Henry C. Adams, "The Slaughter of Railway Employees," *Forum* 13 (June 1892): 500.
23. Goodspeed, *History of the Great Fires,* 614. Quotations are from this source.
24. Ibid.
25. Herman B. Seeley, "The Loss by Fire in the Congested District of Chicago," *American Architect* 87, no. 1524 (11 Mar. 1905): 83.
26. Goodspeed, *History of the Great Fires,* 626–34.
27. Paul C. Ditzel, *Fire Engines, Firefighters: The Men, Equipment and Machines from Colonial Days to the Present* (New York: Crown, 1976), 131 and chap. 16, "Chicago Is in Flames . . . Send Help!" John A. Cregier's story is on 131.
28. John V. Morris, "The Big Burn," in his *Fires and Firefighters* (Boston: Little, Brown, 1953), 195.
29. Ditzel, *Fire Engines, Firefighters,* 122, 124.
30. Mabel Osgood Wright, *My New York* (New York: Macmillan, 1926), 39–40. Michael Schudson, *Discovering the News: A Social History of American Newspapers* (New York: Basic Books, 1978), 207.
31. Wright, *My New York,* 37.
32. Ibid., 40. Both quotations come from this source.
33. Jay Robert Nash, *Darkest Hours: A Narrative Encyclopedia of Worldwide Disasters from Ancient Time to the Present* (Chicago: Nelson-Hall, 1976).
34. Clifford Thomson, "The Waste by Fire," *Forum* 27 (Sept. 1886): 27.
35. *Alexandria (La.) Town Talk,* 23 March 1883, 1.
36. Both incidents were reported in *Alexandria (La.) Town Talk,* 8 May 1883, 1.
37. "A Growing List of Dead: Eleven More Victims of the Wreck at Alton, Ill. Fourteen of the Injured Whose Cases Are Hopeless—Searching For Bodies Near the Scene of the Accident," *New York Daily Tribune,* 23 Jan. 1893, 1:1.
38. *Muncie (Ind.) Daily News,* 10 Dec. 1885, 4:5.
39. Sheahan and Upton, *History of the Great Conflagration,* 371.
40. Wells, *Fire and Ice,* 74.
41. Thomson, "Waste by Fire," 30.
42. Ibid., 28.
43. John Gifford, "The Causes and Effects of Great Forest Fires," *Engineering Magazine* 8, no. 2 (Nov. 1894): 190.
44. G. W. De Succa, *Austin (Nev.) Reese River Reveille,* 29 June 1875, 2:1.

Chapter 8. Fantastic Reality and Realistic Fantasy

1. Colbert and Chamberlin, *Chicago and the Great Conflagration.*
2. Merle Curti, *The Growth of American Thought,* 3d ed. (New York: Harper and Row, 1964), 621.
3. Thomas G. Shearman, "The Coming Billionaire," *Forum* 10 (Jan. 1891): 546. See Lee Soltow, *Patterns of Wealthholding in Wisconsin Since 1850* (Madison: UW-Madison Press, 1971); Garraty, *New Commonwealth*; Sean Dennis Cashman, *America in the Gilded Age: From the Death of Lincoln to the Rise of Theodore Roosevelt* (New York: New York Univ. Press, 1984); and Wiebe, *Search for Order.*

4. Cashman, *America in the Gilded Age,* 78.

5. Shearman, "Coming Billionaire," 547–48.

6. George Juergens, *Joseph Pulitzer and the New York World* (Princeton, N.J.: Princeton Univ. Press, 1966), esp. "A Newspaper for Women," 132–74.

7. "Two Cats on a Satin Costume," *Alexandria (La.) Town Talk,* 1 July 1883, 2:1.

8. Joseph Campbell with Bill Moyers, *Power of Myth* (New York: Doubleday, 1988), 5.

9. "The Little Store," *Austin (Nev.) Reese River Reveille,* 2 Apr. 1875, 3:3.

10. Tompkins, *Sensational Designs,* esp. her introduction, "The Cultural Work of American Fiction," xi–xix.

11. Juergens, *Joseph Pulitzer,* 176 and the chapter "A Gospel of Wealth," 175–209.

12. Orison Swett Marden, *Pushing to the Front; Or, Success Under Difficulties, a Book of Inspiration and Encouragement to All Who Are Struggling for Self-Elevation along Paths of Knowledge and Duty* (Crowell, 1894); and Orison Swett Marden, *The Secret of Achievement: A Book Designed to Teach the Highest Achievement Is That Which Results in Noble Manhood and Womanhood* (Crowell, 1898). William Makepiece Thayer, *Aim High: Hints and Help for Young Men* (New York: Whittaker, 1895); Thayer, *Women Who Win; Or, Making Things Happen* (New York: Nelson, 1896); and Thayer, *Onward to Fame and Fortune; Or, Climbing Life's Ladder, Containing 75 Superb Portraits and Numerous Illustrations* (New York: Christian Herald, 1897).

13. "Keeping Everlastingly at It," *Lewiston, Mont., Fergus County Argus,* Jan. 16, 1896, 2.

14. "Pioneer Printer's Luck: Frank Dallam Tells of His Early Observations. Men Who Stuck to the Printers Trade and Lost Opportunities," *Wenatchee (Wash.) Advance,* 19 Jan. 1895, 2:1.

15. Ibid.

16. "Paralyzed," *Lewiston, Mont., Fergus County Argus,* 27 June 1895, 4:1.

17. *Alexandria (La.) Town Talk,* 22 Sept. 1883, 3:1.

18. "Killed in a Quarrel Over Twenty-Five Cents," *New York Daily Tribune,* 13 Apr. 1893, 1:3.

19. "Romance of a Wig: A Very Simple Trick That Ended in a Tragedy," *Lewiston (Mont.) Fergus County Argus,* 3 Jan. 1896, 4:1.

20. Ibid. "Choosing a Wife," *Lewiston (Mont.) Fergus County Argus,* 10 Oct. 1895, 1:2.

21. "Unable to Stand Good Fortune," *Muncie (Ind.) Daily News,* 31 Dec. 1885, 1:5.

22. Washington Gladden, "Three Dangers," *Century Magazine* 30 (Aug. 1884): 620.

23. "Wealth and Vulgarity," *New York World,* 14 Oct. 1883, 4, qtd. in Juergens, *Joseph Pulitzer,* 769.

24. "Miss Gardner Wants Solace," *Wenatchee (Wash.) Advance,* 9 Feb. 1895, 2d col., probably p. 4 (microfilm indistinct).

25. "Wealth and Vulgarity," 4, qtd. in *New York World,* 14 Oct. 1883, 4, qtd. in Juergens, *Joseph Pulitzer,* 769.

26. Juergens, *Joseph Pulitzer,* 179.

27. "Lazy," *Alexandria (La.) Daily Town Talk,* 1 July 1883, 2:1.

28. Gladden, "Three Dangers," 625.

29. Ibid., 627.
30. *Alexandria (La.) Town Talk,* 17 Mar. 1883, 2:2.
31. Juergens, *Joseph Pulitzer,* 184; on speculation, see 181–84.
32. "The Dude," *Alexandria (La.) Town Talk,* 17 Mar. 1883, 4:1P, qtd. from the *Brooklyn Eagle* newspaper.
33. John F. Kasson, *Rudeness and Civility: Manners in Nineteenth-Century Urban America* (New York: Hill and Wang, 1990), 127–29.
34. "Preaching Without Gloves On," *Muncie (Ind.) Daily News,* 2 July 1885, 1:3.
35. "American Fondness for Titles," *Lewiston, Mont., Fergus County Argus,* 28 Mar. 1895, 4:1.
36. "Marrying and Blacking Boots," *New York World,* 21 Nov. 1883, 4, qtd. in Juergens, *Joseph Pulitzer,* 191.
37. Juergens, *Joseph Pulitzer,* 208.
38. Ibid., 206.
39. Ibid., 208.
40. Weiss, *American Myth of Success,* 75.

Epilogue

1. Daniel J. Boorstin, "Why an Eminent Historian Unequivocally States, 'I Am Optimistic about America,'" *Parade Magazine,* 10 July 1994, 5.
2. Ibid.
3. Erica Jong, "Facing the Fear of Fifty," *Parade Magazine,* 10 July 1994, 8.
4. "Earl Hamner, Coming Home to Walton's Mountain: The Real John-Boy, Walton's Creator, Earl Hamner, Looks Back on the Series that Defined an Era's Family Values," *TV Guide* 41, no. 47 (20 Nov. 1993): 10–14; and Deborah Starr Seibel, "The Other Side of the Mountain: A Waltons 'Where Are They Now?'" *TV Guide* 41, no. 47 (20 Nov. 1993): 18, 20.
5. Alan Loy McGinnis, "Try These Tips for Greater Success and Happiness: Getting the Most Out of Life" (condensed from McGinnis, *The Power of Optimism* [New York: Harper, 1993]) *Reader's Digest* 139, no. 831 (July 1991): 17.
6. "*Star* by Danielle Steel," *Good Housekeeping* 208, no. 2 (Feb. 1989): 143+.
7. "Danielle Steel's *Star,*" *People Magazine* 40, no. 12 (20 Sept. 1993): 12.
8. Tompkins, *Sensational Designs,* esp. chap. 5: "Sentimental Power," 122–46.
9. Salem Press Magill Book Reviews, available on Proquest, a computerized index, are protected by copyright. No reviewer is indicated for the review of Danielle Steel's *Star* (New York: Delacourt, 1989), item no. 9008015379, Salem Press Magill Book Reviews on Proquest. J. K. Sweeney, review of Dawn Powell, *A Time to Be Born* (New York: Yarrow, 1991), item no.: 9202249119, Salem Press Magill Book Reviews on Proquest.
10. *Books in Print (1993–1994): Subject Guide* (New York: Bowker, 1993–94).
11. Irene Brandenburg, review of Melvyn Kinder, *Going Nowhere Fast: Step Off Life's Treadmills and Find Peace of Mind* (New York: Prentice-Hall, 1990), item no. 9104159004, Salem Press Magill Book Reviews on Proquest.
12. Tocqueville, *Democracy in America,* 2:164.
13. Richard Weiss, *American Myth of Success,* 78.
14. Carnegie, *Gospel of Wealth.*

15. Conwell, *Acres of Diamonds,* 13.
16. John Steinbeck, "About Ed Ricketts," in *The Log from the Sea of Cortez,* by John Steinbeck (1941; rpt. New York: Viking, 1951), lxv.
17. Frances X. Clines, "An Unfettered Milken Has Lessons to Teach," *New York Times,* 16 Oct. 1993, 1. The comment on thievery is in "Unhumbled, Milken Flourishes in the Classroom," col. 1, p. 9.
18. Ann Landers, "Being Rich Isn't the Key to Happiness," *Mining Journal,* 29 Jan. 1994, 6:1.
19. Review of Kinder, *Going Nowhere Fast,* in *Publishers Weekly* 237, no. 32 (10 Aug. 1994): 137.
20. Kevin Kelly, "A 'Living Hell' in Indiana," *Business Week,* 9 Mar. 1992, 33.
21. Michael Mandel, "More and More, Joblessness Wears a Business Suit," *Business Week,* Feb. 28, 1994, 22. Also see John W. Verity, "When Benefits—and Jobs—Are Deconstructed," *Business Week,* 23 Nov. 1992, 100.
22. Andrew Bard Schmookler, "The Insatiable Society: Materialistic Values and Human Needs," *Futurist* 25, no. 4 (July–Aug. 1991): 18.
23. Miriam Horn, "Happiness in the Hills: Traditional Goals Guide This Clan—To Farm, to Work, to Be with Our Family,'" *U.S. News and World Report,* 12 Dec. 1988, 84.
24. Schmookler, "Insatiable Society," 18.

Bibliography

Primary Sources
Popular Plots

Alger, Horatio. *Luke Walton; Or, The Chicago Newsboy*, Philadelphia: Porter and
Coates. Rpt. as *Luke Walton*, New York: Winston, 1889.
————. *Phil the Fiddler; Or, the Story of a Street Musician*. Boston: Loring, 1872.

Barr, Amelia. *Jan Vedder's Wife*. New York: Dodd, Mead, 1885.

Baum, L. Frank. *The Wonderful Wizard of Oz*. Chicago: Donohue, 1900. Rpt. as *The
Wizard of Oz*, Chicago: Rand McNally, 1956.

Bellamy, Edward. *Looking Backward: 2000–1887*. Boston: Ticknor, 1888. Rpt. as
Looking Backward. Cleveland: World, 1945.

Burnett, Frances Hodgson. *A Little Princess: Being the Whole Story of What Happened to
Sara Crewe, Now Told for the First Time*. New York: Scribners, 1905. Rpt.
New York: Apple Classics, 1988. This book is an expanded version of *Sara
Crewe; Or, What Happened at Miss Minchin's*. New York: Scribners, 1888.

Cable, George. *John March, Southerner*. New York: Scribners, 1894. Rpt. New
York: Garrett, 1970.

Carter, Nick (John Russell Coryell). "Nick Carter's Mysterious Case; Or, The Road-
House Tragedy." In Robert Clurman's collection of original stories, *Nick
Carter, Detective: Fiction's Most Celebrated Detective (Six Astonishing Adventures)*. Nick Carter Library no. 248. New York: Street and Smith, 1896. Rpt.
introd. Robert Clurman. New York: Macmillan, 1963.

Deland, Margaret. *John Ward, Preacher*. London: Warne, 1887. Rpt. Boston:
Houghton Mifflin, 1888.

Eggleston, Edward. *The Hoosier School-Master*. New York: Orange and Judd, 1871.
Rpt. Bloomington: Indiana Univ. Press, 1984.

Ellis, Edward S. *Wyoming*. Philadelphia: Porter and Coates, 1888.

Green, Anna Katharine (Rohlfs). *The Circular Study*. Garden City, N.Y.: Doubleday
Page, 1900.
————. *The Leavenworth Case: A Lawyer's Case*. 1878. Rpt. as *The Leavenworth Case*,
New York: Putnam, 1901.

Halsey, Harlan Page ("Old Sleuth"). *Fly-Away Ned*. New York: Parlor Car, 1895.
Rpt. New York: Arno, 1974.

Holmes, Mary Jane. *Edith Lyle's Secret.* New York: Burt, late 1870s to early 1880s.

Otis, James (James Otis Kaler). *Josiah in New York; Or, A Coupon from the Fresh Air Fund.* New York: Hurst, 1893.

——. *Toby Tyler; Or, Ten Weeks with a Circus.* Garden City, N.Y.: Doubleday, 1881.

Phelps (Ward), Elizabeth Stuart. *Beyond the Gates.* Boston: Houghton Mifflin, 1883.

——. *The Gates Ajar.* Boston: Fields and Osgood, 1868. Rpt. ed. Helen Sootin Smith, Cambridge, Mass.: Harvard Univ. Press, Belknap Press, 1964.

——. *The Gates Between.* Boston: Houghton Mifflin, 1887.

Porter, Eleanor. *Pollyanna.* Doubleday, Page, 1913. Rpt. New York: Apple Classics, 1987.

Read, Opie. *The Jucklins.* Chicago: Laird and Lee, 1896.

Richards, Laura. *Captain January.* Boston: Estes and Lauriat, 1893.

Rice, Alice Caldwell Hegan. *Captain June.* New York: Century, 1907.

——. *Mrs. Wiggs of the Cabbage Patch.* New York: Century, 1901.

Rinehart, Mary Roberts. *The Circular Staircase.* New York: Grosset and Dunlap, 1908.

Roe, E. P. *Barriers Burned Away.* New York: Dodd, Mead, 1872.

Sheldon, Charles M. *In His Steps: What Would Christ Do?* New York: Burt, 1897. Rpt. as *In His Steps,* Chicago: Ulrich, 1899.

Sidney, Margaret (Harriet Mulford Stone Lothrop). *Five Little Peppers and How They Grew.* Lothrop, 1881. Rpt. New York: Apple Classics, 1989.

Southworth, E. D. E. N. *The Beautiful Fiend; Or, Through the Fire.* New York: Hurst, 1873.

——. *Victor's Triumph.* Philadelphia: T. B. Peterson, 1875. Sequel to *The Beautiful Fiend.*

Standish, Burt L. (Gilbert Patten). *Frank Merriwell's School Days; Or, A Tale of School Life at Fardale Academy.* Ed. Jack Rudman. New York: Smith Street, 1901. Rpt. 1907.

Stephens, Ann. *Phemie Frost's Experiences.* New York: Carlton, 1874.

Stratton-Porter, Gene. *Freckles.* New York: Doubleday Page, 1904.

Twain, Mark, and Charles Dudley Warner. *The Gilded Age: A Tale of Today.* Hartford, Conn.: American, 1873. Originally sold by subscription.

Wallace, Lew. *Ben-Hur: A Tale of the Christ.* New York: Harper, 1880.

Wheeler, E. L. (Edward Lytton). *Deadwood Dick on Deck; Or, Calamity Jane, the Heroine of Whoop-Up: A Story of Dakota.* Beadle's Half Dime Library, no. 73. New York: Beadle and Adams, 1878. Rpt. New York: Beadle and Adams, 1885. Beadle's Pocket Library, no. 5, vol. 57.

Wiggin, Kate Douglas (Mrs. G. C. Riggs). *The Birds' Christmas Carol.* San Francisco: C. A. Murdock, 1887. Rpt. New York: Apple Classics, 1972.

——. *Polly Oliver's Problem: A Story for Girls.* Boston: Houghton Mifflin, 1893. Rpt. New York: Grosset and Dunlap, 1951.

——. *Rebecca of Sunnybrook Farm.* Boston: Houghton Mifflin, 1903. Rpt. New York: Apple Classics, 1988.

Wister, Owen. *The Virginian: A Horseman of the Plains.* New York: Macmillan, 1902. Rpt. New York: Penguin, 1988.

Success Literature

Alger, Horatio. *Luke Walton; Or, The Chicago Newsboy,* Philadelphia: Porter and Coates. Rpt. as *Luke Walton,* New York: Winston, 1889.

Atkinson, William Walker. *The Secret of Success: A Course of Nine Lessons on the Subject of the Application of the Latent Powers of the Individual toward the Attainment of Success in Life.* Chicago: Advanced Thought, 1908.

Barnum, P. T. *Humbugs of the World: An Account of Humbugs, Delusions, Impositions, Quackeries, Deceits, and Deceivers Generally, in All Ages.* New York: Carleton, 1866.

————. *Struggles and Triumphs: The Art of Money Making.* 1854. Rpt. Buffalo, N.Y.: Courier, 1884. Rpt. as *How I Made Millions; Or, The Secrets of Success,* Chicago: Belford and Clarke, 1884.

Bok, Edward W. *Successward: A Youngman's Book for Young Men.* New York: Revell, 1895.

Burns, Rex. *Success in America: The Yeoman Dream and the Industrial Revolution.* Amherst: Univ. of Massachusetts Press, 1976.

Carnegie, Andrew. "The Advantages of Poverty." *Nineteenth Century* 29 (Mar. 1891): 379.

————. *Gospel of Wealth.* London: Hagen, 1889. Rpt. New York: Century, 1901.

Cawelti, John G. *Apostles of the Self-Made Man.* Chicago: Univ. of Chicago Press, 1965.

Chenoweth, Lawrence. *The American Dream of Success: The Search for the Self in the Twentieth Century.* North Scituate, Mass.: Duxbury, 1974.

Conwell, Russell. *Acres of Diamonds: How Men and Women May Become Rich: Examples Adapted to All Classes.* Philadelphia: Huber, 1890. Rpt. as *Acres of Diamonds; Or, How Men Get Rich Honestly,* Philadelphia: Book, 1893. Rpt. as *Acres of Diamonds,* Old Tappan, N.J.: Revell, 1983.

Greene, Theodore P. *America's Heroes: The Changing Models of Success in American Magazines.* New York: Oxford Univ. Press, 1970.

Huber, Richard M. *The American Idea of Success.* New York: McGraw-Hill, 1971.

Long, Elizabeth. *The American Dream and the Popular Novel.* Boston: Routledge and Kegan, 1985.

Smith, Henry Nash. "The Scribbling Women and the Cosmic Success Story." *Critical Inquiry* 1 (Sept. 1974): 47–70.

Southworth, E. D. E. N. *Self-Raised; Or, From the Depths.* Philadelphia: Peterson, 1876. Rpt. New York: Grosset and Dunlap, 1928.

Weiss, Richard. *The American Myth of Success: From Horatio Alger to Norman Vincent Peale.* New York: Basic Books, 1969.

Wyllie, Irvin G. *The Self-Made Man in America: The Myth of Rags to Riches.* New Brunswick, N.J.: Rutgers Univ. Press, 1954.

Other Works Consulted

Adams, Henry C. "The Slaughter of Railway Employees." *Forum* 13 (June 1892): 500–506.

Adams, John. *Harriet Beecher Stowe.* New Haven, Conn.: College and Univ. Press, 1963.

Addams, Jane. *Twenty Years at Hull House.* New York: Macmillan, 1910.

Allen, Frederick Lewis. "Horatio Alger, Jr." *Saturday Review* 18, no. 21 (17 Sept. 1938): 3–4.

Arbuthnot, May Hill. *Children and Books.* 3d ed. Glenview, Ill.: Scott-Foresman, 1964.

Arnett, Ronald C. *Communication and Community: Implications of Martin Buber's Dialogue.* Carbondale: Southern Illinois Univ. Press, 1968.

Ashton, Jean W. *Harriet Beecher Stowe: A Reference Guide.* Boston, Mass.: Hall, 1977.

Atherton, Lewis. *Main Street on the Middle Border.* Chicago: Quadrangle, 1954.

Atkinson, Edward. "Our Enormous Loss by Fire." *Engineering Magazine* 7, no. 5 (Aug. 1894): 603–12.

Avery, Gillian. "The Evangelical Child, 1818–80." In her *Childhood's Pattern: A Study of the Heroes and Heroines of Children's Fiction, 1770–1950.* London: Hodder and Stoughton, 1975. 92–120.

Bales, Jack. "Herbert R. Mayes and Horatio Alger, Jr.; Or, The Story of a Unique Literary Hoax." *Journal of Popular Culture* 8, no. 2 (Fall 1974): 317–19.

Barr, Amelia. *All the Days of My Life: An Autobiography—The Red Leaves of a Human Heart.* New York: Appleton, 1913.

Barrows, John H. *Henry Ward Beecher: The Shakespeare of the Pulpit.* New York: Funk and Wagnalls, 1893.

Barth, Gunther. *City People: The Rise of Modern City Culture in Nineteenth-Century America.* London: Oxford Univ. Press, 1981.

Barthes, Roland. *Elements of Semiology.* 11th ed. Translated by Annette Lavers and Colin Smith. New York: Hill and Wang, 1986.

———. *Mythologies.* Translated by Annette Lavers. New York: Hill and Wang, 1986.

Barton, Bruce. "Conversation Between a Young Man and an Old Man: Bruce Barton at 34, Russell H. Conwell at 78." *American Magazine* 92, no. 1 (July 1921): 13–15, 108.

———. *The Man Nobody Knows: A Discovery of the Real Jesus.* New York: Grossett Dunlap, 1925.

Barzun, Jacques, and Wendell Hertig Taylor. *A Catalogue of Crime, of Mystery, Detection and Related Genres: A Reader's Guide to the Literature.* New York: Harper and Row, 1971.

Berk, Stephen E. *Calvinism Versus Democracy: Timothy Dwight and the Origins of American Evangelical Orthodoxy.* Hamden, Conn.: Archon, 1974.

Blair, Henry William. *The Temperance Movement; Or, the Conflict Between Man and Alcohol.* Boston: Smythe, 1888.

Blonsky, Marshall. *On Signs.* Baltimore, Md.: Johns Hopkins Univ. Press, 1985.

Bloom, Eleanor. *Basic Books in the Mass Media.* Urbana: Univ. of Illinois Press, 1972.

Bloom, Margaret. "George W. Cable: A New Englander in the South." *Bookman* 73, no. 4 (June 1931): 401–3.

Bok, Edward. *The Americanization of Edward Bok: An Autobiography of a Dutch Boy Fifty Years After.* New York: Scribners, 1930.

Bold, Christine. "The Voice of the Fiction Factory in Dime and Pulp Westerns." *Journal of American Studies* 17 (Apr. 1983): 29–46.

Boller, Paul F., Jr. *American Thought in Transition: The Impact of Evolutionary Naturalism, 1865–1900.* Lanham, Md.: Univ. Press of America, 1981.

Boorstin, Daniel J. *The Americans: The Democratic Experience.* New York: Vintage, 1974.

Boyer, Paul *When Time Shall Be No More: Prophecy Belief in Modern American Culture.* Cambridge, Mass.: Belknap Press, Harvard Univ. Press, 1992.

Boyer, Paul S. "In His Steps: A Reappraisal." *American Quarterly* 1, no. 1 (Spring 1971): 60–78.

Boyle, Regis Louise. *Mrs. E. D. E. N. Southworth, Novelist: A Dissertation.* Washington, D.C.: Catholic Univ. of America Press, 1939.

Brooks, Van Wyck. "America's Coming-of-Age." In his *Three Essays on America.* New York: Dutton, 1934.

Cadogan, Mary. *You're a Brick, Angela! A New Look at Girls' Fiction from 1839 to 1975.* London: Gollancz, 1976.

Campbell, Helen. *Darkness and Daylight; Or, Lights and Shadows of New York Life—A Woman's Story of Gospel, Temperance, Mission and Rescue Work, with Hundreds of Thrilling Anecdotes and Incidents, Personal Experiences, Sketches of Life and Character, Humorous Stories, Touching Home Scenes and Tales of Tender Pathos, Drawn from the Bright and Shady Sides of City Life.* Hartford, Conn.: Worthington, 1891.

Campbell, Joseph. *Myths To Live By: How We Re-Create Ancient Legends in Our Daily Lives to Release Human Potential.* New York: Bantam, 1972.

————, with Bill Moyers. *Power of Myth.* New York: Doubleday, 1988.

Carey, James W., ed. "Editor's Introduction: Taking Culture Seriously." *Sage Annual Review of Communication Research* 15 (1988): 8–15.

————. "How and Why? The Dark Continent of American Journalism." In *Reading the News: A Pantheon Guide to American Culture,* ed. Robert Karl Manoff and Michael Schudson. New York: Pantheon, 1987.

————. "Technology and Ideology: The Case of the Telegraph." In *Prospects: An Annual of American Cultural Studies,* ed. Jack Salzman. London: Cambridge Univ. Press, 1983.

Carter, Paul A. *The Spiritual Crisis of the Gilded Age.* DeKalb: Northern Illinois Univ. Press, 1971.

Cashman, Sean Dennis. *America in the Gilded Age: From the Death of Lincoln to the Rise of Theodore Roosevelt.* New York: New York Univ. Press, 1984.

Cawelti, John G. *Adventure, Mystery and Romance: Formula Stories as Art and Popular Culture.* Chicago: Univ. of Chicago Press, 1976.

————. "Portrait of the Newsboy as a Young Man: Some Remarks on the Alger Stories." *Wisconsin Magazine of History* 45 (Winter 1961–62): 79–83.

————. *The Six-Gun Mystique.* Bowling Green, Ohio: Bowling Green Univ. Popular Press, (1971?).

Chatham, Seymour. *Story and Discourse: Narrative Structure in Fiction and Film.* Ithaca, N.Y.: Cornell Univ. Press, 1978.

Chomsky, Noam. *Language and Mind.* New York: Harcourt Brace, 1968.

Chudacoff, Howard. *The Evolution on American Urban Society.* New York: Prentice-Hall, 1975.

Clark, Thomas D. "Virgins, Villains, and Varmints." *American Heritage* 3, no. 3 (Spring 1952): 42–45.

Cockburn, Claud. *Bestseller: The Books That Everyone Read, 1900–1939.* London: Sedgwick and Jackson, 1972.

Colbert, Elias, and Everett Chamberlin. *Chicago and the Great Conflagration: With Numerous Illustrations by Chapin and Gulick from Photographic Views Taken on the Spot.* Cincinnati, Ohio: Vent, 1871.

Comstock, Anthony. "Half-Dime Novels and Story Papers." In his *Traps for the Young.* New York: Funk and Wagnalls, 1883. 20–42

———. "Vampire Literature." *North American Review* 153, no. 417 (July 1891): 159–71.

Conn, Peter. *Literature in America: An Illustrated History.* London: Cambridge Univ. Press, 1989.

Cook, William Wallace. *The Fiction Factory.* Ridgewood, N.J.: Editor Company, 1912.

Coste, Didier. *Narrative as Communication: Theory and History of Literature.* Minneapolis: Univ. of Minnesota Press, 1989.

Cowley, Malcolm "Books in Review: The Alger Story." *New Republic* 113, no. 11 (10 Sept. 1945): 319–20.

———. "The Revolt Against Gentility." In his *After the Genteel Tradition.* Carbondale: Southern Illinois Univ. Press, 1964.

Crane, Stephen. *Maggie, A Girl of the Streets: A Story of New York (1893): An Authoritative Text; Backgrounds and Sources; The Author and the Novel; Reviews and Criticism.* Ed. Thomas A. Gullason. New York: Norton, 1979.

Crozier, Alice C. *The Novels of Harriet Beecher Stowe.* New York: Oxford Univ. Press, 1969.

Curti, Merle. "Dime Novels and the American Tradition." *Yale Review* 26, no. 4 (June 1937): 761–78.

———. *The Growth of American Thought.* 3d ed. New York: Harper and Row, 1964.

Czitrom, Daniel J. *Media and the American Mind: From Morse to McLuhan.* Chapel Hill: Univ. of North Carolina Press, 1982.

Darnton, Robert. *The Great Cat Massacre and Other Episodes in French Cultural History.* New York: Vintage, 1985.

Davis, David B. "Ten Gallon Hero." *American Quarterly* 6, no. 2 (Summer 1954): 111–25.

Denning, Michael. *Mechanic Accents: Dime Novels and the Working-Class Culture in America.* New York: Verso, 1987.

Dinan, John A. *The Pulp Western: A Popular History of Western Fiction Magazines in America.* San Bernardino, Calif.: Borgo, 1983.

Ditzel, Paul C. *Fire Engines, Firefighters: The Men, Equipment and Machines from Colonial Days to the Present.* New York: Crown, 1976.

Dorchester, Daniel. "Liquor in the United States." In his *The Liquor Problem in All Ages,* 392–600. New York: Phillips and Hunt, 1884.

Durham, Philip. "Dime Novels: An American Heritage." *Western Humanities Review* 9, no. 1 (Winter 1954–55): 33–43.

Dunlap, George Arthur. *The City in the American Novel, 1789–1900: A Study of American Novels Portraying Contemporary Conditions in New York, Philadelphia and Boston.* New York: Russell and Russell, 1965.

Eaton, Anne. "The American Family." In *A Critical History of Children's Literature: A Survey of Children's Books in English from Earliest Times to the Present, Prepared in Four Parts,* ed. Cornelia Meigs, chap. 6. New York: Macmillan, 1953.

Earl, Howard G. "Peshtigo's Night of Horror: The Fire That Killed 1200 Souls in a Forest So Remote, On a Day So Famous, That Its Story Was Hidden from History." *Esquire* 225, no. 2 (Aug. 1952): 34.

Eco, Umberto. *A Theory of Semiotics.* Bloomington: Indiana Univ. Press, 1979.

Edward, George J. "Bellamy: Utopia, American Plan." *Antioch Review* 14, no. 2 (Summer 1954): 181–93.

Eggleston, Edward. "Formative Influences." *Forum* 10 (Nov. 1890): 279–87.

Ellsworth, William Webster. *A Golden Age of Authors: A Publisher's Recollection.* Boston: Houghton Mifflin, 1919.

Ely, Richard T. "Pauperism in the United States." *North American Review* 413 (Apr. 1891): 395–409.

Emery, Edwin, with Michael Emery. *The Press and America: An Interpretive History of the Mass Media.* 5th ed. Englewood Cliffs, N.J.: Prentice-Hall, 1984.

England, George Allan. "The Fiction Factory: How a Man Writes and Sells Over Half a Million Words a Year." *Independent* 74, no. 3356 (27 Mar. 1913): 687–90.

Estes, Glen E. "American Writers for Children." *Dictionary of American Biography.* Vol. 42. Detroit: Gale, 1985.

Falk, Robert. "Notes on the Higher Criticism of Horatio Alger, Jr." *Arizona Quarterly* 19 (Summer 1963): 151–67.

———. *The Victorian Mode in American Fiction, 1865–1885.* East Lansing: Michigan State Univ. Press, 1965.

———. "The Writer's Search for Reality." In *The Gilded Age,* ed. H. Wayne Morgan. Syracuse, N.Y.: Syracuse Univ. Press, 1970.

Fiedler, Leslie A. *The Inadvertent Epic: From Uncle Tom's Cabin to Roots.* Introduction by Barrie Hayne. New York: Simon and Schuster, 1979.

———. *Love and Death in the American Novel.* New York: Criterion, 1960.

Fisher, Walter R. *Human Communication as Narration: Toward a Philosophy of Reason, Value and Action.* Columbia: Univ. of South Carolina Press, 1987.

———. "Narration as a Human Communication Paradigm: The Case of Public Moral Argument." *Communication Monographs* 51, no. 1 (Mar. 1984).

Fiske, John, and John Hartley. "'Reading' Television." In their *Reading Television,* 85–100. New York: Methuen, 1978.

Flynt, Josiah. *Tramping with Tramps: Studies and Sketches of Vagabond Life.* College Park, Md.: McGrath, 1969.

Folkerts, Jean, with Dwight Teeter. *Voices of a Nation: A History of the Media in the United States.* New York: Macmillan, 1989.

Freire, Paulo, and Donaldo Macedo. *Literacy: Reading the Word and World.* South Hadley, Mass.: Bergin and Garvey, 1987.

Freitag, Joseph K. "Fire Losses in the United States: A Grave National Question." *Engineering Magazine* 331, no. 3 (June 1906): 321–28.

Frye, Northrop. *The Great Code: The Bible and Literature.* New York: Harcourt Brace Jovanovich, 1982.

Garraty, John A. *The New Commonwealth: 1877–1890.* New York: Harper and Row, 1968.

Garrison, Dee. "Cultural Custodians of the Gilded Age: The Public Librarian and Horatio Alger." *Journal of Library History* 6 (Oct. 1971): 327–36.

Gibbons, Cardinal James. "Wealth and Its Obligations." *North American Review* 413 (Apr. 1891): 385–94.

Gifford, John. "The Causes and Effects of Great Forest Fires." *Engineering Magazine* 8, no. 2 (Nov. 1894): 187–94.

Gladden, Washington. "Christianity and Popular Amusements." *Century Magazine* 29, no. 3 (Jan. 1885): 384–92.

———. "Christianity and Wealth." *Century Magazine* 30, no. 4 (Aug. 1884): 903–11.

Godkin, E. L. "Idleness and Immorality." *Forum* 13 (May 1892): 334–43.

Goetzmann, William H. *Exploration and Empire: The Explorer and the Scientist in the Winning of the West.* New York: Knopf, 1966.

———. *New Lands, New Men: America and the Second Great Age of Discovery.* New York: Penguin, 1986.

———. *The West of the Imagination: The Companion to the PBS Series.* New York: Norton, 1986.

Goodspeed, E. J. *History of the Great Fires: Chicago and the West—A Proud Career Arrested by Sudden and Awful Calamity; Towns and Counties Laid Waste by the Devastating Element. Scenes and Incidents, Losses and Sufferings, Benevolence of the Nations, Etc., Etc., with a History of the Rise and Fall of Chicago, the "Young Giant," to Which Is Appended a History of the Great Fires in the Past, Illustrated and Sold Only by Subscription.* New York: Goodspeed, 1871.

Goody, Jack. "Death and the Interpretation of Culture: A Bibliographic Overview." *American Quarterly* 26, no. 5 (Dec. 1974): 448–55.

"The Gospel According to St. Matthew and the Gospel According to St. Mark." In *The Interpreter's Bible: New Testament Articles*, 483–84. New York: Abingdon, 1951.

Gutman, Herbert G. *Work, Culture and Society: Working-Class and Social History.* New York: Vintage Books, 1976.

(Hale, Sarah Josepha). *Biography of Distinguished Women; Or, Woman's Record from Creation to A.D. 1869. Arranged in Four Eras, with Selections from Authoresses of Each Era. Illus. by 230 Portraits Engraved on Wood by Lossing and Barritt.* 3d ed. New York: Harper, 1876.

Hale, Sarah Josepha. *A Woman's Record; Or, Sketches of All Distinguished Women from the Creation to A.D. 1868. Arranged in Four Eras with Selections from Authoresses of Each Era. Illus. by 230 Portraits Engraved on Wood by Lossing and Barritt.* 3d rev. ed. New York: Harper, 1870.

Handlin, Oscar. *Harvard Guide to American History.* 5th ed. Cambridge, Mass.: Harvard Univ. Press, Belknap Press, 1966.

Harris, Susan K. "'But Is It Any Good?' Evaluating Nineteenth-Century American Women's Fiction." *American Literature* 63, no. 1 (Mar. 1991): 43–61.

Hart, James D. *The Oxford Companion to American Literature.* 4th ed. New York: Oxford Univ. Press, 1965.

———. "Platitudes of Piety: Religion and the Popular Modern Novel." *American Quarterly* 6, no. 4 (Winter 1954): 311–22.

———. *The Popular Book: A History of America's Literary Taste.* New York: Oxford Univ. Press, 1950.

Hassan, Ihab H. "The Idea of Adolescence in American Fiction." *American Quarterly* 10, no. 3 (Fall 1958): 312–24.

Harvey, Charles M. "The Dime Novel in American Life." *Atlantic Monthly* 100, no. 1 (July 1907): 37–45.

Hatch, Mary R. P. "The Author of the Leavenworth Case." *Writer* 2, no. 7 (July 1888): 159–61.

Haycroft, Howard. *Murder for Pleasure: The Life and Times of the Detective Story.* New York: Appleton-Century, 1941.

Hersey, Harold Brainerd. *Pulpwood Editor: The Fabulous World of the Thriller Magazines Revealed by a Veteran Editor and Publisher.* Westport, Conn.: Greenwood, 1937.

Hellman, Geoffrey T. "Mary Roberts Rinehart: For 53 Years She Has Been America's Best-Selling Lady Author." *Life* 20, no. 7 (18 Feb. 1946): 55–61.

Hibben, Paxton. *Henry Ward Beecher: An American Portrait.* Introduction by Sinclair Lewis. American Newspapermen Series, 1790–1933. 1927; New York: Press of the Reader's Club, 1942.

Higham, John. *Strangers in the Land: Patterns of American Nativism, 1860–1925.* New Brunswick, N.J.: Rutgers Univ. Press, 1955.

Hine, Charles De Lano. "Heroes of the Railway Service: Notes from Experience." *Century Magazine* 35, no. 5 (Mar. 1899): 653–63.

Hofstadter, Richard. *The Age of Reform: From Bryan to F.D.R.* New York: Knopf, 1955.

———. *Social Darwinism in American Thought.* Rev. ed. Boston: Beacon, 1955.

Holbrook, Stewart H. *The Age of the Moguls.* Garden City, N.Y.: Doubleday, 1953.

"How the World's Wealth Has Grown." *Literary Digest* 48, no. 26 (27 June 1914): 1567–69.

Holman, C. Hugh, and William Harmon. *A Handbook of American Literature.* 5th ed. New York: Macmillan, 1986.

James, Edward T., III, ed. *Notable American Women: A Biographical Dictionary, 1607–1950.* 4 vols. Cambridge, Mass.: Harvard Univ. Press, Belknap Press, 1971.

Jensen, Richard. *The Winning of the Midwest: Social and Political Conflict, 1885–1896.* Chicago: Univ. of Chicago Press, 1971.

Johannsen, Albert. *The House of Beadle and Adams and Its Dime and Nickel Nov-*

els: The Story of a Vanishing Literature. Foreword by John T. McIntyre. 2 vols. Norman: Univ. of Oklahoma Press, 1950.

Johnson, Elizabeth. "Margaret Sidney vs. Harriet Lothrop." *Horn Book* 47, no. 3 (June 1971): 313–19.

Johnson, Emory R., ed. *Proceedings of and Addresses at the Annual Meeting of the National Child Labor Committee, 14–16 Feb. 1905, New York City.* New York: Arno, 1974.

———. "Proceedings of the Annual Meeting of the National Child Labor Committee, 1905, 1906." *Annals of the American Academy of Political and Social Science* 25, no. 3 (May 1905): 1–189.

Johnston, Johanna. *Runaway to Heaven.* Garden City, N.Y.: Doubleday, 1963.

Jones, Daryl. *The Dime Novel Western.* Bowling Green, Ohio: Popular Press, 1978.

Juergens, George. *Joseph Pulitzer and the New York World.* Princeton, N.J.: Princeton Univ. Press, 1966.

Kaplan, Justin. *Mr. Clemens and Mark Twain: A Biography.* New York: Simon and Schuster, 1966.

Kasson, John F. *Civilizing the Machine: Technology and Republican Values in America, 1776–1900.* New York: Penguin, 1986.

———. *Rudeness and Civility: Manners in Nineteenth-Century Urban America.* New York: Hill and Wang, 1990.

Keller, Morton. *Affairs of State: Public Life in Late-Nineteenth-Century America.* Cambridge, Mass.: Harvard Univ. Press, Belknap Press, 1977.

Kelly, Lori Duin. *The Life and Works of Elizabeth Stuart Phelps: Victorian Feminist Writer.* Troy, N.Y.: Whitson, 1983.

Kelly, Mary. *Private Woman, Public Stage: Literary Domesticity in Nineteenth-Century America.* New York: Oxford, 1984.

Kelly, R. Gordon, ed. *Children's Periodicals of the United States.* Historical Guides to World's Periodicals and Newspapers. Westport, Conn.: Greenwood, 1984.

———. *Mother Was a Lady: Self and Society in Selected American Children's Periodicals, 1865–1890.* Contributions in American Studies No. 12. Westport, Conn.: Greenwood, 1974.

Keylin, Arlenn, and Gene Brown, eds. *Disasters from the Pages of the New York Times.* New York: Arno, 1976.

Krout, Mary H. "Personal Reminiscences of Lew Wallace." *Harper's Weekly* 49, no. 2518 (25 Mar. 1905): 406–9.

Kunitz, Stanley J., and Howard Haycraft, eds. *American Authors, 1600–1900: A Biographical Dictionary of American Literature.* New York: Wilson, 1938.

———. *First Supplement to Twentieth-Century Authors.* New York: Wilson, 1955.

———. *Twentieth-Century Authors: A Bibliographic Dictionary of Modern Literature.* New York: Wilson, 1942.

Larson, Orvin. *American Infidel: Robert G. Ingersoll, A Biography.* New York: Citadel, 1962.

Laymon, Charles M., ed. *The Interpreter's One-Volume Commentary on the Bible: Introduction and Commentary for Each Book of the Bible, Including the Apocrypha.* New York: Abingdon, 1971.

Lehmann-Haupt, Hellmut, with Lawrence C. Wroth and Rollo G. Silver. *The Book in America: A History of the Making and Selling of Books in the United States*. 2d ed. New York: Bowker, 1951.

Levine, Lawrence W. *Highbrow/Lowbrow: The Emergence of Cultural Hierarchy in America*. Cambridge, Mass.: Harvard Univ. Press, 1988.

Lindberg, Stanley W. *The Annotated McGuffey: Selections From McGuffey Eclectic Readers, 1836–1920*. New York: Van Nostrand Reinhold, 1976.

Littlefield, Henry M. "The Wizard of Oz: Parable on Populism." *American Quarterly* 16, no. 1 (1964): 47–58.

Loomis, Lafayette C. "Recent Railroad Disasters." *Popular Science Monthly*. 44, no. 23 (Jan. 1894): 314–19.

Lothrop, Margaret M. *The Wayside House: Home of Authors*. New York: American, 1940.

Lyle, Katie Letcher. *Scalded to Death by the Steam: Authentic Stories about Railroad Disasters and the Ballads That Were Written about Them*. Chapel Hill, N.C.: Algonquin, 1988.

Madison, Charles A. *Book Publishing in America*. New York: McGraw-Hill, 1966.

Maio, Kathleen L. *American Women Writers: A Critical Reference Guide from Colonial Times to the Present*. New York: Ungar, 1979.

Manning, Peter K. *Semiotics and Field Work*. Beverly Hills, Calif.: Sage, 1978.

May, Henry F. *The End of American Innocence: A Study of the First Years of Our Time, 1912–1917*. New York: Knopf, 1957.

————. *Protestant Churches and Industrial America*. New York: Harper and Row, 1949.

McLoughlin, William G. *The Meaning of Henry Ward Beecher: An Essay on the Shifting Values of Mid-Victorian America, 1840–70*. New York: Knopf, 1970.

McQuade, Donald. *Popular Writing in America*. New York: Oxford Univ. Press, 1985.

Mencken, August. *The Railroad Passenger Car: An Illustrated History of the First Hundred Years, with Accounts by Contemporary Passengers*. Baltimore, Md.: Johns Hopkins Univ. Press, 1957.

Minnich, Harvey C. *William Holmes McGuffey and His Readers*. New York: American, 1936.

Morgan, H. Wayne. *From Hayes to McKinley: National Party Politics, 1877–1896*. Syracuse, N.Y.: Syracuse Univ. Press, 1969.

————. *The Gilded Age*. Syracuse, N.Y.: Syracuse Univ. Press, 1970.

Morgan, Shepard Ashman. "The Reader, the Reporter and the News." *Outlook* 98 (3 June 1911): 253–56.

————. *Unity and Culture*. Baltimore, Md.: Penguin, 1971.

Morris, John V. "The Big Burn." In *Fires and Firefighters*, 197–258. Boston: Little, Brown, 1953.

Moseley, Edward A. "Railroad Accidents in the United States." *Monthly Review of Reviews* 30, no. 5 (Nov. 1904): 592–96.

Mott, Frank Luther. *Golden Multitudes: The Story of Best Sellers in the United States*. New York: Macmillan, 1947.

————. *A History of American Magazines*. 3 vols. Cambridge, Mass: Harvard Univ. Press, 1938.

Mumford, Lewis. *The Brown Decades: A Study of the Arts in America, 1865–1895.* New York: Harcourt Brace, 1931. Rpt. New York: Dover, 1971.

Nasaw, David. *Children of the City: At Work and at Play.* Garden City, N.Y.: Anchor/Doubleday, 1985.

Nash, Jay Robert. *Darkest Hours: A Narrative Encyclopedia of Worldwide Disasters from Ancient Time to the Present.* Chicago: Nelson-Hall, 1976.

National Cyclopedia of American Biography. New York: J. T. White, 1893–.

Newcomb, H., with R. S. Alley. *The Producer's Medium.* New York: Oxford Univ. Press, 1983.

Noel, Mary. *Villains Galore: The Heyday of the Popular Story Weekly.* New York: Macmillan, 1954.

Nord, David Paul. "Working-Class Readers: Family, Community, and Reading in Late-Nineteenth-Century America." *Communication Research* 13, no. 2 (1986): 156–81.

Nugent, Walter T. K. *Money and American Society, 1865–1880.* New York: Free Press, 1968.

Nye, Russell. *The Unembarrassed Muse: The Popular Arts in America.* New York: Dial, 1970.

Ong, Walter J. *Orality and Literacy: The Technologizing of the Word.* New York: Methuen, 1982.

Oring, Elliott. *Folk Groups and Folklore Genres: An Introduction.* Logan: Utah State Univ. Press, 1986.

Overton, Grant. *American Nights Entertainment.* New York: Appleton, 1923.

———. *The Women Who Make Our Novels.* New York: Moffat Yard, 1919.

Pachon, Stanley A. "Mary Roberts Rinehart and the Nickel Novels." *Dime Novel Roundup* 31, no. 6 (June 1963): 55.

Paine, Fred K., and Nancy E. Paine. *Magazines: A Bibliography for Their Analysis, with Annotations and Study Guide.* Metuchen, N.J.: Scarecrow, 1987.

Papashvily, Helen Waite. *All the Happy Endings: A Study of the Domestic Novel in America, the Women Who Wrote It, the Women Who Read It, in the Nineteenth Century.* Port Washington, N.Y.: Kennikat, 1972.

Parrington, Vernon L. *The Beginnings of Critical Realism.* New York: Harcourt Brace, 1930.

Payne, Darwin. *Owen Wister: Chronicler of the West, Gentleman of the East.* Dallas, Tex.: Southern Methodist Univ. Press, 1985.

Pearson, Carol S. *Awakening the Heroes Within: Twelve Archetypes to Help Us Find Ourselves and Transform Our World.* San Francisco: Harper, 1991.

Pearson, Edmund. *Dime Novels; Or, Following an Old Trail in Popular Literature.* Boston: Little, Brown, 1929.

Peirce, Bradford K. "The Probable Intellectual and Moral Outcome of the Rapid Increase in Libraries." *Library Journal* 10, no. 9–10 (Sept.–Oct. 1885): 234–36.

Pernin, Peter. "Wisconsin Stories: The Great Peshtigo Fire." *Wisconsin Magazine of History* 54 (Summer 1971): 246–72.

Petersen, William J. *Steamboating on the Upper Mississippi.* Iowa City: State Historical Society of Iowa, 1968.

Peterson, Theodore. *Magazines in the Twentieth Century.* Urbana: Univ. of Illinois Press, 1956.

Price, Warren C., and Calder M. Pickett. *An Annotated Journalism Bibliography: 1958–68.* Minneapolis: Univ. of Minnesota, 1990.

Putnam, George. "Influence of Fiction for Good or Evil in Relation to Public Libraries." *Catholic World* 67 (July 1898): 570–72.

Radway, Janice A. *Reading the Romance: Women, Patriarchy and Popular Literature.* Chapel Hill: Univ. of North Carolina Press, 1984.

Reed, Robert C. *Train Wrecks: A Pictorial History of Accidents on the Main Line.* Seattle, Wash.: Superior, 1968.

Reep, Diana C. *Margaret Deland.* U.S. Authors Series. Boston: Twayne, 1985.

Reynolds, David S. *Faith in Fiction: The Emergence of Religious Literature in America.* Cambridge, Mass.: Harvard Univ. Press, 1981.

———. "From Doctrine to Narrative: The Rise of Pulpit Storytelling in America." *American Quarterly* 32, no. 5 (Winter 1980): 479–98.

Reynolds, Quentin. *The Fiction Factory; Or, From Pulp Row to Quality Street.* New York: Random, 1955.

Ricoeur, Paul. "Narrative Time." *Critical Inquiry* 7, no. 1 (Autumn 1980): 176.

Riis, Jacob. *How the Other Half Lives.* New York: Scribners, 1890.

———. *A Ten Years' War: An Account of the Battle with the Slum in New York, with Illus.* New York: Books for Libraries, 1900.

Roe, E. P. "The Elements of Life in Fiction." *Forum* 5 (Apr. 1888): 226–36.

Rosenberg, Charles E. *The Care of Strangers: The Rise of America's Hospital System.* New York: Basic, 1987.

Ross, Ishbel. *Ladies of the Press: The Story of Women in Journalism, by an Insider.* New York: Harper, 1936.

Rourke, Constance M. *Trumpets of Jubilee: Henry Ward Beecher, Harriet Beecher Stowe, Lyman Beecher, Horace Greeley, and P. T. Barnum.* New York: Harcourt Brace, 1922.

Rowntree, Joseph, with Arthur Sherwell. *The Temperance Problem and Social Reform.* 9th ed. London: Hodder and Stoughton, 1901.

Sampson, Robert. *Yesterday's Faces: A Study of Series Characters in the Early Pulp Magazines.* Bowling Green, Ohio: Bowling Green Univ. Popular Press, 1987.

Santayana, George. *The Genteel Tradition: Nine Essays.* Ed. Douglas L. Wilson. Cambridge, Mass.: Harvard Univ. Press, 1967.

Saum, Lewis O. "Death in the Popular Mind of Pre–Civil War America." *American Quarterly* 26, no. 5 (Dec. 1974): 477–95.

Saxon, A. H. *P. T. Barnum: The Legend and the Man.* New York: Columbia Univ. Press, 1989.

———. "P. T. Barnum: Universalism's Surprising 'Prince of Humbugs.'" *The World* 2, no. 3 (May–June 1988): 5–7, 50.

———, ed. *The Autobiography of Mrs. Tom Thumb: Some of My Life Experiences, by Mrs. Countess M. Lavinia Magri, formerly Mrs. General Tom Thumb, with Assistance of Sylvester Bleeker.* Hamden, Conn.: Archon, 1979.

———. *Selected Letters of P. T. Barnum.* New York: Columbia Univ. Press, 1983.

Scharnhorst, Gary, with Jack Bales. *The Lost Life of Horatio Alger, Jr.* Bloomington: Indiana Univ. Press, 1985.

Schivelbusch, Wolfgang. *The Railway Journey: The Industrialization of Time and Space in the Nineteenth Century.* Berkeley: Univ. of California Press, 1977.

Schlipp, Madelon Golden, with Sharon M. Murphy. *Great Women of the Press.* Carbondale: Southern Illinois Univ. Press, 1983.

Schudson, Michael. *Discovering the News: A Social History of American Newspapers.* New York: Basic Books, 1978.

Scoville, Samuel, Jr. "Rescue, Robbery and Escapes." *Forum* 74, no. 1 (July 1925): 83–91.

Seeley, Herman B. "The Loss by Fire in the Congested District of Chicago." *American Architect* 87, no. 1524 (11 Mar. 1905): 83–85.

Seelye, John. "Who Was Horatio? The Alger Myth and American Scholarship." *American Quarterly* 17, no. 4 (Winter 1965): 751.

Segal, Howard. *Technological Utopianism in American Culture.* Chicago: Univ. of Chicago Press, 1985.

Sheahan, James W., and George P. Upton. *History of the Great Conflagration. Chicago: Its Past, Present and Future. Embracing a Detailed Narrative of the Great Conflagration in the North, South and West Divisions. Origin, Progress and Results of the Fire. Prominent Buildings Burned, Character of Buildings, Losses and Insurance, Graphic Description of the Flames, Scenes and Incidents, Loss of Life, the Flight of the People. Also, a Condensed History of Chicago, Its Population, Growth and Great Public Works. And a Statement of All the Great Fires of the World.* Chicago: Union, 1871.

Shearman, Thomas G. "The Coming Billionaire." *Forum* 10 (Jan. 1891): 546–57.

Sheehan, Donald. *This Was Publishing: A Chronicle of the Book Trade in the Gilded Age.* Bloomington: Indiana Univ. Press, 1952.

Shelburne, Walter A. *Mythos and Logos in the Thought of Carl Jung: The Theory of the Collective Unconscious in Scientific Perspective.* Albany: State Univ. of New York Press, 1988.

Shove, Raymond Howard. *Cheap Books Produced in the United States, 1870–1891.* Urbana: Univ. of Illinois Library, 1937.

Siebert, Fred, with Theodore Peterson, and Wilbur Schramm. *Four Theories of the Press: The Authoritarian, Libertarian, Social Responsibility and Soviet Communist Concepts of What the Press Should Be and Do.* Urbana: Univ. of Illinois Press, 1963.

Silberger, Julius, Jr. *Mary Baker Eddy: An Interpretive Biography of Christian Science.* Boston: Little, Brown, 1980.

Sinclair, Upton. *The Jungle.* 1905. Rpt. New York: Signet, 1980.

Slotkin, Richard. *Regeneration through Violence: The Mythology of the American Frontier, 1600–1860.* Middletown, Conn.: Wesleyan Univ. Press, 1973.

Smith, Henry Nash. *Popular Culture and Industrialism, 1865–1890.* New York: New York Univ. Press, 1967.

———. *The Virgin Land: The American West as Symbol and Myth.* Cambridge, Mass.: Harvard Univ. Press, 1950.

Soibelman, David. "Horatio Alger Goes Greeley: From Wretches to Riches." *Dime Novel Roundup* 48, no. 5 (Oct. 1979): 79–81.

Speed, John Gilmer. "The Great American Showman." *Harper's Weekly* 35, no. 1791 (7 Apr. 1891): 289.

Stannard, David E. "Death and the Puritan Child." *American Quarterly* 26, no. 5 (Dec. 1974): 456–76.

———. "Editor's Introduction." *American Quarterly* 26, no. 5 (Dec. 1974): 443–47. Special issue on the American meaning of death.

Stebbins, Lucy Ward. "Kate Douglas Wiggin as a Child Knew Her." *Horn Book* 26, no. 6 (Nov.–Dec. 1950): 447–54.

Steffens, Lincoln. *The Shame of the Cities.* New York: McLure Phillips, 1904.

Steinberg, S. H. *Five Hundred Years of Printing.* 3d ed. Baltimore, Md.: Penguin, 1974.

Stern, Madeleine B. *Books and Book People in Nineteenth-Century America.* New York: Bowker, 1978.

———, ed. *Publishers for Mass Entertainment in Nineteenth-Century America.* Boston: Hall, 1980.

———. *The Autobiography of Lincoln Steffens.* New York: Harcourt Brace, 1931.

Stowe, Harriet Beecher. "Henry Ward Beecher." In *The Lives and Deeds of Our Self-Made Men,* by Harriet Beecher Stowe; rev. and ed. Charles E. Stowe, with biographical sketch of the author; 509–71. Boston: Estes and Lauriat, 1889.

———. *Our Famous Women: Comprising the Lives and Deeds of American Women Who Have Distinguished Themselves in Literature, Science, Art, Music, and the Drama, or Are Famous as Heroines, Patriots, Orators, Educators, Physicians, Philanthropists, etc., with Numerous Anecdotes, Incidents and Personal Experiences.* Hartford, Conn.: Worthington, 1884.

———. *Uncle Tom's Cabin; Or, Life among the Lowly.* Boston: Jewett, 1852.

———, with Charles Edward Stowe. *Life of Harriet Beecher Stowe.* Boston: Houghton Mifflin, 1889. Rpt. Detroit: Gale, 1976.

Stowe, Lyman Beecher Stowe. *Saints, Sinners and Beechers.* New York: Blue Ribbon, 1934.

Swenson, Grace. *From the Ashes: The Story of the Hinckley Fire of 1894.* St. Cloud, Minn.: North Star, 1979.

Tarbell, Ida. *The History of the Standard Oil Company.* Ed. David M. Chalmers. New York: Norton, 1969.

Taylor, Frederick. *The Principles of Scientific Management.* New York: Norton, 1967.

Tebbel, John. *Between Covers: The Rise and Transformation of Book Publishing in America.* New York: Oxford Univ. Press, 1987.

———. *A History of Book Publishing in the United States: The Expansion of an Industry, 1865–1919.* 2 vols. New York: Bowker, 1975.

Thomson, Clifford. "The Waste by Fire." *Forum* 27 (Sept. 1886): 27–39.

Thomson, Douglas H. *Masters of Mystery: A Study of the Detective Story.* London: Collins, 1931.

Thorburn, David. "Television as an Aesthetic Medium." *Sage Annual Review of Communication Research* 15 (1988): 48–66.

Tocqueville, Alexis de. *Democracy in America.* 2 vols. New York: Knopf, 1945.

Tompkins, Jane. *Sensational Designs: The Cultural Work of American Fiction, 1790–1860.* New York: Oxford Univ. Press, 1985.

Towers, Tom H. "The Insomnia of Julian West." *American Literature* 47, no. 1 (Mar. 1975): 53.

Trachtenberg, Alan. *Brooklyn Bridge: Fact and Symbol.* New York: Oxford Univ. Press, 1965.

———. *The Incorporation of American Culture and Society in the Gilded Age.* New York: Hill and Wang, 1982.

———. *Reading American Photographs: Images as History, Mathew Brady to Walker Evans.* New York: Hill and Wang, 1989.

Trattner, Walter I. *Crusade for the Children: A History of the National Child Labor Committee and Child Labor in the United States.* Chicago: Quadrangle, 1970.

Trowbridge, John. "Great Fires and Rain-Storms." *Popular Science Monthly* 7, no. 9 (Dec. 1872): 206–11.

Waller, Altina L. *Rev. Beecher and Mrs. Tilton: Sex and Class in Victorian America.* Amherst: Univ. of Massachusetts Press, 1982.

Watt, Ian. *The Rise of the Novel: Studies in Defoe, Richardson and Fielding.* Berkeley: Univ. of California Press, 1957.

Wells, Robert W. *Fire and Ice: Two Deadly Disasters, Fire at Peshtigo.* Ashland, Wis.: Northword, 1983.

Westeroff, John H., III. *McGuffey and His Readers.* New York: Abingdon, 1978.

Wiebe, Robert. *The Search for Order, 1877–1920.* New York: Hill and Wang, 1967.

Wilkinson, William. *Memorials of the Minnesota Forest Fires in the Year of 1894.* Minneapolis, Minn.: Norman E. Wilkinson, 1895.

Willard, Frances E., and Mary A. Livermore. *American Women: A Revised Edition of Women of the Century: 1500 Biographies with over 1,400 Portraits: A Comprehensive Encyclopedia of the Lives and Achievements of American Women during the Nineteenth Century.* New York: Mast, Crowell, and Kirkpatrick, 1897.

Williams, R. Hal. *Years of Decision: American Politics in the 1890s.* New York: Wiley, 1978.

Wilson, Forrest. *Crusader in Crinoline.* Philadelphia: Lippincott, 1941.

Wright, Mabel Osgood. *My New York.* New York: Macmillan, 1926.

Zinn, Howard. *A People's History of the United States.* New York: Harper and Row, 1980.

Zuckerman, Michael. "The Nursery Tales of Horatio Alger." *American Quarterly* 24, no. 2 (May 1972): 191–209.

Zurier, Rebecca. *The American Firehouse: An Architectural and Social History with Photographs by A. Pierce Bounds.* New York: Abbeville, 1982.

Index